CORRECTIONAL

ALSO BY RAVI SHANKAR

A Field Guide to Southern China (coauthor)

The Many Uses of Mint: New and Selected Poems 1998–2018

Durable Transit: New and Selected Poems 1997–2017

The Golden Shovel: New Poems Honoring Gwendolyn Brooks (coeditor)

The Autobiography of a Goddess by Āṇṭāḷ (cotranslator)

What Else Could It Be: Ekphrastics & Collaborations

Deepening Groove

Seamless Matter

Voluptuous Bristle: Poems

Radha Says: Last Poems by Reetika Vazirani (coeditor)

*Language for a New Century: Contemporary Poetry from Asia,
the Middle East, and Beyond* (coeditor)

Wanton Textiles (coauthor)

Instrumentality

CORRECTIONAL

RAVI SHANKAR

THE UNIVERSITY OF WISCONSIN PRESS

The University of Wisconsin Press
728 State Street, Suite 443
Madison, Wisconsin 53706
uwpress.wisc.edu

Gray's Inn House, 127 Clerkenwell Road
London EC1R 5DB, United Kingdom
eurospanbookstore.com

Printed in the United States of America
This book may be available in a digital edition.

Library of Congress Cataloging-in-Publication Data

Names: Shankar, Ravi, 1975– author.
Title: Correctional / Ravi Shankar.
Description: Madison, Wisconsin : The University of Wisconsin Press, [2021]
Identifiers: LCCN 2021009788 | ISBN 9780299335304 (cloth)
Subjects: LCSH: Shankar, Ravi, 1975– | Ex-convicts—United States—Biography. |
East Indian Americans—Biography. | Poets, American—21st century—Biography. |
College teachers—United States—Biography. |
Criminal justice, Administration of—United States.
Classification: LCC PS3619.H3547 Z46 2021 | DDC 818/.603—dc23
LC record available at https://lccn.loc.gov/2021009788

Traumatic memory, according to literary theorist Geoffrey Hartman, is as close to
nescience as it is to knowledge, implying that there may be elisions and embellishments in
what we recall. This is particularly true of *Correctional*, which as a memoir is a truthful
recollection of actual events in my life, but as a work of literature re-creates certain events,
locations, and conversations from memory. In some cases, in order to preserve their
anonymity, I have changed the identifying names, occupations, and other signifying details of
certain individuals. In other instances, I may have compressed or attenuated chronologies.
Moreover, if I wrote about you unwillingly, I'm sorry, and if I willingly didn't write about you,
I'm also sorry. Knowing full well the dangers of a single story, if you disagree with my
version of events, I hope you will write your own.

For the memory of my late grandparents,

Chittoor Hariharan Krishnan,
Parvathi Vaidyanathan Krishnan,
Rukmani Sivaraman Hariharan, *and*
Koyalmannam Sankaranarayanan Hariharan

I feel the need to reaffirm all of it, the whole unhappy territory and all the things loved and unloveable in it, for it is all part of me.

—RALPH ELLISON, *Invisible Man*

Contents

CORRECTIONAL

Introduction

Sometimes, as I go about my day, I will unexpectedly see the faces of the men I spent time with in jail. I will be ordering a chai latte at Starbucks, and—for a moment—I'm certain that the barista is Junkie John, the drug addict and kleptomaniac who taught me how to work the "hungry and homeless" hustle. Or I'll be boarding a bus on Broadway and almost swear Amma's *mala* that the driver is Chaos, the toothless convict who had spent as much time inside as out and was a master of facial contortions. Or I will stride up to a park bench to say hello to my old bunkmate Lenny, the badly inked Vietnam vet with a gut as large as his list of grievances. But my hand will freeze in midair because, of course, it's not him.

I'll never see those men again.

Those promises to keep in touch made in privation, those addresses of half-way houses scrawled out longhand in composition books, those damp and earnest handshakes made while sitting on a metal bench in a tan jumpsuit, waiting for a correctional officer to call your name and inmate number for court? They all melt away the moment you walk out the door. Once you're out, you're out.

That is, until you're back in again.

Not me, though. Or at least that's what I thought the first time I went to jail. That time I was innocent and indignant. Slurred a "sand nigger" by the NYPD and wrongfully detained on an erroneous warrant in a city I once considered home, I became another statistic of NYC mayor Michael Bloomberg's infamous stop-and-frisk policing policy, later deemed unconstitutional by US District Court judge Shira A. Scheindlin. At the time, I was a tenured associate professor of English at a state university in Connecticut, a married homeowner, and a father, so my immediate reaction was to get on a soapbox. I told my story on National Public Radio, wrote an op-ed for the *Hartford Courant*, and delivered a sermon on the topic of social justice at a Unitarian Universalist church in New Haven. I even sued the city for racial discrimination and police misconduct, winning a modest settlement from them—a drop in the bucket considering New York City had paid out well over a billion dollars to settle police misconduct and wrongful conviction cases in the previous decade alone.

The next time I was arrested, I was not so lucky. Nor was I guiltless.

Once, as a child in South India, I went to a Nādi astrologer in the dusty streets of Vadapalani, a neighborhood in Chennai, then known as Madras. The wizened old woman told me that, due to my previous life's misdeeds and a rare planetary alignment when I was born, I would have equal parts fame and hardship in this life. When she held my palm to read the lines on it, she decreed that the gaps between my fingers meant that I would earn much money, but it would all slip through them like water. Reckless ambition would cause a deep fissure somewhere along my days.

This is the true story of how, in the middle of a seemingly successful life, I suddenly ended up in jail. My own good self, as we say in India, turned so very, very bad. This is the story of how I became the first known academic in American history to be promoted to full professor while incarcerated, a decision that inflamed the local media and caused controversy among my peers and colleagues. This is me seen through six seasons, each one taking the form of a letter to a loved one, and this memoir is a trace of what the worst years of my life ended up teaching me about the American criminal justice system and mental illness at the beginning of the twenty-first century. This is how I learned to process a generation's worth of racism, sexism, shame, and redemption while at the same time coming to grips with the dark inner mechanisms of my own heart.

This is the song to set all that shit straight. Not a confessional. A *correctional*.

IlaVenil (*Spring*)

Dearest daughters—

This is not a book I ever imagined I would write, nor one that I would have wanted you to read. Like all fathers, I had hoped to preserve the myth of being an all-conquering hero for as long as I possibly could—the hero who piggybacked you up hillsides and spouted off names of flowers and constellations, even when I was unsure of them, like some kind of maverick horticulturalist cosmonaut. Even imagining talking to you about the time I spent in jail paralyzes me with shame, because it is so far from my own self-conception, from the dreams and wishes I nurture for you both. Yet this is why I'm writing this letter. I'm hard-pressed to focus on the lessons of imperfection, of failure shaping progress, of how the scar can be the source of beauty, although they are all accurate, of course. I'm more fixated on missing out on one of your birthday parties or not being able to coach your soccer teams well into your adolescence. I hope that you can forgive me for those absences, as well as my choice to address them in such a public fashion.

Both of you are growing up as beautiful, intelligent, articulate, biracial women in the twenty-first century. You are growing up in a United States of America that has changed from the one I grew up in as a first-generation immigrant son. Yet I see myself and my own childhood world in you, both the good and the bad. I hope you find it easier than I did to navigate multiple cultures and the persistent, pernicious racism (and sexism) that even some of the most well-meaning people unintentionally overlook or tacitly engender. Some of the work I have been trying to do in untangling ancestral legacies and grappling with shame is intended to make your own path forward a little easier. Sometimes I forget that the civil rights movement is only a little older than me and that as a country, and as individuals, we have so far to go before we can claim equal opportunity and social justice for all.

If you might indulge my sappiness for a few moments longer, you are both as worthy as anyone you might ever meet, and nothing peripheral can ever dim the light of your inner lives. In Sanskrit, there are six *ritu*, or seasons, and as you two exit spring, I am approaching autumn. From this vantage, the wisdom I possess feels meager but crucial. I offer it to you as fruit from the harvest. I want you to remember to remain open to new ideas and experiences, knowing that certainty is porous and that black and white are composed of the absorption or reflection of all the colors of the visible spectrum. I want you to see in your own reflection each sentient being as worthy of compassion, no matter whether they are a celebrity or an ex-con, knowing that all of us seek the same goals from life— love, safety, friendship, acceptance—even if we are unsure, or utterly confused, on how best to achieve them. Finally, I want you to be able to let go of grievance and to forgive those who have—and will—hurt us along the way.

Kutty, my little deer, you are immensely loved and treasured by your mother and me, your aunts and grandparents, and your extended family on both sides, stretching all the way to India and beyond. May your days be filled with boundless curiosity and wonderment, and may your passions guide you toward the most fulfilling destinies imaginable. I write to you as I might to my own younger self, except without blame, lacking any predetermined expectation but that you try your hardest and that when you fail, as we all do, you allow yourself to learn from your mistakes so that you can do better next time. Indeed, it is part of my own attempts at self-betterment that I feel so compelled to share this story, which others would prefer I repress and bury deeply where no one might see it. Denial is a dead end, and nothing healthy ever comes from secrecy, nor from the allure of wearing a mask to please others. Be yourselves. But also put yourself in the well-worn chappals of those you don't understand—even those with whom you might vehemently disagree, for that's the only way to evolve.

The world is an extraordinary place, full of countless miniscule and enormous miracles. We just need to know how and where to look for them. Slow down. Pay attention to the details around you. When you cherish the world, it holds you in return. I wish for you gratitude for what you have, pride in what you learn, and the certainty that you possess so much strength, tenderness, and support that you can overcome any obstacle you might ever face. Ever since you were infants in my arms, looking toward you has given me purpose. I hope, in turn, that I might give you my whole self, full of error and resolve, grace and obstinance. In that exchange, there is a gift of authenticity and the chance to live your own lives openly and without regrets. I love you both unconditionally and look forward to talking to you about all of this and so much more over the course of our lives together.

Your dad

Chapter One

The Many Lines
of Lineage

Alo nanbaa! Nalamaa? How are you, friend?

I sit cross-legged in Trivandrum, South India, facing a gigantic opalescent statue of Lord Vishnu made from thousands of fossilized seashells. The Hindu deity considered the protector of the universe reclines in eternal yogic sleep upon a five-hooded serpent carved from a single enormous stone. The world's richest temple, the Sri Padmanabhaswamy Temple, is buried beneath the seven-story structure. It is undoubtedly a marvel to behold, worthy of a place in an Indiana Jones adventure, although it is not the real reason why I have come back to my ancestral land.

Naan nallaa irukéan. I'm fine.

My mother tongue thickens in the effort of recall, the halting return greeting I give to the *vadhyar*, or priest, with his magisterial beard and the yellow sandalwood paste *tilaka* smeared on his forehead. Plus, I am not fine. How could I be? My life has imploded spectacularly, and I'm still picking shards of shrapnel from my skull. Over the last few years, I have been fired from my dream job as a tenured professor of creative writing in Connecticut, wrecked my marriage, been incarcerated, been admitted as an inpatient to a mental health facility, and had my face splashed over the newspapers and local TV newscasts in the most negative light. What is the Tamil word for FUBAR?

I have come to Trivandrum to hit the floor and, hopefully, to bounce, remembering the wisdom of a friend's words that a wise man hits bottom, but a fool falls right on through. I am here to visit my *ammamma*, or grandmother, who recently turned ninety-three and lives perilously with my retired uncle and his two grown sons. I feel blessed to be with her for what feels like—and what will indeed prove to be—one final time. But, sitting in prayer, the real reason I am in India is to chart the seismic quake that has torn up my life, one whose aftershocks continue to resound and might well do so forever. For, as in zen and jurisprudence, you can't just unring the bell.

Thinking of the negative headlines about me from the latest *Hartford Courant* while sitting inside a temple thousands of years old makes Connecticut feel tiny—a puritanical dust mote on one of the mythical lamps illuminating the idea of the shining city on the hill. In my bitterness, it's not hard to lapse into stereotypes of wayward investment bankers on sailboats and Stepford wives having their cutlery and children polished by au pairs, but the facts are much more discrete and damning than that. Connecticut perpetually remains one of the richest states per capita in the country (which means the galaxy), yet over half the population of its largest cities, such as Hartford, Bridgeport, and New Haven, live below the poverty line. They are Black, Hispanic, and unmentionable over bowls of lobster bisque and Red Sox box scores.

Leaf-stem acrimony brews in my belly, and I lean into its sting. If not for my girls and the few dear friends I have left there, I could go a few lifetimes without having to stub my toe again in the Nutmeg State. When I imagine being back there, the word I conjure is *rectitude*. A hardness born of winter squalls squinted at through the narrow slats of righteousness, made manifest by regularly serviced Volvos driven by the descendants of a people who had once meted out whippings for dressing above one's station.

No, definitely not my kind of place. I am South Indian in my genes. I carry generations of *tamasha* and tabla beats, colorful silks, and armloads of the ripest tamarind fruit. I could never stand shoveling snow and didn't give Hanuman's extendable tail that your grandfather's great-uncle once owned the titular tavern in town. Still, as the Bruce Springsteen song goes, I was born in the USA, so knowing how to make a mean lentil dal made me no less American.

I was born in the nation's capital, Washington, DC, on January 13, 1975, one day after Franco Harris and the Pittsburgh Steelers won their first Super Bowl and nearly a year after Patty Hearst had been kidnapped by the Symbionese Liberation Army. As the firstborn child of immigrant parents from South India who had lost three previous pregnancies to miscarriage, my own birth was celebrated copiously. In the scrapbook made by Amma, my mother, there are copies of the announcement cards that were sent around the world with a photograph of my swaddled body and prune face—a wide-eyed samosa set on a mint-chutney-colored shag carpet.

I grew up in Northern Virginia, or NoVA, as it is now known, as the first male child of my generation in my Tamilian Brahmin, or TamBrahm, family— the result, as Amma often reminded me, of many centuries of breeding, which made me feel like a dog-show Pomeranian. Other than my great-uncle, who worked for the World Bank, my parents were the first in their immediate families to immigrate. Their story, like that of so many immigrants, is filled with that bittersweet mix of hard-earned success coupled with enduring degradation.

Appa, my father, was born in Madras, which was later renamed Chennai in a fervent attempt by Hindu nationalists to de-anglicize the names of Indian cities. (Never mind that Madras is a more authentically Tamil word than Chennai, and not to mention that this trend augured the erasure of Muslim legacies in the country.) Although a Brahmin, his father had been a laborer who worked his way up to become the accountant at a cement factory. His mother, a stern woman who lived by the edict that silence exceeded godliness, served as the matriarch for Appa, the eldest son, and his four younger siblings, three sisters and a brother. At the age of fourteen, Appa was sent to boarding school. If he were willing to submit to analysis, we might know more of the trauma he suffered there. To my young self, he resembled a veteran home from war when it came to discussing his own past, not to mention that he would flinch from physical contact such as hugging.

Appa's full name is K. H. Shankar. Following traditional South Indian naming conventions, his first initial represents the village he came from (Koyalmannam in Kerela, Madras). The second represents his father's family name (Hariharan), and his given name is Shankar. By that logic, I should have been M. H. Ravi, for Manassas Hariharan Ravi. Instead, I was encumbered with the name Ravi Shankar, with my parents oblivious to the coincidence that I would forever be in the shadow of India's most famous musician.

In 1960, due in large part to the highly restrictive Immigration Acts of 1917 and 1924, there were only around twelve thousand Indians in the United States, which represented less than half a percent of the total foreign-born population in the country at the time. But in 1965, the Immigration and Nationality Act canceled quotas based on country of origin and created more immigration channels contingent on employability. Appa was among the first wave of South Asians to take advantage of these new policies.

Appa left India in 1966, a scholarship student on a visa sponsored by his uncle. Alone, he headed to Washington, DC, in order to get his degree in mechanical engineering from Howard University. He professed that it had always been his intention to get his degree and then return to India, where he would take on the traditional role prescribed for the eldest son: to provide for and house his parents, get married, settle down in the Brahmin community in which he grew up, and—like his own father—work for an industrial company in the area. But when he got to the United States, his ideas swiftly began to shift.

One of his first acts as a newly arrived American was to ditch his Indian name and take on the moniker of "Sam" instead. Sam Shankar, newly minted American.

I didn't see much of this fellow Sam when I was growing up, glimpsing him only occasionally in sepia-tinted photographs in which he would be sporting butterfly-collared shirts under intricately embroidered polyester suits. Instead, I would more frequently see austere Appa, doling out discipline with his leather belt or the heel of his patent leather shoe if his children disobeyed him by showing any sign of deviating from orthodox Hindu Brahmin life.

A rakshasa in Hindu mythology is a shapeshifting demon, and although I didn't know it on any conscious level back then, I was being schooled in such illusory beasts through the unspoken tutelage of my father. He turned eighty in 2020, and he still remains almost entirely inscrutable to me. He's a study in contrasts, perhaps typified by his ever-changing names and intonations. When he is Sam, he can charm bank tellers to let him use their Xerox machines for free and sell magnetic calendars and logoed coin purses by the carton. He would become one of the best recruiters for and the former lieutenant governor of the Optimist Club of Manassas, a civic organization whose purpose includes the promotion of patriotism, bike safety, and relentless brightness. At home, though, he was always Appa, a strict Brahminical man who stressed the virtues of vegetarianism, teetotalism, asexuality, and self-discipline. Solitary and suspicious of other people's motives, his primary rhetorical modes, even today, are to scold and to warn.

Sam might have projected the image of conquistador back home, but in reality, his life in those early days in America was anything but flourishing. He lived in the basement of his uncle's house in Maryland, out of a suitcase and on a couch, handwashing his two button-down shirts in the kitchen sink, walking a mile to the nearest bus stop. Many of these details have been shuffled and dealt out to me slowly over the years, since Appa's past remains a patchy deck of cards.

"Go!" he would exclaim. "Don't drink out of someone else's water bottle! Don't eat that pizza; it was probably cooked on a meat grill! *Chee Chee!* American sitcoms are very dirty, and you know you should be practicing your maths instead!"

When I put myself in the knockoff black leather wing-tip oxfords he would wear each morning to work, an act that became simultaneously easier and harder once I had stopped living under his roof, I can imagine better what it might have been like for Appa. He was a first-generation Indian immigrant who arrived in America with only his bedeviled pride and dreams of grandeur. Yet, instead of luxury, he found himself a poor engineering student at Howard University, barely scraping by and dependent upon his relations for meals and company. Washington, DC, back then (and even now) was far from anyone's idea of a utopian paradise, but Appa was there on campus during that historical moment when over a thousand students occupied the administration building of Howard University with a set of demands.

What I wouldn't give to be able to borrow his eyes when, just over a month later, Martin Luther King Jr. was assassinated, and Trinidad-born Black activist Stokely Carmichael touched off the riots that left nearly half of DC burned to the ground and entire neighborhoods within blocks of the White House looted. Amma has told me how Appa had to scurry home under cover of night to hide when President Lyndon B. Johnson ordered the army and National Guard to erect machine-gun emplacements around the federal buildings.

It boggles my mind to imagine my serious, orthodox father sprinting down the same streets that Black Panthers patrolled in green field jackets, binoculars around their necks and assault rifles upon their shoulders, while looters carried off transistor radios, televisions, and appliances, and soldiers in fatigues shot tear gas into the streets. He came from India to find the American dream and instead found that dream deferred and then literally exploded outward into the civil rights movement. How might that experience have colored his relationship to this new country and shaped his children, as yet unborn?

Amma, on the other hand, had a very different journey to America. Though she would never see it this way, my mother's is the story of a woman born into a patriarchal society, considered property and consigned to do the bidding of men. By all accounts, including her own, she had been blessed with an ideal childhood. After Madras, Coimbatore is the second-largest city in Tamil Nadu. It is sometimes referred to as the Manchester of South India because of its factories and industrial heritage, but also with a slightly derisive edge. Nearly half the motors, water pumps, and wet grinders in India are manufactured in this city, with all the industrial grime and little of the music or culture of its British counterpart.

Amma was the third of four children, and her father, my *thatha*, or grandfather, was a journalist who worked for the PTI (Press Trust of India), which used to be Reuters, and provided news to all the national newspapers. C. H. Krishnan wrote for the *Hindu*, India's largest English-language newspaper, and there are photographs of him with Winston Churchill, Jawaharlal Nehru, and many other statesmen, cricketers, and actors. He was stationed in Kashmir and East Bengal during partition in 1947, at which point the nation-states of India and Pakistan were created, and family lore has it that when violence broke out, he brought his family back to safety in India and then smuggled himself back to the war zone, dressed as a Muslim woman shrouded in a head-to-toe burka. When I was growing up, Thatha was a larger-than-life figure, a charismatic, boisterous, roaring lion of a man who would have my sisters and I walk on his back to massage him and who, even into his late eighties, would meet us at the train station and insist on carrying all our luggage by himself to a waiting taxi.

The apple of Thatha's eye, Amma, was a precocious student who was already working on a teaching degree by the age of nineteen, a sensitive artist who made watercolors of the surrounding villages, and a natural-born athlete who would spend languorous afternoons playing netball and riding her bicycle with friends. She was a curious, deeply intelligent young woman, and surely marriage was the furthest thing from her mind when suddenly it was being proposed to her. Not by my father, but rather by her own, and "proposed" is probably the wrong word, too, since that verb implies choice.

Like many other TamBrahms, my parents never flirted or dated, never enjoyed a friendship or the slow blooming of a romance, never got together nor broke up, never had premarital sex. Appa had already been in America for a few years and was nearly thirty when his own father thought the time was right for him to be married. Traveling through Kerala to check on some of the rice fields his family owned, my paternal grandfather stopped in Coimbatore on his way back home to see about a potential match. To be fair, it was Appa's younger sister he had in mind, as finding a suitable union for a girl of marriageable age was always more complicated than finding a bride for a man, and he arrived at Thatha's house to inquire about Amma's older brother, my uncle Hari.

The two patriarchs of the family shared a cup of chai before dispensing with the small talk and heading to the town's local Vedic astrologer, a wizened old lady who could read omens from palms and fates from tea leaves. She sat at a table with the two men and consulted her Vedic star charts, trying to pair up my aunt's and uncle's *nakshatras* (which are like zodiacal signs but more specific and ancient, being derived from the Rig Veda nearly five thousand years ago). Vedic astrology is an oracular language of divination, an esoteric reading of cryptograms that are said to contain complex coded messages about each human soul. Matching my paternal aunt and maternal uncle together, the astrologer proclaimed that a marriage between the two would result in absolute disaster.

But ever-intrepid Thatha could not be so easily dissuaded; was he really going to let this eminent Brahmin gentleman from Madras walk away without a betrothal? Certainly not when he himself still had another daughter of marriageable age! So he insisted that they stay to try all the other possible permutations of their children, until *nalla atirṣṭam*! Good fortune! Amma and Appa were discovered to be a suitable match.

So it was written in the stars, and a handshake between the two men sealed the deal. When Thatha returned with the news that Amma was the one ordained to marry, her older brother, who surely by his notion of propriety should have been the one to marry first, stamped his feet in disbelief. Amma, unprepared for this news, was no happier. She ran barefoot from the cement house and climbed the highest branch of the tallest banyan tree in the yard. There she straddled a limb, sobbing. She couldn't fathom the prospect of leaving behind her parents, her siblings, her friends, and the wide riverbanks and the tropical heat to travel across the world to live with a man whom she didn't know in a place where it . . . snowed? It was unfathomable.

In the end, though, she had been raised to be the perfect daughter and would never do anything to displease her father. She had been raised to obey. And yet, when she met her groom-to-be for the first time, she refused to lengthen her hair with extensions or powder her skin to appear lighter. If he couldn't accept her as she was, she would have none of it. Thankfully—and perhaps regrettably, given that her very devotion to her beloved father would be the event that would remove her from his presence for decades at a time—she was nineteen years old and gorgeous. Chaperoned by relatives, my parents met briefly and then quickly departed into their separate lives with the promise of their future nuptials hanging in the air like an omen. If they had been closer in age, would Appa still have felt like he had to keep his own inner life private from her and from all his children, demanding we never question him due to the dictates of his seniority and innate maleness? I sometimes wonder who Amma would be today if she had said no and married someone of her own choosing. Who I would be.

But they married each other.

Who knows what shy words they might have spoken in private for the first time? How large their early misgivings might have been? What their first nervous moments of intimacy were like? For when Amma tells us this story, it is often meant more as a rebuke for our stubborn willfulness than to bemoan her own fate. Her very life was proof of how much she had loved her own father and how she could scarcely have imagined challenging him. If she had been as disobedient as I and my two younger sisters sometimes were, she would never have been blessed with us three children.

"God works in mysterious ways," she would say. If her voice quavered even the slightest bit for everything she had sacrificed, her future and ambitions, her free will, the shape of the life she might have led had she not been so suddenly uprooted, we could detect little of it as children.

There's one photograph from their wedding ceremony that I particularly treasure: the two of them seated next to each other on an *oonjal*, an enormous swing. Appa, the *mappillai* or groom, looks dashing in his suit, tie, and waxed pencil mustache, with an abundant garland of jasmine flowers around his shoulders. Amma, the bride, a lovely *manamahal* in a gilded sari with a nose ring and kohl-lined eyes, emanates both warmth and fierceness. If she was afraid, her eyes don't show it. After Appa tied the *mangala sutra*, an auspicious necklace strung with black beads on a thread yellowed with turmeric, around her neck, and after they had done the *saptapadi*, taking seven steps around the sacred flame, they were officially married. Appa left the next morning to return to America, with Amma following him there nearly six months later.

I've often imagined that journey, a near teenager leaving everything and everybody she ever knew behind, to travel with her griddle and her *anjarai petti* (literally a "five-room box," a set of round tins in which cooking spices could be stored) and her dowry of jewelry bundled in a parcel of handloom cloth. This was stuffed into a well-worn traveling bag, a hand-me-down from Thatha, who had also given her a crisp fifty-dollar bill to help her on her way. What ordinary courage it must have taken to traverse thousands of miles in a plane to live with this stranger, her new husband, in a foreign country. And yes, her fears were confirmed: she landed in a snowstorm.

Appa was stuck in traffic, the roads to and from the airport ground to a standstill. When Amma would eventually deplane, there was no one there to greet her! Alone, cold, and terrified, she burst into tears by the baggage carousel and was consoled by a kindhearted Swedish Pan Am stewardess who sat holding her hand while Appa inched along in bumper-to-bumper traffic on the beltway in his rusty orange Dodge Dart, the chariot for his new bride.

Their fated arrangement is why I—an ABCD, or American-Born Confused Desi, as those in India like to mock us—am here: because Amma joined Appa in my uncle's basement. She traded her *salwar kameez* for a pantsuit so she could work packing turntable stereo parts in a factory while Appa finished his degree in mechanical engineering while also working as a part-time security guard in some of the least desirable neighborhoods in Washington, DC. They saved up and sent money back to India. Eventually, they would return home, bringing their children back to the source.

While he was finishing up at Howard, Appa's own father had to take an extended leave of absence from the concrete factory at which he worked as an accountant because of health concerns (perhaps related to breathing in so much dust). This happened to coincide with Appa's three younger sisters approaching marriageable age, so he decided to stay in America to get a job. Appa and Amma would send back more than half of their paychecks each month to help provide the dowry for my aunts to be married, which they eventually all were, thanks to my parents' sacrifice.

While still going to school at Howard University in DC, Appa got a job as an apprentice mechanical engineer at Washington Gas, a natural gas company. My parents eventually left my uncle's house in Maryland to move into a town-house in Lorton, Virginia, and they traded in the Dodge Dart for a Plymouth Cricket. They saved and scrimped, for once I came along, Amma was forbidden from working any longer—the traditional Indian woman's role being in the house while the husband provided. Otherwise, what on earth would the relatives think? This refrain—*what would they think?*—would echo in our ears growing up.

By the time my middle sister, Rajni, was born, we had moved to a single-family home in Dale City, Virginia. When Rahini, my youngest sister, came into the world seven years later, I was sprinting home from my friend Dave Evans's house to a colonial three-bedroom, whose model we had picked out ourselves, in a suburban neighborhood in Manassas. I have vivid memories of cradling my new-born sister in this house, where my parents still live, and which I had watched being built from the ground up. We had literally seen its foundations being poured and its fixtures installed, each week our family getting materially closer to this tangible embodiment of the American dream, evidence that if you worked hard, saved enough, and lived within your means, anything was possible.

Anything, that is, except being able to assimilate. From a very early age, I sensed the differences between me and the other kids around me. I spoke Tamil at home, an ancient language that held no currency in daycare or preschool. Once when offered some celery and peanut butter by a freckled girl in pigtails, I said "*roomba nandri*" instead of "thank you" and was certain I would shrivel from humiliation on the spot. Sometimes, when we went out to eat, Amma would wear her resplendent sari, and I'd hear the mutters of the diners who would gawk at us and then look away.

I learned a lesson back then, one that I have been trying to unlearn ever since, of how to compartmentalize my identity in order to survive. Adopt an Indian perspective at home and an American one outside. I've since met other immigrants who tell me this is a very natural thing to do—learning to camouflage, to attempt to perfect a social face, playing one role in front of the boss, one in front of the wife, and one in front of the mistress. Tamilian culture is frequently repressive (most movies still won't show kissing, and the sale of alcohol is heavily regulated in Tamil Nadu), but human nature is not, so one way to bridge this divide is to wear masks one can slip on and off. But what lurks underneath all those masks?

Sometimes when Appa worked late, I would accompany Amma to pick him up. In the dimly lit alcoves of Washington Gas, plotting degree days and derivatives on large charts of paper, he watched his coworkers be promoted while he stayed in the same menial position. As a ten-year-old, I had been fascinated by the place he worked: his office with its bins of gears and wires, hazard-orange warning signs, and tomb-sized butane canisters; the machine shop with soldering irons and welding masks scattered on long tables. Occasionally I would glimpse a vestige of Appa's 1960s self, finding it in a college textbook about fluid mechanics or polymers and composites, or some ribald cartoon strip he had cut out years earlier, or a photograph in which he looks like he could have stepped from the doors of a booming disco.

I would peer into his drawers when he was not looking, trying to find out something about this man—my father—whom I only knew at arm's length. He was someone I loved and respected (mainly because of filial "duty," that other ubiquitous Tamilian catchword). But he was also someone whom I feared a little, and who caused me a lot of embarrassment.

It's something of a racist cliché with Indians that they are cheap and a little sneaky, and yet Appa is unabashed in embodying those characteristics. His thriftiness is legendary in our family: how he will reuse his razors until they are dull as an old penny, how he carries in his head a running catalog of where the cheapest gas prices and gallons of milk are within a twenty-mile radius, how he leaves his used paper towels out on the windowsill to dry and reuse. When we went on family holidays, we often had to sit through pitches for time-shares we would never buy. We'd never go out to a restaurant unless we had a coupon, and once there, Appa would bemoan the prices and fill his Siberian winter cap with mints and ketchup packets to squirrel away later in our kitchen pantry. He would encourage us to ask for juice when we went to someone's house so that we might gain the most nutritional and monetary value from what we had consumed. Even as a child, I could sense the vulgarity of this greed, this grasping.

And yet he was always there for my sisters and me when we were growing up, bringing home brainteasers for us to solve and coaching our sports teams. He was never drunk or negligent, never a deadbeat dad, and often full of surprises. Sometimes, unbelievably to us, he would morph into "Sam the Super," a weekend entertainer and amateur magician. I was enlisted to assist him as "Magic Junior," his assistant whom he'd dress in a baby-blue mini tux and a turban with a garish fake ruby at the top. He would be hired to work at someone's birthday party or bar mitzvah, transforming onstage from the stern, disapproving K. H. Shankar to a loquacious impresario who conjured playing cards from thin air and long rolls of colored tissue paper from his mouth. But as bubbly as he was onstage, when the curtain closed, he would revert back to a grimace and fill the air with admonishments, leaving us perplexed at his transformation. Sam the Super, international man of mystery.

Amma's nature, on the other hand, has always been warm, effusive, kind-hearted, generous, sociable, and dedicated—first and foremost—to family. She still sends us handwritten cards for our birthdays and, when I visit, makes *ras malai*, the Indian sweet made from milk and sugar that I love so much. She prays for and advises us when we go through difficult times and helps take care of her own family living in India, as well as the young children in the neighborhood who need looking after. She's well liked by everyone and has always been the person to whom I turn when I want to brag or need to cry. Embarrassingly, she will still sometimes call me her runaway bunny, like the wayward main character of the book she would read to me at bedtime as a child. Julie, my partner, sometimes teases me for being not just a rebel but an unreformed mama's boy.

Growing up, I experienced firsthand how difficult living in America was for my family, though I was myopic enough only to worry about how it impacted me. On more than a handful of occasions, we were treated as unworthy, as less than. Once, in a Denny's, we waited for over an hour for a table, only to see families who arrived after us being seated time and time again. Another time, arguing over a repair bill, Appa was called a "dirty towel head" by a mechanic even though he isn't Sikh (and isn't unhygienic). On our way to Disney World, we stayed at a hotel where a waitress refused to put the bill on our room tab but instead demanded cash for our meal. Back then, I would be deathly embarrassed as Appa would yell for the manager, turning apoplectic, while Amma whispered furiously in Tamil, trying to get him to calm down. I was petrified when he'd leave a dime tip or complain about his meal so that he could get it for free. I was never sympathetic at the time, wishing myself as far from the scene as possible.

What is it like to be packed off to boarding school? To marry someone you had only met once before? To leave behind everything familiar, never to feel independent but always duty-bound to fulfill some familial obligation? To live in reflexive fear of what others might think? I'm still amazed at the grace and tolerance Amma and Appa show when, even today, though they've lived in the United States for nearly half a century, strangers will slacken their speech and raise their volume when they speak to them as if they must be hard of hearing. It churns my insides to think of how they are still treated, and yet one of their happiest and proudest moments was when they passed the examination to become bona fide American citizens.

And me? Born in Washington, DC—a full-blooded American citizen—yet, no matter how hard I tried as a child, I was never American enough. I grew so sensitive to how my backpack would soak up the smell of jaggery, turmeric, *methi* seeds, and green chili simmering on the stove that I would hide it in the garage. I refused to take the delicious *sambar* and dal my mother prepared for lunch, preferring to order cardboard-tasting pizza and milk cartons from the school cafeteria. I spoke Tamil at home but acted as if I didn't understand the language when I was at the mall with my parents. That's how the lines of conformity fishhook in a child. Even elementary school students are awakened to how those who are distinctive get singled out and bullied. And yet I was always marked as both special and different, from only attending kindergarten for a month before being skipped ahead to the next grade, to being required to do multiplication tables after finishing my homework while my friends might be playing Atari or ping pong in someone's basement.

I might not have had a card-carrying tiger mom, but I was raised on a regimented schedule of discipline and the pursuit of unfettered achievement. Amma and Appa made me enter every variety of essay, oratorical, and poster contest known to man. Confirming yet another stereotype about Indians, I was the region's representative at the state spelling bee. Although I was likely tone-deaf, I also powered through years of piano lessons, banging out halting renditions of "Itsy Bitsy Spider" and "Yankee Doodle," all while imagining friends having epic action figure battles and water-balloon wars without me.

Once, in fifth grade, I even won the grand prize in an essay contest for the United Daughters of the Confederacy. I can still picture the open jaws of the seniors in their bustles, corded petticoats, and hoop skirts when the little Indian American boy who had won the annual essay contest stood on stage extolling the military tactics of General Stonewall Jackson. It wasn't all bad, of course— I won a ten-speed bike, a trip to Florida, and a ride on an elephant under the big top tent of a circus—and yet each of these accomplishments made me feel even more at odds with everyone around me.

I was that species of reluctant overachiever, never proud of excelling, keeping secret the contests I was forced to enter, never telling my friends in school how much I had actually enjoyed entering a living chess tournament or solving for the variable x in a math competition.

My inner self may have been some subspecies of nerd, but my external motivation was the pursuit of utter coolness. As a result, each surge of pride was accompanied by a concomitant blast of humiliation.

To compensate, I took risks. I got suspended from the school bus for a week for throwing a paper airplane that somehow got lodged in the back of the bus driver's twisted bun. I played Dungeons & Dragons in the back of the class when I should have been working on my civics project. I played practical jokes and took dares that no one else would, distancing myself from the dutiful son who would spend the next weekend driving with his parents in a station wagon to the Sri Venkateswara Temple in Pittsburgh to sing Sanskrit *bhajans*.

Like a tangerine, my own life was divided into segments that I tried to keep apart, though they were connected by the pith. From an early age, I learned the virtues of secrecy: how, if practiced enough, they could become a handy skill set. I wasn't about to jeopardize my hard-won social integration by revealing any bits of self that didn't fit the narrative I was so meticulously constructing. Yet that strategy, which seemed so shrewd back then, began in time to erode my sense of having any sort of fixed identity at all, rendering me restless and irresolute. Mostly, I just longed to belong.

ꟻ

Seated cross-legged on a stone floor in the sandalwood and armpit-scented air, alone in a Hindu temple a continent away from Connecticut and my immediate family, decades away from being this little boy so desperate to fit in, I've somehow managed to make Appa's worst nightmares come true. On top of publicly humiliating myself, I have broken up my family, and any sustained sense of community has eluded me. I've been outcast. If genuine connections are born from small acts of trust, I've been disconnecting, and I need to figure out why.

I try to cleanse the Connecticut headlines—"Poetry Professor Resigns after String of Arrests," "Time to Throw the Book at Professor Shankar"—from my mind. Had I grown up in India, in the light of this ancient and divergent culture, how different might my life have been? Poorer certainly, but also perhaps less notorious and more certain of myself? Or perhaps sneakier, more craven, sunk even further into a morass of materialism? One breath closer to enlightenment, one day nearer betrayal? Would I even have become a writer? Would I have felt more or less at home in my own bones, living closer to my biological family, to the caste system, to the teeming poverty, the ancient customs, to the insular and prejudiced nationalism of the Hindutva instead of that of American patriotism? In the end, my parents' own struggle to gain a foothold in America had come at a considerable expense, and I had, wittingly and unwittingly, undone their many sacrifices to give their children a better life.

I had truly fucked up.

I sit with the heavy shame of my circumstances, breathing it in and out. My coping strategy of hiding and exaggerating, developed as a cunning defensive mechanism over many years, feels so flimsy out here. The only one I've really tricked is myself. I fear I will never be one of those people whose position in the world is certain. They will always know exactly where and to whom they belong, whereas I have never been quite sure.

Ungal sondha oor edhu? Sorry, I don't know where I'm from.

Via Manhattan *via* Manassas *via* Madras. Through marriage and its dissolution, forever now the father of two extraordinary daughters. A son to my parents' pathologies, even as I gravitated to Amma, who treated me like a little maharaja growing up. I was the divine firstborn, raised to believe affection didn't have to be earned but existed as one's manifest birthright. She looks the other way when those she loves do things they should not have done. She does it out of love. Still, there needs to be a moratorium on blaming our parents. Amma is not wholly benign, nor Appa entirely inflexible, and I am endowed with free will.

Under ancient vaults of immense wealth and Lord Vishnu's gaze, I sit with my fear that the moment will end, that this will be the last time I see my ammamma alive, that I will never be redeemed, that I will lose all that I love, that I will never fit in, that I will not be able to keep my daughters safe, that I am a failure. All the anxiety bubbles up inside me when suddenly, from somewhere inside the inner sanctum of a temple, someone strikes a bronze bowl. The vibrations lap against the cliff's edge of my thoughts until all that exists is pure sound. How odd yet perfectly apt that Tibetan sound is in this Hindu context.

I draw in my breath. Slowly. Reverently. Making it the central fulcrum on which the calmly ongoing earth turns with all of us here on it. I'm here now, fully present, neither tumbling into regret nor rushing toward an unknown future: just sitting with myself. This time when I exhale, the heavy fear lifts, and a new lightness overtakes my body. I greet descriptions of transcendence with skepticism myself, so all I can say is what it feels like in this moment. My separateness ends, leaving me floating above myself, looking down to see my life as a few simple stitches, unfinished yet woven into the fabric of a vast and growing tapestry more marvelous and disturbing, unexpected and benevolent, weirder and beautiful than I might ever dare to imagine. I am there, you are there, and everyone we know is there, the dead and the living and the unborn, all of us woven together in this endlessly unfurling living quilt of time and space.

All of it is home.

Chapter Two

Central Booking

I've called a lot of places "home" over the years—Charlottesville, Madras, Paris, San Francisco, New York City, Sydney—but it was because of my ex-wife that I moved to Connecticut. She doesn't want to be written about, and she is the mother of my children, so I will largely acquiesce. I'll only mention that she is American, of German and Irish stock, the yang to my yin, a good woman who has always been firmly grounded, while I surveyed the shapes and sometimes escaped into the topography of clouds. Because she is also a brunette and said by some to look like the actress Mary-Louise Parker, I'll call her by that surname in this story.

We started out as friends and perhaps should have stayed that way, given how unprepared I was to be in a relationship and how much baggage I carried from my own South Asian family. Still, we moved in together after college, much to the consternation of Amma and Appa, and forged our early adulthood together in New York until it was clear we needed to leave the city. Although it was not the direct reason we left, 9/11 changed our lives for good. I was laid off from my job at a literary agency, and for the first time in decades, I became acutely aware of what being South Asian might mean in modern-day America. As if being stereotyped as a Slurpee salesman or computer programmer wasn't bad enough, now suddenly I was being lumped in with jihadists. I sometimes stayed up at night wondering how it might warp someone's mind to be constantly evaluated as a potential threat.

Soon after the terror attacks, Parker got a job at a liberal arts university along the Connecticut shoreline. It seemed the perfect time to transition to a place where we might afford a house and start a family. However, this meant turning my back on one of the very few places I had ever truly felt at home. I had grown hardened in time but had also been completely remade by the city. Arriving a timid graduate student in 1997, by the time I left in 2002, I knew where to get the best bagels and how to avoid the NR subway line (the Never and Rarely), and had seen everything from the gothic revival ruins of the Renwick smallpox hospital on Roosevelt Island to the bowling alley underneath the Henry Clay Frick museum. I was shattered to be leaving Manhattan and going to a place nicknamed the Nutmeg State.

We first moved to Groton, on the eastern shoreline. Unemployed, I slept in and spent my late mornings skulking around the perimeter of the General Dynamics Electric Boat construction facility, which had been assembling submarine hulls since the 1970s. While Parker worked at a college library, I collected unemployment and ate soggy oversauced penne at Paul's Pasta. I watched the masts of boats clack in the pier. I fed seagulls and drafted poems at the local pub, which I soon realized played almost exclusively country music and was frequented by guys sporting mullets and Boston Bruins caps and drinking tallboys and talking about *mahm's baked cahd* and *wicked lobstah fishing*. Swamp Yankees. It was pure culture shock to move from a Brooklyn walkup where I could eat sushi or bibimbap past midnight, and where the steel drums of the West Indian Day parade would reverberate the floorboards at least once a year, to this place with a submarine base, a town green, and a rash of northern rednecks.

I had never imagined that the East Coast was that provincial, but hearing the Sam Adams clinking in appreciation when "She Thinks My Tractor's Sexy" roared on the jukebox told me all I needed to know. During one of my first weeks in town, I sat nursing a pale ale at the bar when the door opened and a tall, handsome Black man with bronzed crocodile-skin loafers and diamond stud earrings strode in. I had never seen him before, but since everyone was staring at him, from the half-cocked kids playing pool to the whiskered man spitting chaw into an empty pint glass, I stared too. He surveyed the bar and saw me hunched over half a beer and a spiral notebook. Without saying a word, he walked over with a widely spreading grin and, before I could even react, had me locked tight in a bear hug.

"Hey, brother." His breath was minty fresh in my ear. "Welcome to Connecticut."

That was it, and I never saw him again.

Welcome to Connecticut.

Two hours from New York City, and where the hell was I?

Neither the backwater nor "by the banks of the long river" either, as the Algonquin Indian meaning of the state name once conveyed. There was nothing of the customs or memories of the indigenous people readily available in Connecticut, where the oldest things in many towns were statues of Puritan tosspots like John Mason and John Winthrop, or the seventeenth-century thatch-roofed post-and-beam homesteads of families such as the Wheelers and the Bushnells. Instead of birchbark canoes on the rivers, Volvos and Subaru Foresters clogged the roads.

Eventually, we left Groton and moved to Chester, a small, quintessentially New England village on the banks of the Connecticut River. The population there was friendlier and more well intentioned, but still as insistently White. Life had blessed me once again since, after interviewing for a job as an adjunct teacher of composition at Central Connecticut State University, I was informed that the resident poet, Richard Blanco (who would go on to become Obama's inaugural poet), had suddenly resigned. This left a tenure-track opening teaching creative writing. Without even my first book in hand, I was hired as an emergency appointment to take his place and I secured tenure before the age of thirty.

After our years together eking out the rent in New York City, Parker and I were finally able to buy a home together in Connecticut. Like Shakespeare's Cordelia, unhappy that I am, I cannot heave my heart into my mouth to talk about the love that once existed between the two of us. I only know that we shared more kinship than romance and that I wish I could have loved her better. I also know that in those early days, as we settled in town, and as our first daughter was born, I was truly contented, a reality that only appears clear in retrospect.

I was lecturing on sonnets and watching enraptured as my little girl unfurled like the rarest orchid imaginable. So what if I was pulled out of line almost every single time I flew out of Bradley International Airport in Hartford or asked to justify Pakistan's harboring of terrorists by a shopkeeper in New Haven? Those were anomalies and exceptions, bound to happen to lots of people in such charged times, right? The cost of being a Brown man in a democracy. I was just doing my part to keep us all safe. Besides, I was an immigrant success story, an Ivy League–educated, first-generation Indian American who had landed a tenured job teaching writing. Plus, I could always skulk back to the glorious teeming city when I needed my fix of culture and diversity.

The irony, then, is not lost on me that it was during a trip to New York City that I had one of the scariest and most racially charged encounters of my life. It was during the summer of 2008, after a launch party for the magazine I had founded, *Drunken Boat*, in an art gallery downtown. Parker had long ago eschewed attending most literary events with me, finding most writers, yours truly included and probably most indicatively, pompous and self-involved. Therefore, I drove to the city alone, promising my cousin, who lived in New Jersey, a ride home afterward.

Buoyed by good cheer, crème fraîche, and sautéed poblano peppers, the kind of Mexican food impossible to get in Connecticut, I departed the city with my cousin and took a completely legal left turn on green from Thirty-Fourth Street onto Sixth Avenue, when I saw a telltale burst of red and blue lights behind me. Confused, I slowed to a stop, and when the officer approached my car, he held a blinding high-intensity flashlight. There are those traumatic memories that the brain will try to repress, and there are those that one can relive minutely in such vivid detail that it feels like it is all happening again right here, in this very moment, and that it will continue to happen like this, not just then and now, but forever. This experience with the NYPD is one of the latter.

❡

"Is there a problem, Officer?"

My voice strains with politeness, the tone I might use if I were a sommelier recommending a pinot grigio to a patron at a high-end restaurant. It is a well-practiced voice, one intended to dampen confrontation. Until that encounter, it never occurred to me how deeply problematic it is that some of us must scrutinize our tone and gestures for fear of repercussion when it comes to dealing with authority.

"License and registration. Now!" The cop, Officer Murphy, whose name, badge number, and visage are forever branded into my mind, dispenses with the pleasantries and takes a cursory glance at my identification. I try to press my university ID card into his hand as well.

"What the fuck is this? Your lawyer?"

"No, Officer." I falter, trying to compose myself. My cousin looks on from the passenger's side. "It's where I work. I'm a professor in Connecticut, sir, and I'm just trying to get home to my family."

"Care where you work?" Murphy grumbles. "Out boozing, were we?"

I shake my head no, but he orders me out of the car to perform a field sobriety test. I touch my nose with my pinky, balance on one foot and then the other, then walk the length of the sidewalk heel to toe. During this time, three other police cruisers pull up behind us. New York City, even at this hour, a little before midnight, strums with vibrancy, the air electric with nights out just beginning for some and ending for others. I could see crowds of people out of the corner of my eye, some glancing at us with mild interest, but most oblivious, heading steadfastly to their destination. I go through the paces in the shadow of Herald Square, where the bronze hands of the clock holding Minerva, the Roman goddess of wisdom and warfare, turn too slowly for an eye to follow.

"Look pretty steady on your feet, but I got one more test for you." Murphy looks slightly bemused, the corner of his mouth wrinkling into a jagged smirk. "The Breathalyzer!"

The whole exchange has begun to irritate me now, but because this is not my first dance, I'm careful not to reveal any displeasure. Still, my inner core burns hot. All his findings will be invalidated or buttressed by the final test—the one that could have been administered from the beginning to save us from our mutual entertainment on the sidewalks of Manhattan. Though I had drunk two margaritas three hours ago and had been sipping water ever since, the weasels of fear nonetheless begin to gnaw away at the back of my brain. How many drinks does it take to tint the blood past the wrong threshold?

"Do I have a choice? Can I call someone?"

"Yeah, you got a choice. Either blow, or we haul you down to the station."

I close my eyes and blow.

What happens after that is in some respects a blur, and in other respects etched with a chisel onto the tablet of my mind. Murphy has retreated to the cruisers behind us, and I can see him conferring with one of his partners. A police van has pulled up behind the cruisers. Murphy returns to me with a grin he can barely hide.

"Good news, Professor," he says, holding out his hand as if to congratulate me, "you passed the Breathalyzer." He skips an extra beat like a comic onstage. "But there's bad news too." The hand that has been extended reaches suddenly for my wrist, twisting it sharply behind my back. "There's a warrant out for your arrest." Murphy mashes my cheek against the metal grate of the storefront in front of us, before slapping cold handcuffs on me.

"What are you talking about? What did I do? Please!"

My head spins with stars of puzzlement. But my protests land on deaf ears as the gears have been sprung into motion and more officers approach. One barks at me to "stay quiet and walk." Another blue uniform marches me past the cruisers to the police van, palming my head like a basketball to shove me into the back. Yet another is on his walkie-talkie, buzzing with voices in the static. Murphy, an Irishman with a squat face, someone whose own family might have immigrated to America during the Great Famine, can't unblink the mixture of joy and disdain from his eyes. His is the face I can call up on demand whenever I want to curdle my blood and smash something.

"Well," he says, turning to his partner, hocking a stringy loogie out onto the asphalt. "It's always a good day when you can bag a sand nigger!" Those are the last words I would hear before the van doors clapped shut. The last time, besides in my dreams, that I would ever see Officer Murphy again.

¶

According to Daniel Bergner in *The Atlantic*, between 2004 and June 2012, 83 percent of the NYPD's stop-and-frisk policy targeted Blacks or Hispanics. Under

Mayor Bloomberg, those numbers increased exponentially. In 2011, the police recorded 686,000 stops, out of which only about 12 percent ended in arrest or summons. Donna Lieberman, the head of the New York Civil Liberties Union, estimated that between 2002 and 2013, "innocent people were subjected to this by-no-means-minor intrusion more than 4.4 million times." You do the math. My larger question is: what does being stigmatized as a criminal do to someone who is innocent? I can only speak my own answer, but I can't help but wonder how, in the twenty-first century, this level of blatant racism still occurs in plain sight and what effect it might have on our collective health.

Stop-and-frisk is not just bigoted; it is sloppy police work. In 1999, after the shooting of the unarmed Amadou Diallo, the New York State Attorney General's office released a statistical analysis of the reported number of stops perpetuated by the infamous NYPD Street Crime Unit, which was disbanded in 2002. The study showed that the SCU stopped sixteen African Americans for every arrest made. In 2003, the city settled a class action lawsuit for unlawful racial profiling practices in relation to these stops. Furthermore, in 2017, the city settled another class action lawsuit after the NYPD had been disproportionately targeting ethnic minority communities with unjustified criminal summonses. If it were the NYPD being arraigned, it might be subject to the penalty enhancement of being a persistent offender.

But the larger calculus has more to do with the question of what it does to a statistically significant portion of the American population to be judged as criminal a priori, before a member of this population has even done one damn thing, and what effect that might have on larger sociopolitical, interpersonal, and economic conditions. Michelle Alexander lays out the facts in her book *The New Jim Crow: Mass Incarceration in the Age of Colorblindness,* and some of what she reveals should have had us out on the street protesting long ago.

The United States has 5 percent of the world's population but nearly 25 percent of the world's prisoners, more than China, Iran, Russia, and North Korea. There are more Black men in prison, on probation, or on parole than there were slaves during the Civil War. From the 1970s to now, there has been an exponential increase in the prison population—much of this explosion due to drug arrests, a figure disproportionately skewed toward African Americans and Hispanic Americans. According to the Sentencing Project report on racial disparities in the US criminal justice system, which was presented to the United Nations in 2013, "one of every three black American males born today can expect to go to prison in his lifetime."

That's the living, breathing legacy of the civil rights movement? One in three?

As James Baldwin put it in a radio conversation with Studs Terkel in 1961, "all you are ever told in this country about being black is that it is a terrible, terrible thing to be. Now, in order to survive this, you have to really dig down into yourself and re-create yourself, really, according to no image which yet exists in America. You have to impose, in fact—this may sound very strange—you have to decide who you are, and force the world to deal with you, not with its idea of you." How few of us are blessed with Baldwin's wisdom. I'm not. Far from it. In fact, it's become clear to me over time that my own reactions, both conscious and impulsive, have been largely foolish and ill-advised. Yet I can no longer pretend that I am not complicit in the prison-industrial complex, having benefited from its institutional racism for many more decades than I would come to suffer its punishments.

How did America, land of the free, become the world's leader in incarceration, and how did jails become so racialized? Early Puritan society banished criminals into the wilderness and meted out sanguinary punishments as public spectacles, where the brandings, maiming, whippings, and executions were meant to be witnessed by the community as deterrents to aberrant behavior. There was no distinction between what was considered criminal and what was deemed sinful, and the law conflated the division between church and state, considering all acts of deviance the work of the devil. It was not until the Quaker Reformers of the early nineteenth century, the political left wing of their time, that jails began to proliferate as a more civilized alternative to the barbarism of an earlier time. The Quakers thought that criminals could be redeemed and transformed through penance, religion, and labor. That early zeal for shaming and punishment never left the scene but became institutionalized in these isolated, secret, surveilled spaces that the public could not access.

Enter the Civil War, Abraham Lincoln's Emancipation Proclamation, and the Thirteenth Amendment to the US Constitution, which, as documentary filmmaker Ava Duvernay argues, contains within its very language of liberation a justification for the continued inequality to come: "Neither slavery nor involuntary servitude, *except as a punishment for crime whereof the party shall have been duly convicted,* shall exist within the United States, or any place subject to their jurisdiction" (emphasis mine). That's the ultimate get-out clause, a way for the disgruntled former plantation owners in America's Deep South to supplement the abolished institution of slavery with another that would replace the lost free labor. Each convict represented for the state a chance to make money, and so the convict lease system was born, an easy way to help rebuild a war-ravaged economy. Freed slaves could be criminalized under the "black codes," ambiguous vagrancy or apprentice laws, where out-of-work men could be arrested, and where Blacks needed to obtain a license from Whites to practice their trade, or else face a fine. The inability to pay this fine would conscript them again into servitude and allow their bodies to be loaned out to other states to work. These practices disenfranchised and denied African Americans equal protection under the law, restricted their movements, and prevented them from owning land or exercising their constitutional right to public education.

It's no coincidence, then, that the next explosion of the prison population came a century later, right on the heels of the civil rights movement. At the end of Jim Crow and segregation, what better way to reinscribe racist policies but to start a "war on drugs" that disproportionately affected populations of color. Just as the left-wing Quakers of their era exacerbated certain social problems, so too did the "liberal" Democrats of the 1990s. Bill Clinton's omnibus crime bill of 1994, signed into effect even as he was deregulating the financial industry, increased and further racialized the prison population by introducing such concepts as "super-predators," "mandatory minimums," "truth in sentencing," and the federal "three strikes" policy. This led to the growth of privatized prisons and the notorious 100-to-1 sentencing disparity between crack and cocaine users, all of which delivered up more bodies of color for, in the words of Angela Davis, "profitable punishment." Indeed, in Hillary Clinton's own words in her 1996 book, *It Takes a Village*, they had inmates, "African-American men in their thirties," work as unpaid servants in the governor's mansion in Arkansas in order to "keep down costs."

I'm not Black, even though there was little nuance or sophistication in Officer Murphy's appraisal and arrest of me that evening. For him, dark skin was dark skin. He didn't need much more than that to pull me over on the flimsiest of pretexts. But, as a matter of fact, as an Asian American, I am part of the most successful demographic group in America (though even that monolithic notion lumps together communities such as Cambodian, Laotian, Bangladeshi, Nepalese, and Burmese Americans, who fall well below the median household income of all Americans). Likewise, there's no question that the racialization and policing of our communities has been vastly different from that of African American communities. In the past, Asian immigrants have been excluded from gaining entry into the United States and becoming citizens. They have even lost their personal property and been sent to internment camps, as Japanese Americans were during World War II. But that's vastly different from the history of segregation, police brutality, and systematic discrimination that African Americans have endured for centuries.

Still, I don't need to be Black to parse the Supreme Court's decision in the 1968 case of *Terry v. Ohio*: "In justifying the particular intrusion, the police officer must be able to point to specific and articulable facts which, taken together with rational inferences from those facts, reasonably warrant that intrusion. . . . Good faith on the part of the arresting officer is not enough." Yet on the police reports made public about stop-and-frisk encounters, NYPD officers needed merely to check a box labeled "furtive movements," "suspicious bulge," or one implausibly labeled "other" to justify a frisking.

I'm not Black, but, after that traffic stop, I understood just a tiny bit better what it was like to be so in America.

ᛦ

The city glimpsed through the slats of an NYPD transportation van's scratch-resistant polycarbonate window barriers: cinematic, a partial view of streetlight streaks receding into the depthless distance, the stale air pulsing with trails and afterimages, every pothole and crevice irradiating through my spinal column and out toward my extremities where my hands are pinched, immobilized behind my back in handcuffs. Dazed with uncertainty. No clue where we are going.

Turns out it's Midtown South, Fourteenth Precinct. Shepherded through the door, I transmogrify into an object: a footstool or a hydrant. Ordered not to turn around, but I don't need to pivot to hear another kind of stereotype come alive, the station buzzing with the start of the night shift, cops bantering about the Mets and Russian chicks in Coney Island, giving each other slapstick undercuts, disregarding me completely. I'm led to a holding cell and uncuffed roughly. Told to remove my shoelaces and belt. No phone call. Still waiting to be Mirandized.

Sitting alone in a jail cell, time slows to a crawl. Officers come and go into the next cell. Even separated by a concrete wall, I can smell the man next to me dry-heaving, yelling out to no one in particular, "Why you hassling me on that open-container shit? You didn't nab those sorority girls drinking cosmos, but now you got to mess with me! Motherfucker, I know you all, lieutenant on down!"

Eventually, I am led out of the cell by a broad, freckled, wheat-haired officer who seems like he would have been more at home herding steer on an Iowa farm. He appears more tired and officious than the rest of the officers. He leads me to a room to photograph me, digitally fingerprint me one digit at a time, and take an inventory of my possessions.

"What am I in here for, please, Officer? I don't know what's going on. I still haven't got my phone call!"

"Calm down. You'll be out of here in no time. You Sobolewski, right?" He peers at a pile of manila folders in front of him.

"No, Shankar. Ravi Shankar."

"Shankar. Yes, got a warrant out for your arrest. Your license is suspended in the city."

"I haven't lived in the city in almost ten years! And when I lived here, I didn't drive a car!"

"It's right here."

He points to a printout on his desk but doesn't hand it to me. From where I'm sitting, it appears to be a citation for a White male weighing 150 pounds.

"Hey! That's not me! I'm two hundred pounds on a diet and never found a soap strong enough to turn me White. Can I please see that?"

"Sorry. Out of my hands now." He shuffles another folder on top of the pile. "Looks like you got an unpaid speeding ticket. Westchester County. About four years ago. After thirty days, you go into suspension in New York."

"But I wasn't in Westchester then. Listen, that's not me! Do I fit that description?" Incredulous agitation has crept into my voice.

"You'll see a judge in a couple of hours. Nothing more I can do."

"Yes, you can! You can let me go right now. We both know that's not me!"

"Tough luck." He sighs and points back toward the cell. "You can tell it to the judge."

Two more hours? This is when my sense of time spins away. Things happen in jolts of action: cuffed chain-gang fashion, one hand to a Hispanic gentleman wearing a Howard Stern T-shirt, the other to a Black man of indiscriminate age in a navy-blue windbreaker. He mutters to himself as if possessed by Tourette's syndrome. I realize it's the man who has been throwing up in the cell next to me.

We are marched past the front desk, where, this time, the officers take notice of us. Led by a portly, chipper, brunette sergeant with a bob cut and swirly fingernail polish, the night shift serenades us with "Here comes the bride" as we are herded toward the sally port where another larger van waits. The one woman our shared handcuff train has collected is shuttled to one side of the van. We are led toward the other, shuffling our feet in unison like an embodied creature, a centipede made of dark segments. By the time we finally arrive at 100 Centre Street, Central Booking, in the bowels under the financial district, it grows clear that some of the men I am with know the officers and the procedure intimately. Still handcuffed, they joke with the cops, try to cadge smokes, chat amicably with their neighbors. I stare straight ahead and harden my jaw. Another uniformed man has approached to address us.

"This is a house of order, gentlemen. Step out of line, your case won't go in front of a judge for another twenty-four. We'll just drop your folder to the bottom of the pile, and then it might take us every last minute of the seventy-two hours we legally have to hold you to process you. Understand?" He surveys us like an expectant teacher. "But do what you're told and you can get out of here more quickly. It's up to you. For example, you're about to talk to some EMT folks who will ask what's wrong with you. If it were me, I wouldn't say squat. You a little sore, a little strung out? Ride it out. You tell the docs there's something wrong with you, and we're keeping you here longer for observation. Guaranteed. But like I said, it's your choice."

Central Booking. A densely populated urban prison, occupied year-round while tourists and businessmen walk on the sidewalks above every day. As we are led shackled into a dimly lit corridor, I feel like a morsel of meat being chewed and digested. Through many gates and checkpoints, we sit and wait while the Black man in the windbreaker soliloquizes in incessant non sequiturs. "Antennae mean one thing. You must bring me my crumpet with Marmite. Don't flip the mattress for them bugs bite!"

It is around 3 a.m. on a Saturday morning. No one in the world, save my cousin, knows where I am. I hope my car has not been impounded. Would he call my wife? Or think there was no need to alarm her or my daughter in the middle of the night? What the hell was happening?

A ripe urine stench slaps us when we enter the cell, which is nearly empty. A few guys in hoodies lounge along the benches riveted onto the cement wall. An open public urinal stands in the corner, barely blocked from our view by a hinged sheet of metal. In front of us, through the bars, we can see a desk and a swivel chair, the upturned visage of an officer making phone calls.

As early morning lightens outside, more and more people pour into the cell. By seven in the morning, over thirty people are jammed into tight quarters. Some are sprawled on the floor using their shoes as pillows or stretched out along the coveted bench space. I have managed to get a berth and sit surveying the man sitting on the floor on a rag of daily papers. Another lies puddled in what must be his own vomit. Among the crowd, there are only two White guys: a Rutgers student who has blown a DUI, and a Polish bartender with a pierced chin and pupils large as manhole covers. The rest are Hispanic or Black: Mexican, Caribbean, Puerto Rican, or African, such as the big doe-eyed boy called Senegal. He has been busted for illegal vending by the Manhattan South Peddler Task Force, an NYPD unit, I would later learn, that was also responsible for the arrest of a SoHo artist selling pillow art and a Buddhist nun who hoped to swap prayer beads for donations to help rebuild her village's burned-down temple.

"Third time I've been busted for not having a peddler's license to sell CDs. But I can't get a license because the city's got a cap on vendors. There's a waitlist ten thousand people deep, or you can buy one for twenty large on the black market! I'm lucky to make that in a year, bruh!"

Senegal sits next to a large, boisterous Dominican who "reps" DDP (Dominicans Don't Play) and has been through the system before. He laughs uproariously at his own story of being busted cooking meth after banging his girlfriend's mother on the kitchen table. He had been found deep in her *toto* by the cops in front of a pile of striker plates, melting tablets of ephedrine, iodine, and whatever else was lying around. No way to bullshit his way out of that one. He speaks primarily to an angular friend with a blackened tooth who calls himself Ganso. Ganso wears a baseball cap bearing the Dominican flag slung low over his eyes, Jheri curls poking out from behind his ears. His face is a coiled jack-in-the-box with raccoon eyes that explode when he wants to punctuate a point. He looks around the cell, addressing no one in particular.

"So where you all from? How about you, my dude? You from Bangladesh, right?"

I realize with a start that I am the one being addressed. Many dark faces swivel toward me. I'm still in my collared dress shirt from the launch party.

"Me?" I hesitate. "My people are straight from the mothership: India." Inadvertently, I'm slipping into another persona, one whose dialect is street, verging on ghetto. It's my default survival skill to blend in and is not meant to be patronizing, though it probably is.

"Oh, I knew you was Indian. Didn't I tell you he was Indian?" Ganso looks over at DDP, then back at me. "I know you Indian guys like spicy curry, right? I tried Indian food once and it grew hair on my nuts, no joke. We like it spicy in the islands, but not like you guys. What you in here for anyway, India?"

"Driving under suspension. But it was bullshit. Warrant wasn't for me."

"Warrant wasn't for you?" His eyes go large. "You think the warrant was for any of us? Like you something special?"

"Didn't mean it like that. Just that it was for some White guy."

"Doesn't matter. If your skin darker than a grocery bag, you're screwed. It's a city sweep. A little game the precincts play in the five boroughs. First one to a hundred collars wins. Doesn't matter what you've done."

Ganso makes a motion like a fisherman throwing a large net into the water.

"You thought Giuliani was bad? Bloomberg is worse than ten of him! But who cares? These dumb rookies think they'll score a couple of extra stripes on their uniform by filling the jails with what? Shit that clogs up the courts. Please, son. Give me my peanut butter and jelly sandwich and get the fuck out of my way."

He pats DDP on the chest.

"I just saw a Chinese woman being hustled off the street for selling turtles. When I was a kid, we used to see them all over the place, big paint buckets full of them. You'd have to use chopsticks to grab one. I'd let mine go on the block, see it play Frogger with the cabs. Those were the days. Slurping Italian ices and buying turtles. Dancing by the hydrant."

"You could even get scorpions if you knew where to look." DDP flicks out his tongue like a cottonmouth. "Take out the stinger, dip it in barbecue sauce, and damn! Scorpion McNugget."

"That's what I'm saying," Ganso interjects philosophically. "If *viejas* like your grandma been smacked for selling turtles, then you know we done fucked it all up."

The morning creeps by fitfully, ten minutes of bad sleep giving way to conversations about Tupac's and Michael Jackson's fake deaths. Through dreams and fragmentary awareness, I drift, scrunched against a slab of cold concrete. On the other side of the cell, some new Mexicans have been thrown in, and one of them stands in waiter's pants, a red stain along the collar of his shirt, gesticulating to the Dominicans over on my side. He struts and makes out like he wants to whip it out, barking in loud, drunken Spanish.

"*Mi verga, grande y peluda! Mi pinga!*" He points to his crotch. "*Mi verga! Un cohete!*" He dances ever closer, suggestively. "*Pinche Dominicano! Usted no puede manejarla, ¿verdad?*"

"Julio César Chávez motherfucker!" another Mexican from the other side of the jail randomly yells.

"Joan Guzmán. You serious?" Ganso looks bewildered. "And you." He points at the drunk Mexican. "*Cago en tu leche!*"

The Mexican cat-and-mouses ever closer, gyrating his hips, miming like he is stroking himself off and about to unbutton his pants when—*boom!*—Ganso leaps up to uncork a fist into the side of the Mexican's head. After a dazed second, the Mexican answers back with a right cross. And then it is on.

The two of them stand in the center of the jail cell, slugging each other for what feels like hours, the inmates around them swelling in blood lust and fervor, shouting and cheering. This eventually brings a guard, who seems to stand with the rest of us to take in the spectacle before going to break up the fight. Other guards stream in, yelling and telling us to back up as they pull the Mexican off Ganso. The Mexican is bleeding from under his eye, and Ganso's ears are bright red.

"*Loco* fucking Mexican," DDP explains to the officers. "Isn't that right, y'all?" He looks around at us for confirmation. "He started it."

Two officers drag the Mexican off to an adjoining cell, leaving behind only a globular smear of blood where he had been getting pummeled only moments before. Ganso, hat slung low, accepts fist bumps as he slinks back to his seat.

I probably haven't seen a fight this close up since grade school, and the violence is shocking. My own heart bounces loudly in its aftermath. In the silence that has cocooned the jail cell, I miss my daughter. America's secret problems are spread out before me tonight, and somehow I've become one of them.

Time passes fitfully. I sleep minutes at a time until a new cop with a paunch and tired eyes addresses us on the day's protocol.

"OK, so here's the deal. There are fifty guys upstairs waiting to meet the public defender and be arraigned. We know you've been waiting, but they've been waiting longer. Depending on who's on the bench, we might start being called in after lunch recess, say around 2 p.m. If the judge is slow, we might get pushed into night court. You might not be called in the order you were arrested, but you should all be out of here by tonight."

"But we been in here like two, three weeks already, isn't that right?" Ganso nudges DDP. "Two minutes feels like two hours in here. Two days like two weeks. Two months like two years. That's why they say prison is like smoking dust. It keeps us young forever!"

"Fountain of fucking youth," DDP responds for the benefit of us all, "but you still look like you about eighty, Ganso." The cell erupts in laughter.

But soon, there is no more laughter, only the monotony of another meal of peanut butter or cheese and bologna sandwiches washed down with lukewarm skim milk. I trace the cross-hatching of the ceiling with my eyes—there is graffiti over the piss pot (*Mo' Blood, Mo' Sex, Mo' $$$*)—and watch the faint outline of day as it disappears in the corner of the window so high you can only see sky. Samuel Beckett floats up to me in shards. We wait. We are bored. In an instant, all will vanish, and we'll be alone once more, in the midst of nothingness. I pick my nails. Try to meditate. Pray to sleep. Worry. Strain my ear for the footsteps of anyone who might deliver us from captivity.

¶

For the first thirty-plus years of my life, I had little overt trouble with the law—but not for lack of effort. Like Sam Shankar, I had inherited a hustler's heart. In college, I was given the nickname "Fingers" by one of my fraternity brothers, ostensibly for the length of my E.T.-like digits, but really because, according to him, "the ladies love him and the cashiers fear him." Besides a few isolated periods of my life, however, my transgressions were fairly minor acts of civil disobedience foisted on the world by a wily philosophical anarchist, or so I thought. Shoplifting and trespassing: rolling a joint to smoke on a rooftop closed for construction or lifting a pack of gum for sheer dint of how easy it was to take.

There was no honor in it; stealing was stealing. But I realize now that I acted impulsively, not just for the thrill but to prop up my wobbly sense of self-esteem. I longed to create a private space separate from other people's perceptions of me in which I could hide, and I took pride in being someone who could outfox others. I reveled, condescendingly, in a sense of *You think I'm one thing, honey, but really I'm so many others, you wouldn't be able to keep count. No way am I going to fit into your little box.* When you disconnect yourself from yourself, there's no room for anyone else to do it to you. It becomes preemptive. You've shamed yourself.

But to be arrested when innocent?

Much of what I experienced that weekend, relatively mild as it was, echoed the testimony in the case against stop-and-frisk made by NYPD whistleblower Adhyl Polanco. In 2013, he testified in Manhattan federal court that in 2009 his supervisors in the Forty-First Precinct required monthly "productivity" quotas of twenty summonses and one arrest ("twenty and one") and five stop-and-frisks. Officers who failed to meet the quotas were penalized with reduced overtime and shift changes. Polanco also testified that police stop-and-frisks were recorded on forms known as UF-250s, or simply 250s, and that generating more of these was incentivized in the way a company might give bonuses for sales.

Nearly all of what I would hear as an unsubstantiated rumor from Ganso would slowly be proven true. Stories of city sweeps, quotas, and civil rights violations, evidence of racial discrimination, police violence, and harassment have since entered the public record, and they led Judge Shira A. Scheindlin to conclude in her opinion that "the stops, which soared in number over the last decade as crime continued to decline, demonstrated a widespread disregard for the Fourth Amendment, which protects against unreasonable searches and seizures by the government, as well as the 14th Amendment's equal protection clause." After all, even for constitutional literalists, the Fourth Amendment is pretty clear in its language that "the right of the people to be secure in their persons, houses, papers, and effects, against unreasonable searches and seizures, shall not be violated, and no warrants shall issue, but upon probable cause, supported by oath or affirmation, and particularly describing the place to be searched, and the persons or things to be seized."

Yet, rather than apologizing to the tens of thousands of innocent minorities this affects each year, Mayor Bloomberg's response to the decision was to claim that "this is a dangerous decision made by a judge who I think does not understand how policing works and what is compliant with the U.S. Constitution as determined by the Supreme Court. I worry for my kids, and I worry for your kids. I worry for you, and I worry for me. Crime can come back any time the criminals think they can get away with things. We just cannot let that happen."

Emily Bader skewered Bloomberg in *The Atlantic* much better than I can, so I leave it to her.

> There are an awful lot of offensive ideas packed in these five sentences. There is the gross fear-mongering ("I worry for your kids"). There is the unproven implication of cause-and-effect (without stop-and-frisk, crime will "come back"). There is the dangerous idea that a federal judge is not qualified to grasp "how policing works." There is the total disregard for the central fact that this case was never about the effectiveness of stop-and-frisk in the first place. Plenty of police tactics might keep your kids and Michael Bloomberg's kids safe on the streets of New York City, like random home weapon inspections or mass preventive detentions. But, inconveniently, those ideas are [not] constitutional.

¶

I'm glad Mayor Bloomberg was worried for my kids, but while I was sitting innocent in jail, my daughter didn't know where her father was, and another day had started to trickle by. If you had told me back then that I would eventually become even more intimate with the mechanisms of institutional control, I would have laughed in your face. Just being in Central Booking for a weekend was horrific enough, and my experiences pale in comparison to those of many of the men I met there. Unlike the Fourteenth Precinct, which had been populated almost exclusively with White officers, Central Booking was a UN General Assembly meeting. Cops of every gender and ethnicity passed by us, none of them willing to communicate anything directly. They say they're different from the cops who will call us to the judge, and they know no more about the inner mysteries of their protocol than about a witch's coven. "Don't ask us," they say.

Finally, 4 p.m. rolls around. Our door cracks, and we can see a clock leering above the guard's desk, the long hand a middle finger. The first three people from our cell are called. They high-five and stride out. Every two hours, another batch from our cells and the other cells around us are called. Ganso is called. The White boy with the DUI. The crazy soliloquist. And then suddenly it is 10 p.m. I'm still in the cell. So is DDP, and an articulate Jamaican bike messenger with dreads who had been stopped with a small trace of marijuana in his satchel.

"Sorry, boys," the officer calls out, "end of night court. Better luck tomorrow."

Those hours between 1 a.m. and 6 a.m. Sunday are pure agony. DDP's sure he's been left in here because he's got a bond hanging over his head. The Jamaican thinks his paperwork has been lost and that we all could end up a statistic. And I see Officer Murphy in my mind's eye, broad-jawed, grinning. I see myself with my foot on his throat the way Natarja, the cosmic Lord of the Dance, balances his foot upon the back of the dwarf of ignorance in Hindu iconography (after what happened to George Floyd, I'm ashamed of how the rage that welled up in me took shape).

That night, for the first time, I suppress a hot tear welling up in my eye.

Beginning at 3 a.m., the next night's crop begins to arrive: unruly, pissed off, stinking drunk, and encrusted with spatter. We are old heads by then, and I stare hard and vacuously at each new arrival before sinking back into my slumber, legs fully extending along a length of the bench for the first time. At 6 a.m., awakened to another lineup call, I finally hear "Shankar," and I recite back my birthday. I am admitted to the line to leave the isolated recesses of Central Booking. My heart swells just to feel my legs move.

But like in Kafka, one cell leads to another. This one has tall, narrowly slanted walls and benches intentionally engineered to support only half a human body. Some of our companions from the previous day are still in here, having not been seen by the judge when night court ended. There's a haggard pallor among us, tinged with the palpable joy of being this much closer to being free. Finally, nearly two days into my stay, I am given a chance to talk to the public defender, who sweats visibly in a crumpled blazer and brow. I still haven't been given my phone call.

"You Shankar? Looks like you were driving under suspension?"

"That's not me! Look at the warrant. It's for a White guy. Five ten. Please. You've got to get me out of here."

He examines some documents in a manila folder.

"Well, I'll be damned. Sure looks that way. I'll talk to the prosecutor and see what we can do. I think the judge will definitely dismiss this. If they want you to pay a ticket, even though it's not for you, you prepared to do that?"

"Yes. Anything. Why am I in here?"

"Well ..." The public defender won't meet my eye. "It's an officer's right. Something like this, they usually just give you a desk summons to take care of later. But if they suspect something, then ..."

"One of the cops, an Officer Murphy, called me a sand nigger!"

"A what?"

"A sand nigger." I mime like I am wearing a *thawb*.

"Oh dear." He winces. "Well, that's not very nice."

He calls up someone else, and I wait some more. In the cell, there's a phone where I am finally able to collect call Parker to tell her where I am. My cousin has already notified her, but she has, of course, been worried out of her mind. She has been calling the police every few hours and has so far been able to extricate nearly as much information as I have, which is to say, close to nothing.

Waiting. Waiting. Wanting to leave, but unable to do so. A subliminal byproduct of police brutality is the needless waiting at every point in the process, a reminder that freedom is necessarily compromised while the prisoner remains "under investigation." Public defenders breeze in and out, calling out names while more men are deposited into the cell. I sit flanked by a Pakistani man whose visa has just expired and who fears deportation, and a Black man with leather boots, pressed slacks, and a hoof-print goatee. This is a side of America I rarely get to see.

¶

Finally, around 2 p.m. on Sunday, forty-odd hours after being wrongfully detained, I face the judge, Ruth Pickholz, a former legal aid lawyer who once told the *New York Times*, "I consider arraignments the ER of the court system. We triage. Some cases need a Band-Aid. Some of them need major surgery." My public defender, Victor Castelli of Legal Aid, has warned me to wait my turn and not speak at all and to be exceptionally polite to her. He has told me that he has reached an arrangement with the state's prosecutor, Matthew Montana. There has been a misunderstanding. The charges will be dropped.

Judge Pickholz runs an efficient courtroom. When I enter the box, she is berating a prosecutor about not having more exacting evidence about a Black woman accused of throwing a lawn chair through a window. The odorless air-conditioned room stands in stark contrast to the humid jail cell with its human rot and odor. In here, I can smell myself, an animal stench seeping from under my collar. I'm called before the judge.

"The warrant is not him, Judge," Castillo begins. "It says it's a five-ten White male weighing 140 pounds on the description that the police showed him—"

"Yes." Judge Pickholz peers through her glasses at me. "They say he's a White male. Doesn't look like him."

Castillo goes on to tell her he has reached an agreement to have the charges dropped and me released, but something else has caught Judge Pickholz's eye.

"Hold on. It says here he's a professor?" She does a double take on my file. "Why does he have a public defender?" She looks down at Castillo.

"Well, in the process of expediency, he's been here for two days . . ."

"He can come back and talk to me when he has hired an attorney."

"Your Honor, it's already taken care of with the state's consent."

"You know the rules."

"Your Honor." I can't hold myself back. "I have been in jail for the weekend on a false charge! That's not me. Please. I just want to go home. I have a wife and a daughter."

"Don't worry. You *are* going home." She gazes down at me. "The public defender program is not meant for someone like you. Trust me, you'll want to hire an attorney to settle this matter. I can continue this until you've had time to better consider your options. You can thank me later."

"But, Judge!" I protest. The bailiff stands behind me and nudges me in the back. "It's over. Move."

I retreat in a daze. Because I am gainfully employed, the judge assumes that I should hire a lawyer to fight this trumped-up charge that both the defense and the state have agreed to dismiss? Having to return to settle this matter when it could easily have been resolved right there is the rancid cherry on top of the sundae.

¶

After speaking to the judge, I walk out dazed into a Sunday afternoon in lower Manhattan. Lovers stroll arm-in-arm, and groups of tourists pose for selfies in front of the charging bronze Wall Street bull. When I finally make it back home, Parker fights back tears while my daughter crawls all over me. I don't know what to say, so I do what any outraged professor would do: I soapbox. I write an op-ed for the *Hartford Courant* titled "Making a Joke out of Justice." I contact the American Civil Liberties Union. I file a complaint with the Civilian Complaint Review Board and go on NPR the very week in which Bollywood star Shahrukh Khan was stopped at Newark International Airport because his name sounded similar to one on the US government's terrorist watch list. I am invited to give a sermon on intolerance at a Unitarian church, where I speak about my struggle to forgive Officer Murphy. His cold eyes, craggy jaw, and sneering lips spitting a racist invective at me still recur in my nightmares. How was a man like him sanctioned to carry a gun?

I even retain high-profile New York attorney Bruce Baron, who agrees to take my case on contingency, telling me that the city is known for making false arrests. The figures bear him out. An investigation in 2010 by the Associated Press into the Office of the New York City Comptroller found that almost $1 billion had been paid to settle claims against the NYPD.

Baron sues the city of New York on my behalf for the fantastic figure of $10 million, which is reported in the *New York Post* under the brazen headline, "Prof: I'll Sue Cops." According to the lawsuit,

> Claimant Ravi Shankar sustained multiple psychological, mental and emotional injuries, monetary loss, public contempt, humiliation, ridicule, disgrace, prejudice, great mental pain and anguish; and has been irreparably harmed in his good name, business and/or professional reputation, and social standing, and has lost the esteem and the respect of the community, friends, acquaintances, business associates, and/or patients, and of the public generally which have caused the claimant to incur and continue to incur expenses, loss of future income and/or monetary benefits, conscious pain and suffering, loss of services, loss of consortium and caused claimant to be absent from employment with a resultant loss therefrom.

Although, until then, I knew not what loss of consortium might have been, it is the case for humiliation, anguish, and suffering that resounds the most.

Back then, I felt triumphant, almost as if my minor brush with the law had turned me into an inadvertent civil rights activist. At the very least, I had done my small part to throw some light on racist police practices. I was deposed and eventually won a settlement against the city and the NYPD. It was only $15,000, but Baron advised me to take it. I could keep fighting, but, in his view, the time and energy would not be worth it. He tried to convince me that, considered on an hourly basis, what I would earn for forty hours in jail was not too shabby. The more important aspect was that I would be vindicated.

"There's nothing more humiliating than being falsely arrested and falsely accused on an improper warrant," Baron told the press when I agreed to accept my settlement. I continued to do what I could to spread the word of this false arrest, not knowing that my own relatively unexceptional testimony would be but one in an accumulating pile of pieces, that this evidence would be assembled to create an undeniable picture of systematic racial discrimination and police overreach that would finally be determined to be unconstitutional.

Another damning testimonial would be the hundreds of hours of tape, recorded and provided to the *Village Voice* by Eighty-First Precinct police officer Adrian Schoolcraft. The Eighty-First Precinct is in Bedford-Stuyvesant, a low-income, densely populated multiracial neighborhood in Brooklyn with public housing projects and streets seemingly immune to gentrification. Schoolcraft's recordings of everything from precinct roll calls to station house banter prove that quotas exist and that officers are pressured to make their "numbers." But, even more disturbingly, the tapes reveal the inbred contempt the police have for those they are being paid to serve and protect. As one lieutenant exhorts, "We own the block. They don't own the block, all right? They might live there, but we own the block. All right? We own the streets here. You tell them what to do."

That's what we are up against. Regular citizens of the most liberal, cosmopolitan city in the entire country feel like they can't do anything to prevent this because the few oversight boards that exist, such as the Civilian Complaint Review Board, are essentially toothless. They end up making recommendations to the Department Advocate's Office that are usually discarded. That was certainly my experience with the CCRB, where, after nearly two years, I was told that there must be a preponderance of evidence to support a finding and that the outcome of my case was "unsubstantiated," which, according to them, "means the available evidence is insufficient to determine whether the officer did or did not commit misconduct." I never did find out whether Officer Murphy was ever reprimanded, or if he continued to patrol the streets. I know where I'd put my money.

The effect on me was not readily apparent, but, in time, I would discover that I had grown jittery and insomniac after that fateful weekend, that a nameless fear had imperceptibly unhinged me. I would act more compulsively than I had before, subconsciously taking an exit off the highway if I saw a cop car behind me. I found myself looking at Hispanic and Caribbean guys with greater empathy and men in uniforms with unearned anger. This was my first real brush with the criminal justice system. I would never have believed you if you were to tell me that this short stint would foretell a greater intimacy with its modes and apparatuses in due course, and that my true disgrace and the irreparable harm to my reputation and social standing would in fact arrive much later. Back then, I only knew that I was made to feel alien in one of the few places I have ever considered home, New York City, and that it stung. Just as my own story was gaining notoriety, I felt, perhaps even more intensely than since I was a child, foreign to myself and ever more foreign to the world around me.

Chapter Three

Unindoctrinated Wilderness

Although I was born in the United States, I had nonetheless been consigned a foreigner from before my birth. Amma and Appa never lost their connection or obligation to India, nor their intention to pass those Vedic values uncritically onto their children. We were raised as strict vegetarians, taken to poojas at the local Hindu temple, and taught Tamil as our mother tongue. Amma would stockpile tamarind paste, fenugreek, and mustard seeds; buy rice by the forty-pound burlap sack; and put us to sleep by singing us Carnatic bhajans, lyrical Hindu devotional songs, instead of lullabies. We might be living in America, but we were not American.

The first time I returned to India, I was an infant. Family lore claims a case of severe asthma hospitalized me there, but, to this day, I retain nothing of that primordial experience save a vague somatic memory of an Ayurvedic tulsi and ginger paste rubbed onto my chest as balm. Never aware enough to handle being bicultural as a child, that overt pressure to celebrate my heritage pushed me the other way. I felt that my strained attempts at being a normal American kid were waylaid by my odd South Asian parents. Yet I was succeeding.

Then, suddenly, all of that shifted.

Back in 1981, running home after playing two-hand touch football in the neighborhood park, during the summer vacation between my second- and third-grade years in Northern Virginia, I was greeted with some grim news: Appa's mother had been diagnosed with an advanced stage of colon cancer and as the eldest son, it was Appa's duty to take care of her. Yet he had a job on the other side of the world and so could not fulfill his filial duty; instead, in the middle of my third-grade year, Amma told me that we would be packing up to move back to South India to take care of my grandmother. That's what family duty entailed. No questions asked.

In a whirlwind, my little sister, Rajni, and I were swept up with our suitcases and herded into the family's aquamarine Chevy Nova to begin the long journey to Madras, the city where my father had been raised. Thinking now about my own daughters' independence at the ages we were back then, I recall having no say in the matter, or even the illusion that I *might* have had a say. There were no big good-byes to my classmates, no sense of what that journey would hold. I do clearly remember tussling with my sister on the plane over a pair of plastic pin-on wings from the stewardess, as flight attendants were called back then. I remember drinking my first mini can of Coke on the plane. I was dressed in a military uniform with a peaked cap and a holster with a toy pistol that today would never be allowed in an airport, let alone admired by a flight crew.

We arrived at a cavernous, soiled airport where large rotary fans pushed heat from space to space. Numerous men in *veshtis*, the colorful cotton garments men wear tied around their waists in lieu of pants, jockeyed to carry my family's bags. Appa firmly rebuffed them with a coarse brand of Tamil I had never before heard him use. The throng outside the airport, in its sheer mass and press of humanity, was terrifying. There were people everywhere, holding signs and madly gesticulating. Yet somehow, even before my father seemed to find them, I recognized my extended Indian family, whom I had not seen in many years. I had been to India when I was six months and then three years old and had met some of these relatives in the United States, so I felt enough of a sense of connection to wave wildly to them.

They waved back. A group of them stood together, all men, in short sleeves and Brylcreemed hair. They greeted us with backslaps and loaded us into an Ambassador taxi to take us back to my grandfather's flat. The images of Madras at night are dusty and hallucinatory. I stood with my forehead pressed to the streaking taxi window while my sister sat with her hands clapped over her ears, for no noise I can remember.

We slept on the floor of the small apartment in the large concrete building, surrounded by our suitcases. In the morning, we were woken by koel birds and the cleaning woman, who swept the doorsill with a broom made from a straw sheaf. My grandmother, even though she was going through chemotherapy, crafted an intricately looping and geometrically precise *kolam* with ground rice powder on her front stoop to begin the day with auspiciousness. Instead of Cheerios, I had a breakfast of *idlis* and *sambar*. Everything shone with marvelous new sounds and colors. Rather than waiting at the corner for the school bus, I sprinted to the rooftop with my cousins to play soccer and cricket. Our Brown bodies glistening with sweat, we would weave and feint through the antennas and yards of colored cloth that had been hung out to dry. Catching my breath, I wondered what would happen if I were to kick the ball over the parapet, and then considered for a moment where I was, so far from where I had come.

When I think back on first experiencing India as a child, my memories are clichés of exoticism and colorful holy tumult: throngs of naga sadhus, clad only in marigold garlands, chanting into the Ganges; each course of a *thali* served on a banana leaf that could be scooped into the mouth with the hands; naked children pissing outside makeshift shantytowns formed of corrugated tin and cardboard; enormous gaudy golden marriage halls blaring "Baba Ki Rani Hoon" into the night sky; an assemblage of previously unknown uncles, cousins, and siblings all sleeping together in a family bed.

"How can the mind take hold of such a country?" E. M. Forster asks in *A Passage to India*. "Generations of invaders have tried, but they remain in exile. . . . She [India] has never defined. She is not a promise, only an appeal." Or, as Arundhati Roy would put it much later, "In India, the wilderness still exists—the unindoctrinated wilderness of the mind, full of untold secrets and wild imaginings." Both condensations of the country are illuminative and problematic, for India is much more than an appeal or a signifier of an ancient culture—and what is wildness, really? From the standpoint of someone other than Roy, such a description would feel vaguely Orientalist. Yet those qualities of being variegated, numinous, and chaotic certainly differentiate the country, which cannot be captured in swift, turgid generalizations—mine or those of anyone else.

There was something so unspeakably innocent and startling about being in India, a culture where teenage boys strolled the streets holding hands and where the skies darken with a downpour of fierce rain that might sop everything for weeks at a time. There are six seasons in India, the prevernal and monsoon added to the usual four.

I wish I had known back then how to hitch my star to India's *ratha*—one of those oldest chariots in the world from the Rig Veda—and to talk smack back to the pimply-faced rat-tail who had said my feet smelled like rotten curry on the school bus. Sanskrit *slokas* and Bollywood fight scenes had been a source of embarrassment to me. How do you talk to a White kid from Manassas about Vedic pride and the Ashoka Chakra? I wished that kid on the bus could have met my grandfather, who though seemingly ancient was surprisingly strong and would engulf me in a bear hug each time I walked by the wood-and-rope Rajasthani chair in which he liked to spend his afternoons.

"Sorry for Kashmiris," he would boom, his breath a mixture of clove and copper, "*Nalla paiyan uṭkāru!* But India never invaded another country. We invented chess, algebra, calculus, surgery, navigation, zero, even your—how do you say?— Snakes and Ladders! *Erumbu oorak kallum theyum!* An army of ants can wear away the stubbornest stone." While I tried to squirm free from his lap, he held me down tighter.

"Hippocrates? Ha! The wandering physician Charaka had consolidated the earliest schools of medicine known to mankind, Ayurveda, long before the togas. Then we beat the Brits at cricket and found water on the moon."

"Never forget your roots!" he trumpeted before I was able to wriggle free to hide behind Amma. I was utterly unsure why we had traveled across the oceans to take care of my grandparents, for they seemed perfectly able to take care of themselves. How little I knew back then about how my grandmother was losing her hair and in constant pain. Nor did I have the knowledge or prescience back then to push back on his assertions, to bring up the Chola kings whose maritime adventures led them to occupy parts of Sri Lanka, how Punjab king Ranjit Singh annexed parts of Afghan territory in the early nineteenth century, or the fact that the border disputes between India and Nepal and Pakistan persist to this very day. I wish I would have known how the Bharatiya Janata Party (BJP), the right-wing Hindu nationalist political party, would take power in India under the auspices of social conservatism and "Hindu values," leading to the destruction of mosques, mob violence, and the disenfranchisement and criminalization of the country's minority Muslim population. Patriotism is rarely complicated.

And at that age, Indian pride was just as foreign to me as the "Made in America" trucker caps and belt buckles that proliferated during the Reagan era in the United States, or the red "MAGA" hats that show up at political rallies these days. Being neither Indian nor American enough, I tended to regard any outbreak of nationalism with a healthy dose of skepticism. Plus, I had been acculturated in the era of the "grand melting pot" and taught to liquefy those rich differences that prevented me from being a "true" American. *To blend in.* I never suspected that the act of folding those six seasons into four would carry its own trauma. Now, however, the pressure to conform to an idea of Indianness while also trying to assimilate to life in Virginia had been inverted. I was now in India as an American and possessed with a sense of intoxicating adventure.

Since we had left America midway through the school year, I was almost immediately enrolled into the M.A.K. Convent, a bilingual school for the locals, where I was sent sweating in knee socks and myrtle green shorts held up with suspenders, swinging a tiffin carrier with Rajni, walking the two miles to school from my grandparents' flat. I was a gangly third-grader, the youngest in my class by virtue of having skipped kindergarten. My sister was in preschool. I had just started acclimating to the American school system, so being uprooted to the motherland and made to take classes in Tamil in a dusty, ramshackle schoolhouse run by a stern headmaster and unsmiling teachers was not the best way to help me fit in. I found that they had little tolerance for the novelty of me and my sister, the only two American transfer students. Within a week of being in the school, we were expected to know all the rules, or else face the repercussions.

Corporal punishment was a daily part of life at the M.A.K. Convent. It was meted out in the form of a swift ruler to the knuckles or a rough grain sheaf to the backside. We arrived each morning to sing "Tamil Thaai Vaazhthu" (Praise for Mother Tamil) and "Jana Gana Mana," the Indian national anthem, before our classes began. We learned, by rote, multiplication columns enumerated in a journal, and tedious entries about Indian independence copied out in English and Tamil in our composition books. Class participation was frowned upon, so you kept quiet unless you were called. The only time a little buoyant energy was allowed to be released was after lunch, when, under the watchful eye of teachers in austere blue saris, the girls plaited one another's hair under the *kattumalli*, or cork tree, and the boys grappled in the yard and played cricket with a discarded desk leg.

From the first day there, I was challenged for my difference. For coming from America. For sounding like John Wayne, according to Mahesh, a mousy little big-eared boy with a uniform made threadbare by vigorous handwashing. Luckily, weaned on a diet of pasteurized milk, peanut butter, and whole-wheat bread, I was bigger than him—bigger, in fact, than almost all my classmates. Though normally shy in America, I found I could go into beast mode here when I was threatened. Turned out I was a rangy dervish that the other boys could not bring down, much as they'd try to corral me in the yard, clutching at my suspenders or piling on top of me, screwing on my head and double-teaming me, derisively calling me the names of American pop stars and movie stars—but never managing to rub my nose in the dust. At least, not literally. Instead, after an afternoon of pursuing me, it was they who would routinely lie scattered around me like sacks of rice, while I was the one to be scolded by a nun and pulled into the classroom by the ear, where I might have to spend an hour after school sitting on my knees on a desk. Begrudgingly, and due to brute force more than to any commendable principle, my fellow students began to respect me.

Even back then, in third standard, there was a sense of the stratification of the classes, a kind of social inevitability about who would succeed and who would recede into the fields as a laborer, into the river as a launderer beating shirts on a stone, or under trays of sambar as a *paan*-stained waiter. The rural kids would dutifully take their punishment, even grinning through their grimacing as if they couldn't believe their luck to be away from their family's poverty and with other kids their age all day. So what if the nuns droned on, the lesson plans were soporific, and there was the occasional beating? No matter how the politicians stumped on about the caste system being dead, the rural kids were steamrolled into centuries of familial destiny.

Then there was someone like Vivek Mithranandran, whose father was a pediatrician and who wore distinctive bow ties with his uniform: one embroidered in fine gold thread, another floppy and oversized, yet another made of satin or velvet. He was paler than the rest of the boys, almost like he had been powdered ever so faintly with some mysterious talcum. He looked slightly sickly, which would normally keep one away, yet I was compelled to get that much closer to him. I smelt the faint tinge of sandalwood and dusky lavender under his nails. He spoke with a stutter, and it was clear that he was badly spoiled—such a rarity in this climate that someone who by all rights should have been mocked was overtly respected and whispered about in secret.

Vivek had never come less than first in class. In India, even at the earliest of ages, everyone is ranked according to region-wide, and increasingly nationwide, examinations, and these records are posted for public consumption. From early on, there's a clear sense of who might have a shot at the Indian Institute of Technology (IIT), the Ivy League of Indian universities, and who might end up as a night watchman at a paper factory. So imagine his surprise when the exam scores were posted at the midterm and Vivek found himself second. To the American.

I usually tried to get along with everyone, my playground skirmishes notwithstanding. I loved both the sons of chai wallahs and the daughters of memsahibs alike. I roughhoused with the twin brothers who had flunked different grades, as if having one stay behind fated the other to eventually join him. I stayed back some lunches at Amma's insistence to help Mahesh subjugate irregular English verbs such as "misunderstand" and "crossbreed." Certainly, I didn't understand the culture of competition at a school in Tamil Nadu. I simply saw my name at the top of the list and was inwardly pleased and outwardly dismissive, just as I had been when I won the regional spelling bee back in Virginia.

Vivek, on the other hand, was furious. I began hearing from some of the other boys that he was going to call a big-time mobster, or *Dada goonda*, to scare some sense into me. His parents spoke to the headmaster to allege possible cheating. How else could a foreign transplant, having joined a school year already in progress just months before, be able to perform so admirably, especially when he spoke his native tongue laboriously, knew next-to-no Hindi, and couldn't read or write the Indic scripts? Even I didn't know how I had done it and shrugged when the headmaster congratulated me for scoring so highly on my exams.

I thought that was that until I returned one afternoon from lunch to find my satchel missing. My textbooks and composition books all gone! Amma would be furious. Hot spikes of tears gathered at the ducts, and in the concerted effort to keep them there, I sprinted from the classroom. My classmates stared, but I ignored them all.

That evening, over admonishments about my scabby knees and mud-splattered uniform, I told Amma what had happened. Even though the great majority of other students were in much more desperate need, the only person I could think to suspect was Vivek. Amma listened to me, asking me when I had seen the bag last, wondering if I might have misplaced or forgotten it. I shook my head. She soothed me not to worry and that she would pray God.

That night, never one to flinch from unfairness, Amma called Vivek's parents. The next evening, she informed me that we would be having a rickshaw ride instead of dinner. We zipped by Ezhumbur, the Madras central station with a platform where cars can be driven nearly to the side of the train, and the statue of Manu Needhi Cholan tending to a cow whose calf had been killed under a chariot's wheels. We arrived at the fashionable district of Mylapore, whose name was derived from a phrase roughly translatable as "the land of the peacock scream," and scream they did in my prepubescent mind—the hot *aathas* in tight-fitting *salwar* pants and the bangled *bajaaris* hooting and hooking elbows with anyone who strode by their storefront. Amma pulled me by them quickly.

We entered a concrete flat screened in by corrugated steel and took an elevator up to the top of a modest tower. There Amma knocked, and I stood behind her, bashful and inquisitive. A portly woman in a sari opened the door. Her hair was in a tight bun, her bulgy midriff exposed. I stepped in tentatively behind Amma. The room we were in was all-purpose. There were large bureaus against the wall, a chapati griddle, a pressure cooker, and a *masala dabba* emanating a trail of scent from atop an ironing board. There was a doctor's anatomical skeleton in one corner of the room, a plastic skull wearing a Yasser Arafat kaffiyeh and an eyepatch. There was a desk piled high with books and there, in the center, was my spirited-away satchel.

A bespectacled, rail-thin Dr. Mithranandran looked warily at our entrance. Behind him, Vivek looked like he had been crying, and, behind Vivek, two younger children—a boy and a girl—peered out curiously at us. Vivek took one look and turned his back on us, either in embarrassment or in anger. I didn't want my bag any longer. But my mother smiled and warmly introduced herself to Vivek's family.

I can still recall the compressed action of that evening. Chai and biscuits were brought out with photo albums. The doctor spoke of a novel remedy for curing piles and fistulas. There was laughter as Vivek's siblings sprinted around the house, and eventually our mothers pushed Vivek and me together on a piano, positioned atop a stack of Kashmiri rugs. They wanted us to duet out our petty rivalry and, amazingly, it worked.

By the end, I had my arm around Vivek, promising him I'd help him with his English grammar if he would help me with Indian history and Tamil pronunciation. Thanks to Amma, we were briefly two tamarind seeds in a pod, though we never really did study together again. I remained in Madras for the rest of that winter and turned eight during the Tamil harvest festival of Pongal, after which I was named. Ravi means "sun" in Sanskrit, and the festival pays homage to Lord Indra, supreme ruler of the sun and the clouds that bring the rains to help produce the crops. There's a communal ritual where useless or broken household articles are thrown into a bonfire made of wood and cow-dung cakes.

During Pongal, I attended a temple pooja, a ceremonial ritual of worship where, alongside offerings of sugarcane and bananas, fresh rice is boiled with milk in an earthenware pot tied round with a turmeric plant that is to be offered to Indra. Another festival day, cows paraded the streets garlanded with colored beads, tinkling bells, corn sheaves, and cut flowers.

Slowly, over the course of that year, my grandparents seemed revitalized. My grandmother wore a head scarf and accompanied us to the beach one afternoon, and my grandfather was able to leave his Rajasthani chair and go for walks with my sister and me, clutching at our arms with a vicelike grip. I can still conjure the scratchy bristles of my grandfather's cheek and how he hid rock candies in a small jar in his bureau, which I would filch to crack my teeth on.

How different my life was in this flat of homes, where there was a security guard who slept on top of his chappals in front of the complex, and where a cook and a cleaning person would come a few times a day to prepare meals and tidy up. At first, the way my grandparents, not rich themselves, employed servants embarrassed me, but over time, I got accustomed to them as members of the family, which is a lie, of course. The servants had pet names but were not allowed to sit on the furniture or use the air conditioner. If the cook wanted to join us when we watched TV, she would squat on the floor.

There's no such thing as personal space or privacy in an Indian home, and so the servants would generally be ignored, as if they were another one of the appliances, whirring around like a fan blade, making ambient noise like static from the transistor radio. I don't mean this to imply that my family was cruel; I would often see my grandmother slip a hundred-rupee note into the folds of the cook's sari, or give them leftover sweets from our dinner. I'm sure my grandparents actually saw their employment of servants as a kindness, for they provided sustenance and accommodation to those who would have otherwise been without those human necessities. However, what they didn't see—what I myself learned not to see, until I could eventually erase my own blindness—was the structural inequality woven into the very fabric of Hindu culture.

We ended our stay that year by pilgrimaging to a few temples. Appa had my head shaved at Tirumala Venkateswara, a famous Vedic temple in Tirupati, a hill town in Andhra Pradesh. It was sometimes called the "world's largest barbershop" for the five hundred tons of human hair collected there each week. The act of tonsure in Hinduism is for auspiciousness and rebirth, and I can recall being a new *mottai*, my bare, tingling scalp rubbed with sandalwood paste, my hair in clumps upon a bronze scale. I felt free and savage. How little I was able to gauge that it might not be the ideal hairstyle for reentering a life in progress in a Northern Virginia suburb.

When I returned to my American elementary school in the spring of 1982, my hair hadn't grown back, and so I was greeted by my classmates with guffaws and cancer patient jokes. Slowly my hair grew in, and I started loving Sting's band, the Police, the World Wrestling Federation, and monster trucks. My sister and I spoke sometimes about India, then less and less frequently, and my memories of our year away began to fade to small details: the scolding string of invectives from my grandmother, who considered me too loud and too little devout (she would pass away a year after our visit; we returned to India in 1983 to perform her sacred rites and my own *poonal*, or sacred thread ceremony); Vivek's lavender odor and Mahesh's gentleness; the rawness of knuckles freshly rapped on by a ruler; the dusty wrestling with smaller boys whom I might have more closely resembled, physically and emotionally, were it not for my own parents' immigration nearly a decade earlier.

I passed through that time in Madras, and that time passed through me, and if you could freeze that moment of my life at a cross-sectional slice, you might be able to see—what? A boy desperate to fit in? Someone who had learned all about the ease of making and discarding friends? Or someone who had learned to navigate a world that contained Viveks? Would I elude, as Homi Bhabha writes in *The Location of Culture*, the politics of polarity to emerge the other of myself?

I'm not sure. I do know, though, that when I was back in America, I possessed knowledge that the other kids in school did not, which made it a secret and convinced me of the very notion that Amma was always telling me: that I was special. The very qualities that made me unlike Tommy and Billy did not have to be a liability but could heighten my sense of superiority, especially during those moments when the world seemed particularly harsh and judgmental. The marvelous dislocation of my year abroad grew in me a sense of difference, even as I longed to assimilate. The outsider learns to observe, and the cohesive self begins to disintegrate.

Back home in Virginia, I prayed to Hanuman devoutly and then derided myself for spending even an iota of energy on a monkey god. Ridiculous. I spoke Tamil with Amma and Appa and perfect American English at school. I remained a vegetarian but sometimes pretended that I ate meat. I lied about my age, wanting to be thought the same age as the kids in my class. I began to take silly risks on the school bus or on the playground, believing it made the other kids admire me more. I nurtured a shadow within myself and projected another face to the world. Sometimes, unbeknownst to me, those selves would switch.

As I grew older in America, I pushed the Indian part of myself farther and farther away. "Jana Gana Mana" wasn't going to help me make the soccer team or talk to girls. It wasn't until much later, perhaps graduate school, that I began to understand that the anxiety of my predicament might have been a boon all along, giving me two rich cultures from which to forge an identity. That I could choose the best and leave the rest, make up a mash-up of American self-reliance and Indian satyagraha, a mosaic of Muhammad Ali and Mahatma Gandhi, Jimi Hendrix, and Parshuram, the ax-wielding avatar of Vishnu. I, too, could partake in the American ideal of continual reinvention and, in a bastardization of Dale Carnegie, could mobilize my "exotic" heritage to win friends and influence people.

I used to think that identity was a little like Amma's *anjarai petti*. You have separate compartments for cumin and mustard seeds, for turmeric, fenugreek, and red chili powder, for ground cumin or coriander, for star anise or whole dried red chilis. You have little boxes for your identity as a jock, a chess champion, a skater, and a dutiful son. You have a few dashes of Desi and a heaping tablespoon of Yankee, and depending on who you were dining with, you could apportion out these elements in just the right proportions and flavors.

I know now that identity doesn't quite work that way. Even when we are trying hard to project a certain self into the world, all that we have pushed away still lurks unseen, like dark matter, gaining in power. All of us inherit complicated legacies and generations of trauma, and all of us are alienated, at some point, from someone or somewhere, and very often from ourselves. In such a way, we create the others of ourselves and the tidy compartments to keep ourselves in; thus, the feeling of being in exile remains virtually universal, though knowing that does surprisingly little to make us feel any less alone.

C. H. Krishnan (Thatha), journalist in Patiala, Punjab, riding one of the horses of the Maharaja of Patiala, circa 1942

Marriage of C. H. Krishnan (Thatha) and Parvathi Vaidhyanathan (Ammamma), Ottaplam (Kerela, India), 1941

Marriage of Rajeswari Krishnan and K. H. Shankar, Ayyana Gowder Kalyana
Mandapam, Coimbatore, India, 1970

C. H. Krishnan (Thatha) reporting on Indian prime minister Jawaharlal Nehru for *The Hindu*, New Delhi, India, 1947

C. H. Krishnan (Thatha) interviewing General Louis Mountbatten, the last viceroy of India, during the partition of British India into India and Pakistan, New Delhi, India, 1948

Appa and Amma after Amma first landed in the United States with one bag and one suitcase. Photo taken in Appa's uncle's basement room, his accommodations while studying at Howard University, Kensington, Maryland, 1971.

Amma, Appa, and Ravi at the Sri Venkateswara Temple, which was then still under construction, Pittsburgh, Pennsylvania, 1976

Shankar family portrait at Olan Mills Photo, Woodbridge, Virginia, 1980

Ravi and Rajni after the installation of a new swing set, Dale City, Virginia, circa 1981

Ravi and Rajni childhood photo, Manassas, Virginia, 1981

Ravi at his preschool graduation,
Lorton, Virginia, 1978

Ravi and K. H. Shankar at Ravi's poonal (sacred thread) ceremony, Vadapalani Murugan Temple, Madras, India, 1983

Ravi at his poonal (sacred thread) ceremony, Vadapalani Murugan Temple, Madras, India, 1983

Ravi in his room as a high school junior at Thomas Jefferson High School for Science & Technology, Manassas, Virginia, 1991

MUTHU VENIL (*Summer*)

Dear *perrōrkal̤,*

How strange that Tamil word for "parents" feels in my mouth, though equally odd, I suppose, as the word *pil̤l̤ai,* for "son." Still, it's also because you are, and have always been, Appa and Amma to your children. Gnarled branch and plum fruit. My two younger sisters and I dropped from your boughs as seeds in this earth, and we owe you our lives. How much I love you for standing by me through the utter *avamāṉam,* the shame that your son, who could do no wrong, brought down upon our entire family name. Yet though some among us have committed far greater crimes, the only way forward is to forgive.

You helped me walk when I was bowlegged and pushed me to excel in school. You provided me with a stable, loving home—crippling me with every advantage a boy could hope for. Through tacit understanding, you taught us to project onto a world gone awry the rosiest aspects of ourselves. I know you only wanted to protect us, to provide better lives for us than you had, to shield us from disappointment and from the foreign corruptions of America that you didn't really understand. In return, you just asked that we do our duty, as you had done for your own parents. But we came through—not from—you. We were never your possessions.

How secretive you are, Appa. You hold secrets so deep and so dark that you have to fill up whole locked basement rooms with them. Whatever it is that you are holding that is so concealed and frightful, I wish you relief. I only longed for a *guru/shishya* relationship from you, while you wanted a master/servant dynamic from your children. Much of that comes from generations of conditioning. Yet all my life, I've been looking for a mentor to give me the companionship and guidance that I lacked from you, though I've tried now to drill myself back through your soles so that I might begin to fathom the depth of the darkness and confusion in myself. Now I have nothing but compassion for you, for those depths inside you that will go unspoken, for the ways you may not be able to integrate fully in this lifetime, for the scars that you've left for us to pick over and heal.

Amma, your love has been a crucial strand in the web that has kept me suspended from the void. I owe you so much of my openness, my wit, my curiosity, and my sparkle. It would be easy to make you everything Appa could not be, though you are not blameless, and our blindness, real or willful, cannot grant us immunity from enabling others. How hard you have worked to make the world all that it is not. You renounced your life for us, and that duty to make you proud will always propel me forward. Your lessons and unconditional love are what has kept me strong in the face of all I've been through. I still remember the Tamil proverbs you taught me, such as *Āṟiṉa kañci paḻaṅ kañci*. Cold food is soon old food.

Your *sambanthi*, my grandparents, live in me. Thatha's lion will, Ammamma's warm eyes, Pāṭṭi's circumspection, and Pāṭṭaṉ's courage. In light of everything that's happened, I've had to lean on those ancestral traits, even while I try to undo some of the more ancient patterns braided from Brahminism and Hindu constructs of superiority. We are no better—and no worse—than anyone around us. We just need to forgive ourselves for thinking otherwise, and I know I've found forgiving myself much harder than forgiving everyone else.

Why fear when I am here? Cast all your burdens on me. I will bear them. Those were the words of Shirdi Sai Baba that Thatha taught you, Amma, and what you taught me. It's the promise that, through devotion, the universe will sustain you, even when you've spectacularly failed or lost your way. When I sit in contemplation with Hanuman or Sai Baba, I can almost touch the edge of that feeling, the strength we all possess.

However, my conscience demands the truth, because anything less prolongs our suffering. Our family trauma is deeper and more mundane than mere emotional or physical agony. Rather, it's akin to the vague, unlocalized unsatisfactoriness that hovers on the edges of our perception, before erupting out into the open as rage or despair. It's the accumulation of a lifetime's worth of birth, aging, and death. It impairs us, suppressed in the carceral space of the soul, rather than being released out into the open.

I cast away my burdens and am left with gratitude. You have done well by me and my sisters, and your grandchildren. That's precisely what gives me the courage to try to dismantle what went wrong in me, and how it might have been shaped by what went unspoken in our family. There's no blame in that conversation, just as there's no judgment from me about the men and women I have met in jail and in a mental facility. I know you would rather I had not written this book, but I'm done with repressing. There's a part of all of us in hiding, but I want to see and embrace my shadow. Our shadows. For in the light of such clear seeing, may our connection to each other only deepen.

Love,

Your *piḷḷai*

Chapter Four

The Three Poisons

Though my parents are devout Hindus, Buddhism has always had a greater resonance with me, perhaps because it is more of a philosophical investigation into the nature of reality than a religion per se. In Buddhism, the *triviṣa*, or three poisons, refer to delusion, greed, and hatred, which are the leading causes of *dukkha*, or suffering. In Tibetan art, the forces that drive us are represented at the center of the wheel of life as three creatures: the pig (delusion), the cock (greed), and the snake (hatred), spinning round and round in an inexorable cycle, each one endlessly biting the next one's tail. They are driven in mad pursuit of the one in front, while being consumed by the one behind.

In such a way, my own days were consumed. I was eaten from within by all the forces I chose not to see, which explains how, as a fully grown man, a tenured professor of English in Connecticut, I might come to suffer from all three.

The Pig

Indians are often stereotyped as sneaky. Shrewd. Mutable. Perhaps to survive in a country of more than 1.2 billion people, you need to leverage some kind of evolutionary advantage over others. Parker never understood this, but I was raised to believe that if you can find a way to get free cable or cut in line, why not? In my family, there was always some sense that our vegetarianism, our Brahminism, our family bond, and our fervor for education, while not making us better than other people, made us different. Truth be told, that kind of difference might as well be a euphemism for better, never mind the ways in which we might actually be worse. Appa certainly felt this way, and, even while he looked down on others for being "dirty" and "derelict," he filled his water cup with soda at fast-food restaurants and encouraged us to "sample" grapes at the supermarket.

My own reflexive, thoughtless behavior over the years might have derived initially from the pathology of these Brahmin supremacy constructs, from the dual sense of deprivation and entitlement they evoked: privation, on the one hand, gluttony, on the other. As Atul Ketkar, a spokesperson for the Chitpawan Brahmins, insists in the documentary film *Jai Bhim Comrade*, his caste—my caste—is superior because of the "uniqueness of [our] genes." Plus, as is often the case, there's the scripture for subjugation. The ancient Rig Veda claimed that society was one unified body, breathed into being by Brahma's divine manifestation, and composed of different classes of people intended to do different tasks to keep that body healthy. When you feel that way, you feel you can get away with anything because everything is due to you.

Though almost universally condemned as racist, the remnants of the caste system, which relegated individuals into a stratified social hierarchy, remains in place in parts of India. Shrouded in premodern ideology, its origins are murky, but its racist implementation over time is clear. People were born into four major castes and ranked in order of prominence. My lineage, the Brahmins, were the priests and lawmakers, the mouth of the collective body; the Kshatriya, the warriors and nobility, were its arms; the Vaisya, the farmers, moneylenders, and artisans, were its thighs; and the Shudra, who served as the tenant farmers and servants, were its feet—laborers barred from such activities as studying the Vedas.

This taxonomy left out a great number of people who were born outside the caste system. These were the Dalits, or "untouchables," who lived under the feet of society, doing such jobs as dealing with sewage, disposing animal carcasses, and cleaning out latrines and funeral pyres. The echoes of Jim Crow are evident— Dalits were forbidden from attending the same temples, drinking from the same cups in chai stalls, or even wearing shoes in front of someone from an upper caste. Brahmins were an embodiment of purity; untouchables, pollution. Even when this pernicious form of social organization was outlawed by the Indian Constitution of 1950, the discrimination didn't cease. Dalits were prevented from voting and had their property stolen, their houses burnt down, and were sometimes made to parade naked in the street, or were forced into prostitution, or compelled to consume their own excrement. In 1989, the country passed the Prevention of Atrocities Act in order to outlaw what had remained commonplace in parts of rural India. It remains stupefying that, in a modern democratic society, it took the enactment of legislation to prevent people from forcing their neighbors to eat their own shit.

When Michelle Alexander describes the American criminal justice system, she compares institutional racism to the Indian caste system, writing that "it is fair to say that we have witnessed an evolution in the United States from a racial caste system based entirely on exploitation (slavery), to one based largely on subordination (Jim Crow), to one defined by marginalization (mass incarceration). While marginalization may sound far preferable to exploitation, it may prove to be even more dangerous. Extreme marginalization, as we have seen throughout world history, poses the risk of extermination."

It would take a sociologist and a scholar to measure the similarities and untangle the differences between the two systems of oppression, but at the root of both is the fear and demonization of the other, a conscious or subconscious effort to exploit difference to one's personal advantage. Appa grew up in a family where this resonance of the caste system was still in the air, if not spoken about explicitly. From the west coast of South India to the American east coast, he carried with him a false sense of purity and genetic superiority that he passed on to his children. Perhaps, because he was not accepted by them, he felt that most Americans were lower caste. And in some ways, as desperate as I was to assimilate, I suppose I did too.

The Cock

Growing up with Amma and Appa, I never got an allowance like the majority of my friends, which meant I had to beg to get those things I felt back then were absolutely essential: G.I. Joe and Star Wars action figures, a BMX bike, classic Air Jordans, parachute pants. Due to his penuriousness, it was useless to ask Appa for anything, but Amma could be more malleable if I appealed to her kindlier nature. I would cajole and whine, wheedle and cry, until finally, on my birthday or Diwali, the Indian new year, I'd finally get one of these longed-for toys or faddish articles of clothing. By then, however, the trend would have inevitably shifted and moved on to Atari and portable Walkmen, leaving me a few steps behind in my parachute pants.

When I turned thirteen, I was allowed to get a job. I would traverse the neighborhood on a Huffy BMX, chucking copies of the *Journal Messenger* onto lawns. However, even in this instance, I was not allowed to keep my salary. Instead, I had to donate it to help pay for "family expenses." It was a policy that didn't exactly increase my keenness to wake at 5 a.m. to deliver papers. What it did do was increase my longing for those forbidden items I couldn't buy, even with the money I had earned myself.

Still, there was a trade-off. Thanks to Amma and my status as the eldest, only son, I never had to wash a dish. I'd eat, and magically my plates would disappear and reappear clean for my next meal. I'd spill pencil sharpener shavings all over the shag carpet and, abracadabra, they vaporized when I left the room. Much to Parker's chagrin, I went to college not knowing how to operate a washer or a dryer, let alone an iron. It was certainly not Appa, the house's resident magician, doing this conjuring, but I was too self-involved to notice how hard Amma worked to keep the household together.

I know now that my parents did the very best they could, framing the American dream through immigrant thrift. But back then, despite being coddled, I grew furious that my basic liberties were being denied, that I was being caged from the siren call of sensation. I craved all that I thought I was missing more and more.

I never wanted for anything growing up, but still, I wanted everything.

The Snake

When I used to get mad, I yelled and broke stuff. The Shankar household gave me plenty of opportunities to kick walls and snap my hated glasses. If only I could have foreseen in those clouds of rage that Amma would just tape them up and force me to wear them to school anyway. The unfairness of my life would descend on me in such moments, like a demon's scaly wing.

I had plenty at which to seethe because my requests were not over the top. I wanted to go to the shopping mall and to watch MTV. I wanted to try a hamburger, go to prom, and get my driver's license. Yet these aspects of normal American teenage life would set Appa off.

"*Chee, chee!*" he would exclaim, making a cackle of disgust, "why do you want to do such dirty things? Stay at home to study. Set a good example for your sisters."

But I was already a good student. I had entered and won contests I hated entering and winning. I would probably still have rebelled even if Appa had been more reasonable, but being given only stern prohibitions made me go berserk. Under cover of night, I'd break littered beer bottles in the cul-de-sac to blow off steam.

The Pig

Decades later, one rain-speckled night in 2011, after meeting some colleagues to kvetch at Elmer's, the university's local dive bar, I retired to my office to finish marking papers. I loved my students at this state school, many of them first-generation college students, often from working-class backgrounds, who took their education seriously. However, the bureaucracy I could do without. My fellow faculty members were constantly convening committees on assessment and grade norming, and, when I had gone up for tenure, a colleague had asked me to slow down my research output because to continue to publish profusely would make them all look bad.

Still, it was my dream job. As one of the only faculty members of color in the entire English department, I felt compelled to stay involved. I served as the faculty advisor for the student literary magazine and ran the state's largest writing conference. I had taken to the habit of going into my office early and staying there late—which must have been, though I didn't realize it at the time, a clear harbinger that my marriage was in serious trouble. We had given birth to another daughter, but Parker and I had grown distant in time, our differences magnified. I was discontented with domesticity and obsessed with being a "writer." I got drunk on the taste of publishing success and supplemented the feeling in real life by downing vodka gimlets straight from Raymond Chandler's novels.

That fateful night, I had drunk more than my share. Walking back to the office to sober up, I began to surf the web and discovered that the Argentine men's soccer team, featuring Lionel Messi, possibly the world's greatest soccer player, would be playing a friendly match in the new Meadowlands Stadium in New Jersey. Convinced that the game would sell out, and since reselling tickets online had become legalized, I decided to order a dozen tickets. I'd go with some friends and sell the rest at a profit, not the first time I had hatched such an entrepreneurial scheme.

Online, I scoured the different sections of the stadium—the club seats and the bleachers—and tried to order the tickets to no avail. My web browser had frozen. I refreshed it and tried again. Nothing. I rebooted my computer, staring at the screen and pushing down on my mouse until my eyes burned blue. I accepted defeat, shut down my computer, and dozed off in my office chair.

In the fitful sleep before waking, I dreamed of a game without players. Just a ghostly ball, thundering its way up and down a silent pitch.

The Cock

A few weeks later, I found our mailbox at home bulging with envelopes. Each one was from Ticketmaster, and they all contained soccer tickets. Sometimes a pair of them. Sometimes four. Sometimes just one. Sometimes a dozen. What the hell? By the time I was finished counting, there were over two hundred tickets spread around me like oversize confetti.

I went online to check my credit card statement, and I couldn't believe my eyes. Over the course of those two hours in my office, I had been charged by Ticketmaster for over $25,000, and my credit card had somehow allowed the transaction!

The Snake

Thank you for calling Discover Card. One of our representatives will be with you momentarily. In the meantime, did you know that you could get a low-interest mortgage

in just a matter of minutes? Please visit Discovercard.com or ask your customer service
representative for more details.

"Operator."

Thank you for calling Discover Card. Please enter your credit card number at the
sound of the tone. One of our representatives will be with you momentarily.

"Operator. Operator. Operator." *oo, ##, o#o#o!* "Operator!"

Thank you for calling Discover Card. One of our representatives will be with you
momentarily. This call may be recorded for quality and training purposes.

"Hello! Who do I have the pleasure of speaking with today?"

"This is Ravi Shankar."

"Thank you, Mr. Shankar. Can I please get your mother's maiden name or
password?"

"Harihan."

"Thank you for that. And what can I help you with this afternoon?"

"I'm calling because my credit card was charged over $25,000 in a matter of
two hours the other day. What on earth is going on?"

"Well, that does seem highly irregular. Have you contacted the merchant in
question?"

"Ticketmaster? No, you're my credit card. I thought to call you first."

"Are you calling these charges fraudulent?"

"Yes! I mean no. What I mean is that I tried to buy a dozen tickets but not over
two hundred of them! How could all those charges go through? Why wasn't I
contacted or the card flagged or something?"

"Might have been due to a computer glitch. Generally, this is very suspicious
behavior, and we'd shut down your card immediately. I'll have to look into why
that didn't happen. Can you please hold?"

"How could over twenty grand worth of charges go through in two hours?"

"Do you wish to claim the purchase as fraud?"

"What the hell do you think? What are my options?"

"I'm afraid that's all I can suggest. Otherwise, I would suggest calling the merchant to see if they can reverse the charges. Please hold."

The Pig

In the end, like creatures eating one another, Ticketmaster blamed Discover Card
and Discover Card blamed Ticketmaster. I found out the hard way that tickets to
a sporting event had a seventy-two-hour return policy, so, unfortunately, they
could not be refunded under any circumstance. Caveat emptor. When I once

tried to buy an iPhone, the very same credit card company had declined the charges because they wanted to speak to me to verify that it was a valid purchase, but, somehow, they allowed tens of thousands of dollars' worth of charges to go through without any compunction? What happened to me stretched the bounds of credibility for anyone to whom I would later tell the story, but I have the credit card statements to prove it.

I made many phone calls, raging at whomever I spoke to. When that didn't work, I wrote an angry letter to the Federal Trade Commission's Bureau of Consumer Protection, from whom I never heard back. Nothing seemed to help. At the time, I didn't confide my misfortune to anyone, not to Amma or Appa, not to Parker, nor to my best friends, because I felt like such a fool.

Then, in the midst of the storm, a lightning bolt. What if this was not a problem at all, but an opportunity in disguise? What if I sold the twenty-five thousand dollars' worth of tickets for thirty thousand? Fifty thousand? What if I could turn this unfortunate error into a tidy profit?

Under the spell of such magical thinking, I listed all the tickets on StubHub, eBay, and Craigslist at various levels of markup.

The Cock

The game was still a couple of months away, so I had time to sell off my stash. In the first week, I sold two for a profit. In the second, four more. In the third, another two. But then, as the game approached, rather than skyrocket, the sales slowed to a dribble. Distressingly, I noticed that the game had not, in fact, sold out and that tickets were beginning to sell for less, not more, than face value on StubHub. There were still hundreds of tickets available on the secondary market, and I still had nearly two hundred tickets to sell. Panic set in.

I drastically slashed the prices of the tickets I had remaining so that they would sell, and I would get something back in return. I reduced the price of those that didn't sell further, until I was only getting back a fraction of their cost. By the time the game rolled around, I had lost nearly $15,000 and still had nearly a dozen left that had not sold at all. How could I have been so delusional?

The Snake

It was amazing that I attended the game with any modicum of composure. Sitting with my friends in the stadium, a mob of weasels gnawed my heart, and my mind felt submerged in brine. What was I going to do? In the match, Messi was less effervescent than usual, and the game ended in a dull draw. As we walked out

of the stadium and into the din of the boisterous crowd, I burned with indignation and made the decision that would change my life forever. I would claim the
purchase of those tickets as fraud.

The Pig

Cops are cops, whether they wear berets on a bicycle or wear full riot gear and
swing a baton. In India, as a small child, I can remember a *thulla* in military
fatigues asking my thatha for baksheesh, a bribe, to allow us to pass a roadblock.
The origin of that slang North Indian term comes from the word for a sack made
of jute fiber, which resembled a cop's brown starched uniform. In time, thulla had
come to mean someone incapable of doing honest work.

I never meant to involve the cops, but it had been such a painless process to
declare the purchase of those soccer tickets as fraud. A representative took your
call, and the charges were reversed. You were re-credited the entire amount in
question and mailed out a new credit card with a new number. As the spring
semester ended, I pushed the debacle with the soccer tickets to the back of my
mind. I hosted my students at an open mike in Bristol, and they presented me
with a leather-bound journal that they had all signed in gratitude. Soon after, I
had my next book of poems accepted for publication. I spent that summer playing with my daughters and hanging out with friends.

During this time, I also fell in love with another woman. Nothing about this
relationship made sense—though she had been separated from her husband for
years, we were both married, plus she was older than me with four children of her
own. Julie and I met in a church pew during a literary festival, where she shared a
sandwich with me. We talked about poetry and community, and soon we were
sharing stories of our parents' immigration and the names of our children. That
night, under a canopy of the most stars I have ever seen, we kissed; and if errati-
cally at first, we have been kissing ever since. The electricity between us was
undeniable and magnetic. Life is messy and unpredictable, and much as I tried to
resist it, I found in her arms a solace and sensuality that I had never felt with
Parker and in her presence true companionship and a deeper understanding of
empathy and myself. In addition to teaching writing classes, Julie brings college
accredited classes to homeless shelters in the greater Boston area, and I owe
much of my understanding of the crippling effects of shame, toxic masculinity,
and how to deal constructively with the vicissitudes of life to her. Our connection
is profound, but at the time, I felt I couldn't be open about our relationship. Julie,
for her part, was always open. But for me, my feelings of secrecy and hiddenness
only deepened.

The Cock

Then, nearly three months after the soccer game, I received a phone call from an investigator at Discover Card. They had been researching my claim of fraud and needed to ask me some questions. I was caught off guard, and the litany began innocuously enough. But when the investigator began to ask me for the names and phone numbers of the friends with whom I had attended the game, I demurred. Why? The next day the same investigator called back to say I needed to file a police report in order to continue with my claim. Then suddenly, as in a nightmare, the $25,000 in charges reappeared on my credit card bill.

Since the charges were made from my office, the credit card company referred me to the campus cops. I told the Latino desk cop on duty what happened: how I had tried to order a dozen tickets and had instead been charged for ten times that; how my credit card statement showed the improbable record of transactions, multiple charges of the same amount being made one after the other in mere milliseconds. However, I left out one crucial fact—how I had resold many of the tickets at a loss.

Why this lie of omission? This failure to tell the truth in a situation requiring full disclosure? Because I was scared that admitting to selling the tickets would be seen as intentionally taking possession of them; because I imagined the police report was simply a pro forma document that the credit card company would process before reporting it to their insurance provider, who would cover their losses; because I was pissed off at being victimized by a predatory lender who had admitted to a computer glitch and advised me to declare the charges as fraud; because I didn't think the campus cops were real cops and I wanted to get away with it.

The Snake

What began as a mistake then became intentional. Not intentionally criminal, because I had no larger plan, nor any fear of getting caught. I was convinced that I had been wronged and blindly assumed that the credit card company would ultimately be forced to pay for their error.

The next day a detective called me back.

If I could have seen myself clearly back then, I might have seen my arrogance, my belief that I was exempt from the rules of society. While I seethed inside at the unfairness of the situation, I spoke coolly to the detective. The story in its retelling had begun to adopt the heft of reality. I began to believe what I spoke, even if I was conscious of what I was leaving out.

While fall foliage is most extolled in New England, I believe summer's the best season, the moment to swim in lakes and pick blueberries. In the weeks that followed, I was swaddled in sunshine, and a hazy breed of cognitive dissonance bloomed in my mind. I played soccer with my girls and mowed the lawn. I went out to dinner with pals who would stop returning my calls just a few months later. Like William Wordsworth, I took long walks along the shoreline with a notebook to recollect my emotions in tranquility.

Then the detective called again.

He was a former Hartford cop serving out his glory years on a sleepy university force. I had grown to like him and regretted that we could not have met under different circumstances.

"Hey, Professor."

"Yes, Detective?"

"We traced those credit card charges to Bridgeport and Danbury."

"Where? I haven't been there in years!"

"Not surprising. Listen, identity theft is big. You got to protect yourself. What do you do with your old phones and computers?"

"Sell them?"

"No, you got to drill through them. Right through the motherboard. Otherwise, your data's still there. Never just get rid of a computer. That's probably how they got you."

"Really?"

"Yeah, any drill will do the trick. Me?" He chuckled. "I'd use a standard-issue firearm."

The Pig

After speaking to the detective, I grew convinced there were other forces at play. I wanted so badly to believe my own con that I began magically to imagine it to be true. I researched identity theft and, remembering that they had worked on my computer, I called the university's IT department to ask them to delete any old files of mine that might remain on their servers. Maybe they were at fault. I felt trapped by the process I had put in motion.

Then, a week before the fall semester was set to begin, I got another call from the detective.

"Professor? We're really close to breaking the case. I think we know who stole your identity."

"You do?"

"Yes. Just got to verify a couple of things from you. Call me when you get home."

It was a lustrous August evening, the kind that empurpled the sunset in peacock streaks across the sky. A day for an open sunroof, for short sleeves and flip-flops. Golden. Nonetheless, when we turned onto Main Street, some imperceptible warning jangled. I wanted to turn the car around but was driving home with my wife and our daughters. Not surprisingly, given all that I was being furtive about, I had barely shared any of what had been happening with any of them.

The Cock

When our house came into view, I saw three cop cars in our driveway: one Ford Explorer SUV and two cruisers. A uniformed man was perched insouciantly on the rail of our front porch, swishing his foot through the day lilies. I was stunned, though admittedly not as much as Parker.

An officer I knew approached the car. He was a lieutenant with whom I had served on the parking and transportation committee some years ago. For the first time, I noticed that he was wearing a gun in his holster. I reached reflexively for my infant daughter, hoping subconsciously that she would provoke some warmth in these visitors.

"Professor, Professor. Sneaky Professor." The lieutenant wagged his stump of a forefinger. "Afraid we got a warrant to search your house and seize any electronic devices."

The Snake

Looking past him, I could see that our front door, which we never locked, was slightly ajar. Inside, two officers sat on our couch, stretching their booted feet on the coffee table. Another was walking down the stairs. The wash of violation was immediate, swift and furious, though tempered with the cold sweat that had begun to trickle down my back.

"What do you mean, Lieutenant?"

"We traced the IP addresses. They came back to your office."

"But what about Bridgeport and Danbury?"

"No crime to lie to a suspect. We call it good police work." He winked. "Now you're going to want to come talk to us. You don't have to, but we think you better."

The cops had already begun to carry out our computers and other personal items in plastic bags. My daughters had erupted into sobs, and Parker was protesting. They were taking her things too, and she had nothing to do with any of this. I wondered if our neighbors were peering at us through their shades.

"Officer, please!" I intervened. "The credit card company admitted they screwed up!"

"That's what we can talk about. Just come down to the station for a quick chat, and then you can get all your and your wife's stuff back."

I followed the procession of cops back to campus in my own car and told them the full story. They empathized, gave me collegial advice, and patted me on the back, thanking me for cooperating. Then I drove myself back home to fill in Parker. It was not the first time I had deceived or disappointed her, and she could barely look at me. The whole time while I was blubbering my apologies, I was wishing inside that I could have been comforted by Julie instead, and hating myself for feeling that way. I felt myself a selfish asshole. Thankfully my little girls were asleep.

Two weeks later, I was arrested on two misdemeanor counts of false statement, one felony count of tampering with evidence, and one felony count of attempted larceny in the first degree. Just the latter crime itself carried with it a recommended sentence of seven years in prison.

The Pig

What do you know from every cop show on TV? Zip thy lip. If you're accused of a crime, never say anything to anyone without a lawyer present. However, in my fear and desperation to get Parker's computer back, not only had I talked, I had even signed a statement. Soon after, I was asked to come into human resources, where I was informed that, since an arrest warrant had been issued for me, I would be put on administrative leave at CCSU. I had also been teaching in the low-residency MFA program at Fairfield University, and they fired me immediately. Of the many things for which you might be able to fault the Jesuits, thoroughness and expediency are not among them.

The Cock

This could have been a glorious period, since I was literally being paid for doing nothing. No classes. No committee work. No office hours. No students. Still drawing my full salary. A kind of paid vacation or bonus sabbatical. But, in reality, I was a mess. I couldn't think straight. I hid out at home, not calling anyone, staving off each morning in bed for as long as possible.

I had to hire a lawyer, of course—one recommended to me by the union whose retainer was quadruple what I would make in a month. When I met her, she berated me for having spoken to the cops without a lawyer present. I should have watched enough episodes of *Law & Order* to know that, at least! I also had to borrow money from Amma in order to pay off the credit card bill and legal fees, which was galling. Parker was irate, and my parents were upset and confused, not anticipating how much worse it would get.

The Snake

The writer Anne Lamott once wrote that "not forgiving is like drinking rat poison and then waiting for the rat to die." In the course of these next few years, there would be many people—some of whom I considered friends, others who didn't know me at all—who would bad-mouth me and try to take advantage of my own misfortune for themselves. In the throes of insomnia, I would sometimes stay up at night, mourning my lost friendships and reputation, plotting a grand revenge on all those who had abandoned and besmirched me. I would stick pins in the voodoo dolls of my mind. Then suddenly, like air hissing from a balloon, my hatred would deflate, until all I would be left holding was a limp string.

The Pig

As fall's vermillion embers gave way to barren branches and the season's first frost, I slowly emerged from my ostrich oblivion. I would quickly learn that the legal process proceeds glacially and that my case was just going to be continued time and again. During this time, I barely confided in anyone about what I was going through. The only good that came from this was that I could spend more time with my daughters and try to shake my funk. I began to move, to rake leaves, to make a compost heap, and to chop wood. When I could not find solace from my mind, I could still try to lose myself in my body.

I was also playing on a soccer team in an indoor arena just down the road from Quinnipiac University. I played with a group of Irish and British lads, who claimed they were "a drinking team with a soccer problem." One night in October 2012, just a couple of weeks before Halloween, I scored our team's winning goal and retired to the pub for a pint. Connecticut had been hit with an early freak blizzard, one that had piled the yards with snowdrifts and knocked out power in dozens of towns. Many of the streetlights on the roads and highways had yet to be restored, and, as I finished my beer and stepped into the bracing night, the stars shimmered overhead like an overturned jewelry box.

The Cock

It was pitch black when I left the pub that night. I knew the route by heart and was headed home when I found myself next to a tractor trailer hogging the left lane of the highway. In order to overtake him, I briefly accelerated. By the time I saw the car jutting from the breakdown lane, it was too late. I slammed on the brake pedal but could not swerve out of the way.

I clipped the hatchback while traveling at highway speed, and instantly an airbag deployed in my face, blinding me so that all I could see was the periphery of the windshield. Up ahead, the lights of Interstate 84 pulsed with menace, and I tried my best to pilot my car toward them, edging up the on-ramp and off the road as soon as it seemed safe.

When I got out of my car, I saw the damage was extensive. My fender had been jammed into the engine block, and a neon green liquid pooled on the asphalt. The rims of my wheels twisted and the axles bowed. As I surveyed my wrecked car, the enormity of what had just happened dawned on me. I had just had a few beers but remained terrified. I turned on my cell phone but couldn't get a signal. Should I walk back toward the other vehicle?

Instead, I walked down a steep embankment next to the highway, twenty yards or so from my car, and, seeing an enormous oak tree, its arms outstretched to the sky, I collapsed under it. I leaned against its thick trunk and started to weep.

When I finally looked up, the air up above was tinged with the telltale bursts of red and blue. I picked myself up, brushed myself off, and began to trudge slowly back up the incline to face the authorities. Suddenly, a movement from the woods adjacent to my path caught my attention. I heard guttural noises I could not process—a snarl. Then, swiftly, a set of slavering fangs burst from the dark.

It was a German shepherd, more wolf than dog, that leapt onto my chest and clawed at my sweatpants. Slavering on my face, it dug its incisors into my thigh, and I bellowed. By the time the police came to pull the dog off me, I was bleeding in three places, a deep puncture wound gushing blood from my thigh.

The Snake

"Stay on the ground! Hands where I can see them!"

"Please pull that dog off me!"

The officers grabbed the glowering German shepherd off me and helped me to my feet, escorting me to the police cruiser, where I was asked to sit for further questioning.

"You own that car?"

"Yes."

"Eyewitness said you struck another vehicle a few hundred yards back?"

"Yes, I believe so."

"What you doing down in the woods? Running?"

"No, Officer, trying to find a phone signal."

"You been drinking?"

"A couple of beers after playing soccer, but that was hours ago. I'm fine."

"Follow this light with your eyes. Your pupils look dilated. Listen, I'm going to need you to blow for me."

"I'm sorry, Officer. I'd like to speak to my attorney before I do anything else."

"I'll make this real simple. Do what we say, or we're going to arrest you. Understood?"

"Can I call someone?"

"Not now. Hey, stop that!"

"Stop what?"

"You're dripping blood in my cruiser. Why *are* you bleeding in my cruiser?"

The Pig

After an ambulance arrived, I was strapped, handcuffed to a gurney, and put in the back connected to an array of vials, tubes, nozzles, and a blinking defibrillator. We sped off to Yale New Haven Hospital with sirens blaring, and I was given a tetanus shot after the paramedics confirmed the dog bite. While I was kept overnight for observation, even though I would never be tested for my blood alcohol content, I was given a summons for operating under the influence (OUI), evading responsibility, and failure to maintain my lane.

It turned out that there had been a driver and a passenger in the other vehicle, and I would later find out that the two of them were high on methamphetamine and passed out in their car on the side of the road, which was jutting out akimbo into the highway. But, ultimately, that would prove to be irrelevant because I was the one who had struck them from behind. Thankfully, the doctors told me, they suffered from nothing more than minor contusions.

Had I been flying under the radar before, my situation now went nuclear. I was on the front page of the *Hartford Courant* and also appeared on NBC, ABC, and FOX-CT. Though I didn't see the coverage, a friend would tell me that I had been portrayed as a wild animal escaped from the zoo: a criminal running a credit card fraud scheme using state-issued computers; an alcoholic who had drunkenly struck a vehicle and fled, needing to be hunted down in the woods by police dogs; a reprobate gambler with massive credit card debt; an addict whose deviant behavior was being subsidized by the good taxpayers of the state; a Brown pawn on a Black-and-White chessboard.

The Cock

Refusing a Breathalyzer in Connecticut is tantamount to admitting guilt, so, for this latest charge, I hired a different attorney. She was articulate and maternal, soliciting character references from my friends and family and writing an eloquent brief on my behalf, outlining all the good I had done in the state. She argued that I had never had an alcohol-related offense before, so I should be eligible for the Alcohol Education Program, or AEP, meant for first-time offenders, which would have cleared the charge from my record. But, because I had been involved in an accident and had other pending charges, the prosecutor refused my request.

The Snake

The Germans have some of the best words when it comes to describing internal states of consciousness. Like weltschmerz, the Platonic depression caused by comparing the actual state of the world with an ideal one. Or *fremdschämen*, which I felt as a young boy with Appa—the incredulity, verging on pain, that one feels when they realize that someone is oblivious to how embarrassing they truly are. How many times had I wished to belong to another family?

When it came to some of my colleagues at CCSU, however, there was only one appropriate word: schadenfreude—taking pleasure in someone else's misery. When the news of my arrests broke, the dean told me that the English department didn't want me back in the classroom. They wished to excommunicate me. Having been celebrated in the news before, I was finally receiving my just deserts.

The Pig

The months stretched on. Winter thawed to spring, and each court date meant yet another continuance. Then, finally, after nearly a year, there was a resolution to both cases. Like over 90 percent of those accused of crimes in America, I was advised to plead guilty. First, to the OUI on the motor vehicle charge, and then to one misdemeanor count of making a false statement in respect to the credit card. Neither outcome was ideal, but I would avoid jail time, and according to my union contract, hold on to my job.

I stood in front of the judge and pled no contest in both cases under the Alford doctrine, meaning that, while I disagreed with the facts as presented by the state, I was willing to take the deal so as not to expose myself to more serious charges. I was sentenced to two years of suspended jail time and eighteen months of probation. In addition to my legal charges, I also had to face the consequences from the Department of Motor Vehicles. Refusing to take a Breathalyzer meant that I lost my license for six months. When I finally got it back, I would have to put an ignition interlock device, or IID, in my vehicle, which demanded I blow into it to be sure I had not been drinking before I could even start my car. Now my wings had truly been clipped, and I was enmeshed in the system.

The Cock

That first meeting with my probation officer, I sat in a waiting room at the Old Saybrook police department for over two hours before I was finally called in to see my probation officer. She turned out to be an attractive middle-aged White woman, well dressed and coifed with an enormous diamond ring on her finger. What might have compelled her to take this job? Before she had even properly introduced herself, she pointed to my crotch with a pen, indicating I would need to take a piss test. I had smoked a celebratory joint with a friend when my court cases had been resolved only a few weeks before.

"Sorry, I just peed."

"You're going to be randomly drug tested during your entire probation period. I know it's not a condition of your probation, but it's our office's prerogative. You fail, you could be subject to the entire time you have hanging. Let's see." She peered at some papers in a manila folder with my name on the tab. "Two years. You know I could put you away for two years right now for refusing to take this test?"

"I'm not refusing," I protested. "Just can't this very minute."

"Okay, well, here's what we are going to do. The Charter Oak drug rehabilitation facility is right down the road. Speak to the counselor there. She'll test you for us. Do this by the end of the day. We clear? Otherwise, we will have no choice but to violate you. Which would be a shame"—her ruby lips curled into bemusement—"since we just met."

I left, shaken, and made a beeline for a health food store to buy a noxious-looking blood purifier and an even viler system cleanser, which looked like antifreeze for a car's radiator. Then I chugged a gallon jug of water for good measure, followed up with chalky medicinal herbal supplements meant to flush the THC metabolites out of my system. By the time I arrived at Charter Oak, I was a dam about to burst.

In the waiting room, I began to feel worse and worse. The minutes crawled by while I shifted and re-shifted myself. Finally, when my name was called, I sprang from my seat. A counselor gave me a specimen jar and indicated a bathroom stall. Unfortunately, she was not quick enough. Because even before the door closed behind me, the levees had been breached. And not in the way I was expecting.

I undid my belt and saw that I had not pissed myself. Much worse. I had shit my pants. Watery fecal matter ran down the back of my thighs, into my pants, and squished around in my socks. I felt like throwing up. Instead, shaking like a wind chime in a storm, I filled the specimen jar. Then I balled up and chucked my underwear and socks in the garbage bin. I cleaned myself off and wiped down the bathroom floor as best as I could.

Leaving a snail-trail behind me, I shoved the jar on the counselor's desk and didn't look back. My sample came back clean.

The Snake

Journalist Sadhbh Walshe argued in *The Guardian* that the probation and parole system is supposed to offer incarceration alternatives for eligible nonviolent offenders, "but because the system (or, more accurately, a lack of a system) is overburdened, underfunded and haphazardly managed, it frequently functions just as well as a feeder system, ensuring prison beds do not stay empty for long." He reported that the Pew Center for the States found a third of prison admissions are parole violators, and "half the US jail population is the consequence of failure of community supervision."

Almost three million people are in American prisons, and another five million are on parole, probation, or some other form of institutional supervision. Overlay that statistic with the racial demographics of *who* ends up in prison, or is on parole and probation, then add in felony disenfranchisement laws in many states, which bar people with past criminal convictions from voting. Then include the fact that the prison-industrial complex, which includes privatized, for-profit prisons, is a multimillion-dollar industry that is often incentivized to lock people up who then work for substandard wages. It's the convict lease system from a century ago remade to fit late-stage capitalism. How do we, in the land of the free, reconcile ourselves with the fact that there are now hundreds of prison factories that make everything from military fatigues and lingerie to processed meat where the prisoners are paid, in some cases, just twenty-three cents per hour?

The Pig

In Buddhism, ignorance emanates from the idea of separateness, from the perception that there is a "me" that is not also connecting to everything else that is "not me." Over the course of my life thus far, I had never realized how much I had in common with so many other Americans caught up in the criminal justice system. But now I *knew*. Once a week, I had to show up at probation. If I wanted to leave the state, I had to get permission. I could be randomly tested for drugs or alcohol. A probation officer could show up at my house at any time and search me without cause.

However, there was a slight problem with my mandatory visits to probation or anywhere else for that matter: since my license had been suspended and I had to wait six months to install the IID, I was barred from driving. In the meantime, I had to rely on rides from friends, from a driver I found on Craigslist, and from Ubers. Sometimes, though, I took my chances. What could possibly happen on a five-minute trip to the supermarket?

One afternoon, because my pride couldn't imagine telling her to take a cab when she had just gotten off a plane from Cyprus, I set off to pick up a visiting family friend with my young daughter in tow. I was just a few miles down the road when I heard a bang beneath the car. Coaxing the car to the side of the road, I realized to my dismay that I had just blown out my rear tire. I didn't have a jack in the car, so I called roadside assistance.

That's when I noticed a state trooper pulling up behind us. I stepped out to indicate that we had a flat tire and that a tow truck was on its way.

"Get back in your car! Now!"

The officer who stepped out to meet me had on mirrored shades, a tasseled and peaked cap, and his hand was on his holstered weapon. I slid back in the car and placed both hands in plain view on the steering wheel. I soothed my daughter.

The officer walked around to the passenger side of the car, tapping on the window with a gloved hand until I opened it. He spoke in plosive imperatives, his face sallow and indrawn.

"License and registration!"

"Sorry, Officer? It's just a flat. Already called AAA and a tow truck is on its way. We're all taken care of here."

"License and registration. Now!"

Just as I have wondered so often since then why I felt myself above the law, I have also regularly pondered why power manifests itself in the pathological need to bully. I swallowed hard and opened the glove compartment. There, among the sheaf of registration and insurance cards, was my cousin's driver's license. He had left it behind when he had to drive my car home after my fateful encounter with the NYPD, and I had been meaning to return it to him. Years had passed, and glimpsing it in this instant seemed like a divine gift, something put there for a purpose. Swallowing hard, I offered the papers and the license to the officer.

He inspected what he held in his hand.

"Hold on. How come this vehicle is not registered to you? This you?"

He waved my cousin's ID at me. Mechanically, unthinkingly, I nodded one of those Indian ambiguous head nods. *Maybe yes, maybe no, I do not know, kind sir, shall I be on my way?*

"All the way out here from New York? How you pronounce your last name? You WENK-a-TRA-what?"

This was the moment my darling girl chose to pipe up from the back seat.

"That's not our name! Our name is Shankar. S-H-A-N-K-A-R."

Ever precocious, my eldest. Her interjection spurred this ever-vigilant servant of the peace to demand that I exit the car with my hands atop my head and to stand spread-eagled behind my car. The trooper patted me down, and, just as he was fishing my actual driver's license from my wallet, the blinking lights of the tow truck appeared behind us.

I was charged with driving on a suspended license and criminal impersonation. My daughter stood in tears on the side of the highway. I had hurt no one, but I had violated my probation. Now I faced all the suspended jail time that I had hanging.

The Cock

Nāṉ oru muṭṭāḷ! I'm an absolute imbecile. When I tried to explain my thinking to my friends, my explanations sounded more like justifications. Why would I give the cops a fake ID? Why was I driving in the first place? I really couldn't explain it either. My actions may have been born of panicked desperation, but they were deceitful. In truth, there was no excuse for me not hewing to the letter of the law, given all that was at stake. My friends looked down at their shoes when I tried to elucidate how and why I unraveled. It didn't help that none of them had ever been racially profiled or slurred, and soon I spoke to some of my oldest friends less and less. After a while, they stopped calling me altogether.

The Snake

The media spotlight reignited then, demolishing all that I had been trying to rebuild. I raged inside when I thought of the adjunct whom I had gotten a job for, who now disseminated the word of my disgrace, hoping she could take my position on a full-time basis. I saw the chest-beating, bar-owning Republican legislator Kevin Witkos, who wrote an open letter in the *Hartford Courant* demanding that I be fired, and who tried to mandate background checks on all the state's educators because of me, even though his own body of publicly elected officials held no such requirement. I saw the jowly face of Kevin Rennie, bearded Jon Lender, and the rabble of other predominantly White, conservative journalists for whom my life had become sensationalistic fodder. Then I would stare at my own face in the mirror, for if I hated the world and the world hated me, I hated myself more.

The Pig

I had to borrow more money and take out a cash advance on my credit cards to afford my new legal fees. Poor Amma and Appa. Having lived their lives convinced that appearances were everything, they now had a criminal son who was being lambasted in the media. Each time I spoke to Amma, she would break into tears.

Parker simply ignored me. I was less than a roommate, and our marriage, which had been on the rocks for a while, had now irrevocably ruptured. My daughters, young as they were, could sense that something was amiss. My sisters, Rajni and Rahini, called to check up on me and to encourage me, but they were busy with their own lives far from Connecticut. Thankfully I still had Julie in my life, but because we were afraid the media would find out about our relationship and further complicate my case, we saw each other irregularly. Plus, all that I was going through was bound to raise red flags for her about who I might actually be. I was a mess and steeped in self-pity.

"Probation violations are serious, my friend," said my attorney, a former prosecutor and chief state's attorney, "because they can hit you with all of your suspended time—two years in jail. Driving on a suspended license is a minor infraction. Even criminal impersonation is just a misdemeanor. But a violation is a violation, doesn't matter if you're jaywalking or swinging a machete at someone's head. Just hold tight. I'll talk to the state, but no one is very happy with you right now."

The stretching out of my court case over many more months seemed to work in my favor this time around. The initial media hubbub died down, and the news cycle moved on from me. Each time we went to court, the case was continued, so I was glad to put it out of my mind. I had even been allowed to start teaching again and was elated to be back in the classroom, even if my colleagues wouldn't meet my eyes in the hallway. If I had been alive and Puritan in seventeenth-century Connecticut, I might have been branded or made to stand in a public place with my tongue upon a cleft stick. Three hundred and fifty years later, my stigma had been broadcast in the news but was invisible to the eye. Still, like a bad odor, it led people to keep their distance.

The Cock

Then, one late spring day, just as the semester was about to end, my attorney asked me to come in. He had worked out a deal. In exchange for having the probation violation dropped, I would agree to do ninety days in jail. I would not be convicted of anything but would serve that time as pretrial detention, which would satisfy the state and do away with my probation violation.

"Ninety days?" I protested. That was as much time as Brock Turner, the Stanford swimmer convicted of sexually assaulting an unconscious woman, had served. "But I teach summer school. I'm supposed to teach in Hong Kong this summer."

"You want to do two years? Listen, I'm calling in a favor on this. I've talked to the state, and they're willing to split up your time, so you go in this summer for a few weeks. Come out and teach your classes. And then go back in to finish your time. I'll keep grinding. I'm sure we can get that ninety days reduced. You're a big boy. It's time to swallow your medicine."

The Snake

That's how I would come to find myself back inside the courtroom in Middletown, Connecticut. Over the last few years, I had been in and out of here enough times that I had memorized the backdrop and the rituals, the grain of the wood paneling, and the drape of the ubiquitous American flag furled in the corner. I could conjure the Latina court reporter, the fat, bearded bailiff who asked for everyone to rise when the honorable judge walked into the courtroom, and the Spanish translator who always had takers. I knew the whole cast of characters by heart. However, this time would be different from all the other times I had been there.

Sitting silently in the gallery, I waited for my name to be called. The whey-faced judge went through the regular docket, calling up the accused one by one, listening to the prosecutor's account of the facts, and then alternately gently chiding or harshly reprimanding him or her as he saw fit. Most of the people who faced him were allowed to walk out of court. I knew I wouldn't be so lucky.

Parker had to work. My daughters were in school. Amma, Appa, Rajni, and Rahini lived in other states, and, given our paranoia, we still felt that Julie shouldn't be seen with me publicly. I sat alone with a stack of books next to me—*The Collected Works of Shakespeare*, Seamus Heaney's translation of *Beowulf*, and the *Essential Rumi* among them—because I was still naive enough to think that I would be able to bring them into jail.

When my name was finally called, I approached the bench to stand beside my attorney. The judge looked down. All parties had already agreed, so there was no theatricality in the moment, much as I might have wished for some dramatic music to be piped in. Mozart's *Requiem* perhaps, or Franz Schubert's *Winterreise*—a prelude to some surprise witness entering the courtroom to exonerate me. Instead, the judge addressed me in a disinterested monotone.

"Mr. Shankar, do you stand before me, voluntarily, and of sound mind, knowing that we are going to temporarily raise your bond, and you're going to choose not to pay it, thereby entering into an arrangement that will satisfy the state?"

"Yes, Your Honor."

With those words, I gave up my freedom. Two marshals sporting blue latex gloves materialized behind me to spread and shackle my legs and to cuff my hands behind my back.

The handcuffs ratcheted tightly around my wrists hurt more than I imagined they would, and the leg irons jangled. Though I found my mind wandering back to my weekend years ago in Central Booking in Manhattan, my prior experience was no preparation. As I was being steered by the elbow from the courtroom to a caged elevator, what I had feared in the abstract for months suddenly became manifest. I had crossed the social threshold from citizen to criminal, and the shame that washed over me was tidal.

Chapter Five

An Unexpected Commencement

I emerge from the caged elevator to the basement of the courthouse, where my freedom has officially been surrendered. I'm searched for the first of many times that day by a brisk marshal who pats me down like a furniture appraiser looking for defects in an antique bureau. He confiscates my silk tie, my books, and my shoelaces, none of which I will ever get back, and leads me into a communal cell that smells of sour milk. I'm about to begin my time in jail.

The only other person is a Black man, sitting on the floor. In his ripped sweatshirt and camouflaged fatigues, he looks attired for a street war. I'm not eager to gauge what he thinks of me in my collared herringbone shirt and wool slacks. He doesn't bother to lift his head when I enter but sings his greeting nonetheless.

"We headed to HCC, bruh. That's Hartford Correctional. Don't get it twisted, and keep it professional. Done me two bids up there. Nothing but clown shit, that's county jail."

We will have to wait until court ends and more disconsolate prisoners file in before we will be transported to HCC. I perch on my length of metal bench, screwing my face into an imitation of fierce. Five more Black men, three Hispanic men, and a White plumber's apprentice have filled the barred space with their curses and odors. We are given rubbery bologna sandwiches on white bread and processed orange drink, and, as a lifelong vegetarian, my first act of communion with these other men is to share the wealth.

When it feels like I can't wait a minute longer, the marshal appears. He seems to know many of my fellow cellmates, if not by name, then by crime.

"Yo, Narco, you back here?" he shouts. "And you, Restraining Order?"

One by one, we are lined up single file, our palms flat against the wall, and our legs spread so we can be searched again. This marshal removes our individual leg irons and fastens us together chain-gang style, our right ankle attached to the left one of the man in front of us. We are marched into the sally port, where a prison van waits.

The Black man in camos begins to hum a tune recognizable from ice cream trucks in the suburbs. His outburst earns him a "Shut up, you dumb fuck!" and all of us a sharp tug, causing us to stumble into the back of the man in front of us.

To step into the truck, we have to synchronize. Lift our legs up and scoot together. It's a grudging exercise in humility. Once inside, I understand why they called this the ice cream truck. The air-conditioning blasts the metal seats icy as the truck lurches out of the sally port. Shoulder to shoulder, we smash into one another on lurching waves of pavement. The outside world beckons in tiny pinpricks in the reinforced steel of the back door.

"Probably be midnight before we see the dorms. Straight want to bet? Give me odds. Ten to one? Last time, it took four hours to process us. No joke."

I would later wish camo man had more hyperbole in him.

We arrive at Hartford Correctional Center and are led up a ramp and into a brightly lit hallway dotted with cells, the faces of shadowy men pressing up against them. I try to shift the ordeal into an aesthetic experience, an act of immersion journalism, but I fail. Waiting on another length of bench to be un-shackled, I'm panicked and exhausted, barely holding it together.

Once we are uncuffed, we are thrust into a bullpen filled with men in no mood to talk. My head swims in a fog of exhausted unknowing. After a long while, I am called forward, identified, fingerprinted, photographed, and, like part of a cattle herd, stored in another bullpen. Then, I'm told to strip, to trade my laceless shoes for a pair of black martial-arts-style slippers, which I'd learn were called Jackie Chans or Skippies. I stand naked in front of a correctional offi-cer, or CO, in an open cubicle. He asks me to spread my ass cheeks and to lift my balls.

"Check him out, Ramirez." The CO processing me sniggers, seeing my hairy body. "This one comes with a built-in sweater." My court clothes go into a box, and I'm given a tan uniform, a little too tight and short.

When I sit down outside a set of double doors marked Emergency, a skinny guy with rasping breath and horn-rimmed glasses sits beside me. "Hey, I'm Jay. You're new here, right?" He speaks as if we might be officemates at a corporate law office. "I'll let you know what's about to go down. We're not headed to the dorms or the blocks.

"Summertime in Hartford, you know, shit be crazy! Never seen it so crowded in here. My boy said they are putting guys on the gym floor now."

We wait to speak to the male nurse, who takes my vitals disinterestedly and asks me very few questions. The mental health counselor asks even fewer. I hesitate when asked if I have ever contemplated thoughts of self-harm.

By the time we are given a bedroll and directed to follow a CO, I don't know the hour. After all that waiting, we are through a gauntlet of metal detectors. We walk past what looks like a mural of the world begun by children and then abandoned so that Eastern Europe trails off into cinderblock.

"Wait behind me in single file," the CO commands. He searches his utility belt for a key. When he opens the double doors, the yawning space before us is indeed a poorly lit gymnasium. Dozens of dark shapes loom on the floor, resolving into the shapes of men—a small village's worth.

"We sleeping on boats! Holy mother, no!" Jay groans. "Worse than I thought! They got us on the gym floor!"

Around me is a mass of fellow human beings in jagged rows. A few are covered completely, wrapped in blankets like corpses, and others are on their mattresses shivering, snoring, or going through what might be termed mild seizures. Some men are huddling together or gesturing in the air with unmistakable, inscrutable resolve. Others are splayed out prone, eerily motionless.

Near the rear of the gym, I'm given my own flame-retardant mattress and a gray plastic boat—a stackable bunk without any component parts that could be weaponized. I anchor next to a hundred other men. This can't be legal under the city's fire code.

I'm exhausted. It's the middle of the night, but the fluorescent lights are still on. It's pure pretense that they give COs some light for medical emergencies, because their main purpose is to create sensory deprivation. I spread my sheet and blanket atop the mattress on the plastic boat, rolling the extra T-shirt into a lumpy pillow. What I see around me looks like a makeshift shelter after nuclear fallout.

I notice some of the other men around me have somehow acquired possessions that spill over the sides of their beds: pyramids of balled-up toilet paper or mildewing Styrofoam cups from which the stub ends of pencils stargaze. Others have flipped their bunks to make an impromptu card table and sit in knots throwing spades and diamonds. One man, shrouded in his blanket like a bedouin, stares expectantly at a television housed in Plexiglas, even though it is not turned on. Two COs sit behind a glassed-off area accessible only by intercom, next to a bathroom that looks like a busted-up mouth with two of the three stalls missing doors.

Jay crouches next to me conspiratorially. "Just you wait. Some senator or fire inspector comes through, and they'll send us out to the rec yard to hide the boats.

This shit is straight illegal. But summertime in Hartford! Gold coast to broke ass, who cares what's legal?"

I'm thankful Jay's boat is many quadrants away since, in the few hours I've come to know him, he has asked me for tissues, to make a phone call for him, and whether I could help him buy some pills. His manner of asking for something reflexively presupposes assent—a junkie trait I will come to recognize in time.

For now, engulfed in a miasma of fear, shame, and humiliation, balled up on state-issued sheets trying not to think about the grim reality of the next months, I can only sense the world in terms of relative danger. For the most part, Jay seems innocuous, even intelligent, and is a source of perpetual new information, so I would be glad to have him as a confidant during the day. But, for now, I need to sleep with an eye half-open and wish him away.

It's the summer of 2014.

Right now, I would be asleep in my own queen-sized bed after having spent the afternoon outside riding bikes with my daughters, or swimming in Cedar Lake, or dining out with one of my restaurant-reviewer friends. I could walk in socks to the fridge for a cold drink of water or turn earth over in one of my raised bed gardens. Instead, I'm scared and sleepless where the night snakes slither.

From where I lie, I can see more unfinished murals: the outline of a spindly man with African features hoisting a basketball midair with his legs bent in classic Jerry West fashion, his body not quite colored in; the glinting almond eyes of a heavily furred and growling Siberian husky dog, its body curved into a sickle that trails off at the forepaws; a half-begun rendition of the great seal of the state of Connecticut with only the first twining of a grape plant visible under the Latin motto of the state, which is rendered in full.

Qui Transtulit Sustinet.

He who transplanted sustains.

Transplanted, I had not sustained. I would never have the steel or judgmental streak of those Puritan forbearers who still lived today. Yet how could I be one of the men I'm surrounded by? I'm Ivy League–educated, a college professor, a homeowner. A recurrent thought-wave for the ego to surf, but when I look down at my raft, at my chest, I know I am no different than these other men.

Inmate #396964, designated by the Department of Corrections laminate ID clipped to my tans. My outside credentials don't mean squat in here.

I am indubitably one of them, awake in the middle of the night, looking perplexedly at the rafters of the ceiling and what seem like four spotlights bearing down on the row of Brown and Black faces, in whose continuum mine surely fits.

Still, I'm not one of them. *I'm not!* Impossible. I want to convince myself. I want to fall asleep, like Rip Van Winkle, and to awaken on the other side of this sandbar of time on which I've suddenly been beached. My new home a post-industrial dugout. I stare at the lights until an uneasy sleep overtakes me.

On any given day, Hartford Correctional Center has about a thousand inmates in residence. It was opened in 1977, two years after I was born. It's one of the twenty-odd jails in Connecticut whose names I will gain familiarity with from listening to the other inmates' stories: Osborn; Northern; Carl Robinson; the mythic Gates on the banks of a lake in Niantic, where on a good day you could see the girl prisoners from York taking their morning stroll.

HCC is located on a stretch of urban ramble, next to various car dealerships, fast-food restaurants, seedy-looking motels, and an enormous post office, where much of the state's mail is sorted. Driving by on the road, you might not even notice it, except for the glinting barbed wire encircling the grounds.

According to the Department of Corrections website, HCC is a "level 4, high-security urban jail [that] holds primarily pretrial [male] offenders and serves superior courts in Bristol, Enfield, Hartford, Manchester, Middletown, New Britain, Rockville and West Hartford." In short, it's a county jail, not the real thing—not the place hardened criminals go to do real time, where you have to walk around with two sharpened shanks at all times because you never know who is going to jump you.

"Place like Cheshire," Jay informs me, "hero doing straight life ain't gonna think twice about slicing you up on account of you reach over his plate to pass your bread. Real talk."

I am being housed with the low-level offenders in Level One, those incarcerated for breach of the peace or criminal mischief, along with those still waiting to be sentenced. Jay assures me that I will have nothing to fear here.

"Not in this correctional," Jay spits dismissively. "Pure carnival joke shit."

Joke shit or not, my mind obsesses over the sequence of events that has landed me here. I veer from astonishment to self-pity, seeing the shadowy center that lurked beneath my philosophical anarchism and the vestiges of Brahmin exceptionalism.

In modern-day America, adding together the number of people in prison and jail with those under parole or probation supervision, one in every thirty-one adults, or 3.2 percent of the country's population, is under some form of correctional control. Call us the three percenters.

I rue not taking probation more seriously.

I rue not having kissed my daughters one last time. I rue booze. I rue my impulsivity. I rue the forty-six and a half days I have left to go.

Rue, rue, rue your boat.

I awaken only to close my eyes again. Lying adrift in the stench of men, slowly passing time, I worry about how I will survive the full three months' worth.

When morning scuttles in, it's way too soon. We are awakened by a CO braying into a megaphone, walking the length of the gym floor, kicking toilet paper wads from his path.

"Rise and shine. Time to clean your asses, ladies. Let's go. Up, up, up."

I rise with the men around me slowly from the dusty floor, blinking hard in the gym lights. The more intrepid heave themselves into push-ups or jumping jacks. Pulling on our prison jumpsuits, or tans, we are shepherded to a bathroom with two showers and take our turn waiting to wash the stink from us. If we don't have soap, we don't have soap.

Then, in batches, our inmate numbers are called for orientation. We shuffle to what looks like a derelict cafeteria. Along the walls are cells with inmates pushed up against the bars of the window. We are made to sit at long tables and face a Hispanic man called Sánchez. He has a droopy mustache and a stack of pamphlets.

"Welcome, gentlemen," Sánchez begins. "Most of you know this place too damn well, but who knows? There's a first time for everything. So the rules are very simple for today. Shut up and pay attention, even if you heard all of this before. Do what you are asked, don't talk to your buddy, and you'll walk out of here with a state care package and, most importantly, your PIN number. You need that to make phone calls.

"If you don't do what you're asked, you will be escorted out"—he points to the door we entered from—"and you're going to have to wait a week before you get what you need. No PIN number. No toiletries. Your ass is gone. Got it? Good."

An inmate has begun passing out packets of paper and stubs of golf pencils. Among them is the Inmate Handbook, which lists the Connecticut Department of Correction motto as P.R.I.D.E.—Professionalism, Respect, Integrity, Dignity, and Excellence—an acrostic that puts me in the mind of those NYPD cruisers that trumpet C.P.R. (Courtesy, Professionalism, and Respect) along their sides. The joke with my friends of color, years before I had been stopped-and-frisked, conjectured that CPR, cardiopulmonary resuscitation, was the least they would do to you once they got done Abner Louima–ing your ass.

The second page of the handbook lists the HCC administration: from Warden Walter Ford to the Lieutenants and Commanders, from Classification & Records to Caseload, from Mental Health Supervisor to Telephone Monitoring. The code of regulations begins with instructions on how to address the staff: "Staff should be addressed by title. 'Officer (name),' 'Captain (name),' 'Warden,' (etc.) If you do not know the title, address the staff as 'Mister or Ms. (name).' If you do not know their name, use 'Sir' or 'Ms.' You must obey an order issued to you by a staff member. If more than one order has been given, obey the last order given, and notify the other staff member of the conflicting order. Failure to comply with an order will result in a disciplinary action."

Another part of the handbook addresses conduct: "You are required to conduct yourself in a reasonable manner. You are not permitted to engage in behavior that disrupts the order of the facility, threatens security, endangers the safety of any person or imperils state or personal property. You are not permitted to make sexually suggestive remarks or gestures to any person. You are not permitted to make excessive noise or use profanity. You shall be given a copy of the Prison Rape Elimination Act zero-tolerance policy."

Now that gets my full attention.

Sánchez tells us to fill out some paperwork that will be collected, including what size T-shirt and boxers we want. The size request begins at 1 XL and goes to 8 XL, which I begin to suspect is another component in the plan to create maximum dissonance. Nothing will ever quite fit in here. We can list two names on the Courtesy Visiting List, with the caveat that they have to be related to us by birth or marriage. We can also fill out a Request for Religious Services, which includes Christian, Catholic, Islam, Jewish, or Native American. Hindu is not an option. I'm intrigued by the prospect of learning how to do a sun dance in a sweat lodge in prison, but decide, because I have always been interested in kabbalah, that I will become Jewish for the next month and a half.

When Sánchez is done talking, a pretty nurse in scrubs takes his place to tell us that we can request HIV or other blood tests. If we ever have a medical issue, we put in a Medical Request. There's guffawing up and down the row when she says this.

"Put you in the turtle suit when you make too many brown snowmen." Jay jokes a few seats down. He means an anti-suicide smock, those tear-resistant, single-piece collarless and sleeveless gowns with nylon fasteners designed to prevent you from turning it into a noose.

The nurse wears a thick coat of makeup, a tight-fitting lab coat, and black stockings, which I find curious given her job. She plays us a video about the dangers of nicotine addiction. Onscreen, an elderly man smokes out of his tracheostomy. Another lies dying on a hospital bed. Then she hands it over to Sánchez.

Sánchez returns to the front of the room. Now it is the last item on the personal conduct checkbook he wants to address—the one that has elicited much of my fear in anticipation. Signed into law in 2003, the Prison Rape Elimination Act zero-tolerance policy is the first bit of federal legislation passed to deal with the sexual assault of prisoners. Any concerns would be dealt with swiftly and confidentially, and, by all accounts, this policy has been working exceptionally well. True enough, throughout the time I would spend at HCC, I would see very few suggestions of sexual misconduct or be propositioned in any way, though Sánchez makes a joke out of it.

"Just don't take that Snickers bar, gentlemen. It's that simple. Someone giving you something wants something too. Human nature." He puts his hand up to stop the cascading laughter. "But seriously, gentlemen, they make me tell you this, but if you believe you have 'been witness to or a participant in any sort of inappropriate act,' there's a number you can call to report it anonymously. Any questions? Anything in the handbook? Speak now or forever hold your peace."

I do have questions, tons of them, but Sánchez doesn't leave much time for anyone to formulate their thoughts. His manner is efficient yet thorough, and he leaves just a heartbeat's pause before launching onward to the rules of phone usage. We are each going to be given our PIN number, which is the way we will manage our telephone accounts. The first week of each month, we can add or remove up to ten approved individuals to call. These people have to prepay to fund their accounts through Securus, the exclusive inmate phone service provider in a number of states.

In the multimillion-dollar prison-industrial complex, there are many individuals and companies profiting from the incarceration of individuals. Bob Barker—contrary to urban legend, not the former *The Price Is Right* host—owns a company that sells commissary goods at a steep markup in prisons, but his business is not nearly as lucrative as the Securus monopoly's price gouging. Inmates, and their friends and families, are charged roughly five dollars for a fifteen-minute phone call interrupted by beeps and warnings. Sánchez tells us not to misuse our PIN number and not to let someone borrow it because, if we are found doing so, it's a Class A ticket for both parties and a loss of phone privileges for a month, maybe longer.

Finally, we are accorded our property. We get two state-issued envelopes and can write correspondence that will be opened, read, and checked for contraband. We receive two white T-shirts (size 2XL for me), two pairs of starchy white boxers, two pairs of white tube socks, and a plastic package that contains shampoo, a bar of soap, a disposable foldable washcloth, a tubular cylinder of deodorant, a toothbrush that will fray to bristle upon first usage, and fresh mint toothpaste that tastes like tile grout.

In order to receive the state's "care package," we are meant to return our golf pencils, but I find I am willing to incur the wrath of Sánchez and risk further punishment for the chance to write. I hide my pencil in the pocket of my tans and grab my bundle when no one is looking. Old habits die hard.

Now owning a pencil, a sheaf of blank inmate request forms, and a roll of toilet paper I have cadged from the bathroom, as well as my fresh state property, I am a considerable step up in caste from many of the men on the gym floor, including those still detoxing and writhing in spasm, and those who will doubtlessly arrive tonight with no possessions at all. I am figuring out how to guard my pencil in my pocket at all times, and it's incredible how quickly such a minor victory feels triumphant.

According to the state of Connecticut's Department of Corrections Frequently Asked Questions webpage, the average daily cost of incarcerating an inmate is "approximately $95.16 per inmate." One hundred dollars a day! That's the cost of staying at a Courtyard by Marriott. And what do taxpayers get for their money? Based on my unscientific calculations, given the possessions we were given, the cost of housing men in dorms and cellblocks, the barely digestible meals, and our meager access to schooling and medical care, I would be shocked if the inmates themselves saw even a quarter of that figure.

So where does the rest of it go?

After orientation, I trudge back to the gym floor while Jay chirps in my ear.

"See the new guy? Bald head White guy? Name Jones?"

I shake my head.

"Dude's a diaper sniper." Jay can't contain himself; his face lights up like a Christmas tree. "He a straight slot badger pedo. My boy Batman"—nearly everyone I would come to meet in time would have a nickname, and I myself would be called India, 7-Eleven, Abu Dhabi, Bin Laden, the Terrorist, or simply the Professor—"know him from the block. He tried to pick up a little girl from the playground. Batman has four little girls himself, and he's not happy. By the way, you going to use your envelopes? Because, if not, I could trade them for some soups. Take your socks and T-shirt off you too. Good looking out, right?"

Through two metal detectors and back down the hallway with the partial map of the world painted on the wall, I escape from Jay into the bathroom of the gym. On the back of the one stall that still has a door, there's some jailhouse humor. Someone has scrawled a desperate plea in wavering letters, "I need hope." Someone else has crossed out the *h* and replaced it with a *d* so that it reads,

"I need dope." Someone else has altered that sentiment even further, turning it into "I need rope," with a noose alongside. Finally, in large bubble letters, the kind used to tag the underside of a bridge with spray paint, someone has written a coda to the entire conversation: "Nope suckers, you need soap!"

I can't piss, so I return to a King James Bible on my boat. I have borrowed it from Bill, a red-nosed White dude who just got his fifth DUI. I'm flipping through the pages at random, and my eyes stop at Psalms 22:14–20. I write down one of the verses on the back of an inmate request form, the first words I would write down during my stay at HCC: *I am poured out like water, and all my bones are out of joint: my heart is like wax; it is melted in the midst of my bowels.*

Poured out in waves of anxiety, I feel like I've swallowed a candle. Slowly, I grow pliable and drowsy, but just as I'm about to plunge into sleep, I hear my bed number and name blared out of the megaphone.

"Bed number thirty-one, Hernández. Bed number thirty-eight, Lloyd. Bed number forty-seven, Shankar. Bed number forty-eight, Montrelle. Move your ass, fellas. Line up at the door. Bail commissioner time."

The bail commissioner, when we arrive, has a printout that lists:

(a) Name
(b) Inmate Number
(c) Date of Birth
(d) Status—Sentenced or Accused (Unsentenced)
(e) Primary Offense (also referred to as Controlling Offense)
(f) Current location
(g) Admission date
(h) Sentencing date (if applicable)
(i) Minimum sentence (if applicable)
(j) Maximum sentence (if applicable)
(k) Minimum release date (if applicable)
(l) Maximum release date (if applicable)
(m) Estimated release date (if applicable)
(n) Detainer (if applicable)
(o) Correctional History
(p) Disciplinary History

She's a woman of about forty-five, hair coiled in a tight bun, who looks familiar to me—as if I might have met her in the library. If she recognizes me, however, she doesn't show it. Instead, she runs a fingernail down my documentation.

"Looks like you're a level two, low-risk assessment, with two detainers on you. But your bond is only fifteen thousand dollars. Can you pay that? You only need ten percent, probably even less, like three percent. A bail bondsman could put you on a payment plan. You could be out of here for a few hundred bucks. Can't you find somebody to post this for you?"

I shouldn't even try, but I try to compress the improbable sequence of events to her, ending with the pretrial confinement of ninety days that I am in the midst of enduring. She listens without any expression on her face.

"So, you could pay the bond if you wanted?"

I nod.

"But you prefer to remain jailed?"

I nod again.

"Well, good luck."

The next inmate replaces me on the bench.

When I return to the gymnasium, there's a pheromonal odor in the air. Against the wall with the murals, I see two COs straddling the back of a large Black man with an inked tear frozen under his left eye. Next to him, a bald White guy slumps. He's already in cuffs; his left eye socket scraped purple, his pug nose dripping blood in large globs onto his tans. A small cadre of COs encircles them, one of them pointing a camera at the bleeding man. All the inmates have gathered around with interest, but the COs are keeping them away. Jay is exactly where I'd expect to find him, right in the middle of the action. When he sees me, he gesticulates wildly.

"Told you, bro!" He waves as if cheering a touchdown. "The pedo got beat down. Just like I said! Batman pounded his face. You missed a good one. Sweet mother. Right cross! Holy Jesus. Left uppercut! Now they both off to Seg." He means administrative segregation, also known as solitary confinement.

"Back to your beds. Now! Nothing more to look at here!" a CO snarls after Jay's animated broadcast. We disperse back to our boats to lie stretched out once more on the floor, something I have not done regularly since I was a child in India, when I would spend summer nights sleeping on a straw mat on the floor or on some uncle's rooftop. Under the mats, there's a streak of fresh blood. To my surprise, I find that I am disappointed to have missed the fight, and then instantly horrified at my disappointment. Less than a full day into my time at HCC, and the place has already begun to disfigure me.

Chapter Six

Browning the Apple

When I used to think of the word "freedom," I would imagine Central Park in the summertime. Now, I can't help but think of the "Central Park Five," the five Black and Latino Harlem teenagers who were wrongfully convicted of raping a White woman in 1989. But, back then, I would picture myself walking hand in hand with Parker over the cast-iron Bow Bridge to the fountain spouting from the center of the sandstone Bethesda Terrace, the faint scent of cloves, which I would later find out was due to the organic herbicide sprayed on the trees, lingering on the periphery of the sunny afternoon. The bronze neoclassical sculpture at the center of the terrace, the *Angel of the Waters*, carries a lily in one hand and stands above four small cherubim who hold her up in the triumphant pose of a bygone era. Watching her pour out her healing waters, someone may well have cued the orchestra, because we were here on our own. Making it in New York City! The future lay glittering before us, like the city itself, which offered us a million new possibilities every waking moment.

I left my first job out of college, as an assistant editor at a large trade publisher in San Francisco, to move back East for graduate school. Like much of the rest of the world, I didn't know much about NYC save through representations on screen and in books. In my mind, the imaginary city was a Cubist collage of Nick Carraway's West Egg, Holden Caulfield's Central Park ducks in winter, *American Psycho*'s Wall Street, James Stewart's view of Greenwich Village in *Rear Window*, and Mookie chucking a garbage can through Sal's pizzeria in Spike Lee's *Do the Right Thing*. I could close my eyes and better see the Invisible Man in Harlem, or hear Gershwin's "Rhapsody in Blue" in black and white—the soundtrack overlaying the East River in the opening sequence of Woody Allen's *Manhattan*. Like that film's neurotic narrator, I romanticized the city out of all proportion.

I arrived there with Parker, who was then my girlfriend, in the summer of 1997. Beyond our differences in race and temperament, our challenges were compounded by the fact that Appa considered us to be living in sin. He tried to keep the fact of our cohabitation secret from our relatives and forbade my sisters from visiting us in New York. When I look back, even at our early happiness together, it was evident we were not particularly well suited to be partners. We'd have that glorious afternoon in Central Park, followed by a rancorous row at dinner. We'd fight on the subway and not make up until the next day. I had already learned subconsciously to compartmentalize the love I had for her, like that which I had for my family, far away from the persona I hoped to enact in the city.

I was in New York for one thing: to become a writer. I was studying for my MFA at Columbia University, which abutted Harlem to the north and the Upper West Side to the south. That's the sort of demographic bracketing I had come to recognize as the epitome and underside of the American dream. Walk for less than a half hour uptown from Lincoln Center, and you'd end up in front of a housing project. Walk east, and you'd need to *hablar en español*. That was then. Now, of course, nearly all of Manhattan has become an unaffordable enclave.

Through the magic of the Off-Campus Housing Registry, within an afternoon of being in the city, Parker and I had found a place with a posh address: 410 Central Park West, at the intersection of CPW and 101st Street, a first-floor one-bedroom in a prewar apartment building with hardwood floors, crown molding, large casement windows, high baseboards, and even a doorman in a gray bow tie. I still regard with amusement our shock at debating whether or not we should take the place, which seemed astronomically priced at $1,250 a month. But, feeling flush with student loans, we took the plunge. We furnished the place from IKEA, set out houseplants, and lived the next two years within skipping distance of Central Park's North Meadow.

The neighborhood we lived in, despite its desirable address, was still considered, in the euphemism of urban planners and realtors, "in transition." The locusts of gentrification—of which we were an indicator—had just started to devour the ethnic communities that had lived all over the city for a generation. When we first moved to the neighborhood, there was still a Latino bodega on the corner, groups of young Puerto Rican men hanging out under the streetlights at all hours, unofficial "plate lunch" and beauty parlor shops run out of random apartments, and Sri Lankan and Bangladeshi cab drivers taking naps before heading to the Museum of Natural History or through the park to Madison Avenue to collect their fares.

Many of the landmarks were over a century old, such as the château turrets of the onetime New York Cancer Hospital, converted into condominium units, or the Church of the Ascension, built by German immigrants in the nineteenth century. There was also a large tract of public housing, the Frederick Douglass Houses, that took up a few blocks, and the closest grocery store was a soiled C-Town, with sentries of empty malt liquor bottles in brown paper bags girding the perimeter.

The neighborhood has a name to subdivide it even further from the Upper West Side: Manhattan Valley. According to the 2000 census, this neighborhood might be a cross-section of what much of America will look like in the next century. Nearly half the population back then was Hispanic, and another third African American—many of them hovering around the poverty line with a median family annual income of less than $15,000, and nearly a quarter of the neighborhood living on social security and public assistance. The muckety-mucks mainly lived west of Broadway and East of Manhattan Avenue, but this little valley was like the drought-parched village in a country that has been drenched by rainfall.

Part of that has historical roots, of course. In the late nineteenth century, the neighborhood was focused on care for the ill and aged. The cancer hospital was designed by architect Charles Haight, whose signature round towers and gothic windows were an attempt to keep germs from accumulating in the sharp corners of a regular-shaped room and prevent air from stagnating in the wards. This palliative air is surely what deterred the nouveaux riches from taking up residence nearby.

Instead, Irish and German immigrants settled there, followed by Puerto Ricans who played stickball in the streets. When Robert Moses's urban renewal project in the 1950s demolished several city blocks to construct the housing projects before the related graft and corruption eventually helped bring him down, Manhattan Valley's epitaph had already been written. In the 1970s and 1980s, it primarily became known as a good spot to score smack.

By the time we moved in, there was both a palpable sense of desperation and righteous outrage, but also the kind of community you don't usually find in Manhattan. We had few tourists and fewer transients. I got the sense, walking through the projects or hearing the cop cars casing the streets, that this was a land outside time. Squeezed by fingers of immense wealth on all sides, Manhattan Valley felt like a persistent zit about to burst. How do you explain to a family on food stamps in subsidized housing that, a mere block away, a new set of luxury condos is about to be constructed that will cost more to rent for a month than their family of eight might earn in a year?

And yet, in spite of this sheer, absurdist discordance, there was also a sense of solidarity on the streets that I never found elsewhere in the city: women playing cards on their stoop, girls jumping double Dutch, and boys clutching Italian ices bought for a dollar from the pushcart where the ice was shaved in front of your eyes by a glinting razor. Even the little knots of young men who seemed to have no vocation other than hanging out were a family. My destination, walking up the Park or taking the subway two stops uptown to Morningside, was a far planet from the world of my neighbors.

Jimmy, one of our doormen, was young, Latino, and handsome. A new father of twins. He always stood in front of the building with patriarchal pride, arms crossed, chest puffed out. One got the sense even as he held open the door for a septuagenarian widow with a yipping poodle, or carried packages from the back of a cab for the investment banker who lived on the top floor, that some essential aspect of him could never be cowed or owned. He would talk about the apartment building as if he had built it with his own hands. Though he was one of thirteen doormen and maintenance workers attached to the building (a number seared into my mind from the number of envelopes we would have to stuff with cash each Christmas), Jimmy was the one we got to know the best. We grew to appreciate his candor and his conjunction of Old World dignity and youthful exuberance.

One day, coming home from classes, I walked under the green awning of the building to see two paramedics sharing a laugh with Jimmy, and a heap of hat boxes and rolled parchment in the hallway. The musty odor of a tannery left open to the rain permeated the lobby.

"What's going on, Jimmy?"

Jimmy motioned toward a neighbor's apartment, that of an elderly Parisian woman we had infrequently encountered.

"Mademoiselle Oiseaux"—he chewed the syllables cautiously as if negotiating a piece of bony shad—"done flown off to paradise."

"Miss Bird?" I looked quizzically back at him. "That was her name?"

"No, she just asks us to call her that. Her real name . . . well, I collected her mail for the last five years. Let's just say she's a real-life heiress. You'll probably read about her in the *Post* tomorrow." I looked away and went to our own apartment. Miss Bird was leaving Manhattan Valley on a stretcher. In true NYC fashion, I never did check the obituaries to find out her real name or family history.

Parker worked downtown at a market research firm, but I had most of my classes in Dodge Hall on the Columbia campus, two stops on the 1/9 train, or a twenty-minute walk uptown. The world shifted dramatically in the classrooms of one of the world's most expensive graduate programs. With so little financial aid available for its students, yet crawling with rumors of agents who would give fiction writers six-figure book contracts, there was always a brand of unhealthy competition when I was there. Indeed, I find that anyone who has gone to

Columbia for creative writing will pause for at least a beat before describing their experiences.

This atmosphere made for shifting alliances within our class, though a handful of my former classmates remain dear friends today. I was one of two South Asians in the program. The other was a Kashmiri American poet and photographer, Rafiq Kathwari, who was a childhood friend of Agha Shahid Ali and the brother of the CEO of Ethan Allen. He and I were the whole population of color in class. India would sometimes come up when someone wrote a poem about an elephant or a fakir lying on a bed of nails. The class would collectively swivel to us both to verify the accuracy of the details. Did a mahout use a hook, a pole, or both to control an elephant? Could you really meditate on a bed of nails?

My poetics were more aligned with order and disorder, the philosophical pangs of Wallace Stevens, or Hart Crane's iridescent furrow of voyages. I knew the Hindi word for "cobra" as much as I knew the square root of -304, and yet, whenever something verging on the Asiatic would appear—an allusion to curry powder or kohl-lined eyes—I was always the one to whom the class, professor included, would refer. And amazingly, instead of resisting the typecasting or getting upset about it, I internalized the demand, thinking to myself that I damn well better know more about the Vedas than some Protestant parochial school graduate from Scarsdale. This was the moment I began to see how my bifurcated identity could be a strength. It differentiated me from my classmates and could help me find a way into publication, even as it ghettoized me by creating othering expectations about what my subject matter should be.

I was still learning immense amounts. The great redemptive virtue of being in graduate school in New York was the city itself. There was never a lack of things to do, whether it was seeing a Nobel laureate at the Ninety-Second Street Y, or taking part in a poetry marathon at the St. Marks' Poetry Project. Just over the course of one weekend, Parker and I might visit a jazz club in Harlem, a Sigmar Polke exhibit at MoMA, or watch a free outdoor movie at Bryant Park after eating the world's best bagels on the Lower East Side. The late nineties in NYC were throbbing with such overwhelming vitality that, on many nights, we would be overwhelmed by the choices at hand and retreat instead for a pint at the Night Café—rumored incorrectly to have provided Joyce Johnson the title for her retrospective novel about living with Jack Kerouac and the Beats. On other occasions, I might go alone for a coffee at Tom's, the diner made famous by Seinfeld and Suzanne Vega, or spend an entire afternoon sitting in the pews of the massive Gothic revival cathedral of Saint John the Divine, hoping to glimpse a peacock when I emerged.

I was making headway as a writer, studying with such professors as the late Lucie Brock-Broido, with her streaming hair and mystical sensibilities (I remember her telling us that she could only write poems during the winter months in a "chamber hung with red velvet curtains, candles, and at least two cats"), or the great translator and poet Richard Howard, who might well be the most erudite, catty, and mischievous man I will ever encounter. Richard would lecture in his workshop "Sermon on the Mount" style, and then we would have to go to his apartment on Waverly Place in the Village, where, under floor-to-ceiling shelves of books and penile sculptures, he would tinker with our line breaks while his French bulldog Gide humped our legs. If we were lucky, he just might accept one of our poems for the *Paris Review*, for which he was the poetry editor.

It was after studying with him that I was asked to be a reader at the *Paris Review*. Seeing firsthand how a serious magazine operated was one of the great learning experiences of my life and instrumental in helping me start my own literary magazine, *Drunken Boat*. And back then, George Plimpton was always around: a kindly, lanky, loose-limbed man in his seventies, usually wearing a sports coat, who was always encouraging the staff to scuttle their labors and shoot pool with him upstairs or join him for a cocktail and spaghetti Bolognese at Elaine's. The iconic restaurant across the street was where Hunter S. Thompson once set himself on fire drinking flaming rum shots and where you could dine with Plimpton while a plaster bust of the man himself looked down on his flesh-and-blood head across the table from you.

The Plimpton memorabilia on display in the *Paris Review* offices was impressive. Here was a framed photo of George and Muhammad Ali ringside before the famous Rumble in the Jungle in Zaire. There was a scarred chair nailed to the ceiling as a souvenir of Plimpton's time as a lion tamer. Here was a certificate signed by former New York Mayor John Lindsay, naming him the city's fireworks commissioner. Another photo showed a dusty, enormous bedouin encampment dotted with a few camels and Panavision cameras. I always wondered about that image. One day George offered us an explanation.

"That's on the set of *Lawrence of Arabia*. Largest bedouin encampment ever established since the First World War. You wouldn't know by looking, but I was one of the bedouins on set. In fact"—he paused theatrically for the small group of starry-eyed interns and staff members in earshot before pointing to an undistinguishable shrouded figure—"I'm that one. First and last time I stepped foot in Wadi Rum Jordan."

Being exposed to the professional amateur was a revelation. Here was someone who had played professional football, baseball, basketball, hockey, golf, *and* bridge (yes, I would learn from Plimpton, there was a professional bridge circuit), not to mention having played with the New York Philharmonic Orchestra, worked as a high-wire circus performer, performed at Showtime at the Apollo, spent time as a famed ornithologist, authored an oral biography of Truman Capote, written a libretto, and appeared as a character on *The Simpsons* and as a psychologist in the movie *Good Will Hunting*.

This was the romance I had always dreamed existed in the literary world. I'd be invited to his notorious parties, which would inevitably be sponsored by a single-malt scotch company like Macallan's (how one gets a liquor company to sponsor a private party in your own home is one of those rare Plimpton feats that will always remain well beyond my ken), where you might well rub elbows with a candidate for mayor, a prize fighter, a supermodel, and a Pulitzer Prize winner, while someone would be tinkling away on the baby grand piano. His apartment would swell with the hard-drinking conviviality of a bygone era, a few hundred people jammed into every nook and crevice of the brownstone, madly conversing, and Plimpton presiding over it all as the consummate host and gentlemen, looking slightly bemused and full of rumpled vivacity. *This*—I was probably not alone in thinking—*is exactly why I moved to New York City*.

Plimpton might have been a revelation, but he also embodied the paragon of a certain kind of WASP effortlessness that, try as I might, I would never possess. He was someone who had been born with the opportunity to pursue his tastes in whatever eccentric way he chose. All around me, affluence swirled, but I didn't come from money or privilege, and I didn't know anyone, except for those whom I had endeavored to meet. There was a part of me that took this as a challenge, and I vowed to become somebody at any cost: a Faustian bargain to be sure, but one that appealed to my inner hustler. If I had shoplifted as a gawky teenager, I now "class-lifted," trying desperately to make myself fit into that upwardly mobile and urbane literary set.

At the end of our lease in Manhattan Valley, Parker and I moved down to Brooklyn. She had a job at a market research firm in Chelsea, so the move didn't require her to wake up any earlier. The late nineties were the time of exodus; writers and artists pulling up stakes in Manhattan and moving to the borough rhapsodized by the Beastie Boys. Though well on its way, Park Slope had not yet been totally infiltrated by baby buggies and gourmet markets, and warehouse space in Greenpoint and Williamsburg was still relatively affordable.

We found a brick walk-up in Prospect Heights, which at the time was on the sharpened edge between sketchy and safe. Prospect Park replaced Central Park in our lives, and the proximity to the public library, the Brooklyn Museum, the botanical gardens, and the farmers' market at Grand Army Plaza all made the transition more palatable, even if the commute up to Columbia took close to an hour. Prospect Heights had been predominantly Italian, Jewish, and German in the first half of the twentieth century, though after World War I, more African Americans moved in, making it a multiethnic neighborhood of the working class. Unlike more recently named neighborhoods, such as NoMad ("north of Madison Square Park"), or ViVa ("Viaduct Valley," West 125th to 132nd to the Hudson River), the name Prospect Heights can be traced back to 1889, where it appeared to describe the "rapidly growing part of Brooklyn near Prospect Park" in a letter to the editor published in the *Brooklyn Eagle*.

We grew to love the diversity. We'd get bagels on Flatbush Avenue, take bike rides to Coney Island, toss a Frisbee with friends in the park, shoot darts and pool at Brownstone Billiards, and eat thin-crust pizza. The streets would light up during the annual West Indian Day parade, where the sound of steel drums and the vision of sashaying women dressed in the plumage of tropical birds and *moko jumbies* on towering stilts would resonate for hours. For the most part in Brooklyn, I felt the opposite of what I would come to feel in Connecticut, safely residing in a body of color and never looked at askance for having a White girlfriend.

In the few years we lived there, we saw ethnic communities slowly get pushed from Flatbush Avenue into Crown Heights and Bed-Stuy, and the wave of gentrification overran the shores of the Slope to lap against the Heights. The Caribbean barbershop on the corner disappeared, and where there had once been carpet stores and off-track betting, the bright awning of a gastropub now glinted.

Parker and I watched the turning of the millennium in Times Square. If we were going to ever participate in this clichéd ritual, this seemed to be the moment. For the purposes of television broadcast, the celebrations were synchronized around the world, and those countries closest to the International Date Line argued about who was the first to enter the new millennium. In New York City, we were one of nearly two million people crowded on the street, which thronged with dancing and screaming revelers, swinging streamers and wearing oversize glasses shaped as "2000." At the top of each hour, as we waited, a live feed from whatever region was celebrating its midnight moment (London, England; Ponta Verde, Brazil) would arrive on screen, and a mad cheer would go up in some pocket of the crowd. It amped up the excitement, as these periodic false peaks and moving images of other people celebrating put us in the mood to outdo them when our own moment arrived.

The ball that would drop at midnight was the first to be made entirely of Waterford Crystals, replacing an aluminum and rhinestone ball, which in turn had replaced a wrought iron one adorned by light bulbs. As the final countdown approached, it throbbed with reflective color and sparked like a star being birthed. The massive crowd in Times Square was jumping and hugging, deliriously happy, as a giant storm of ecstasy rained collectively over us. It was so loud and neon we could barely hear or see the news helicopters overhead. We were really here. Y2K! Alive in the epicenter, having hundreds of millions of people across the world watching us partying as part of their own party. Representative humans opening the door onto another thousand years of history.

When the ball dropped, I kissed Parker in a swirling blizzard of confetti.

"I can't believe we made it. The new millennium!"

"I'm glad you dragged me out. I thought this was going to be the cheesiest New Year's ever."

"Look, Times Square is still lit up. And nothing seems to have exploded. What Y2K?"

"Happy new year, Ravi."

Vast crowds celebrated around us, and I was momentarily lightheaded, overwhelmed by sensation. Indeed, the world had not come to an end, as evinced by the news continuing to scroll along the Dow Jones zipper. I was overjoyed and saddened simultaneously, a pinprick in a vast throng of happy people, squeezing Parker by my side, and yet still feeling deep down very much alone.

I graduated from Columbia in May 2000, having stayed an extra year to teach Logic and Rhetoric to the undergraduates. Bill Murray addressed the arts graduates at our commencement in a coconut bra. When the bell rang from Saint Paul's Chapel to indicate the conferral of degrees, the graduates from the different schools threw different representative items into the air: shredded newspaper for the journalism school, travel toothbrushes for the school of dentistry, Monopoly money for the business school. The school of the arts folks must have missed the memo, because our airspace remained conspicuously empty, though the running joke was that we would throw a party, because what else could you do with the muses, massive debt, and no real job waiting?

Finishing graduate school meant contending with the real world, which changed my relationship with the city. It meant I had to get a job. Poetry was certainly not going to pay the bills. I had bartended while at Columbia as part of their Bartending Agency, which is known throughout the city as providing reliable, if not wholly professional, service. Armed with a basic knowledge of jiggers and liquors, we Columbia bartenders would disseminate into the world to work a variety of gigs, from art and theater openings to private parties, from corporate functions to poolside revels. In my time, I bartended a bris, a bar mitzvah, a Thanksgiving meal, numerous weddings, and Robert Rauschenberg's seventy-third birthday party at the Gagosian, where I served Chuck Close a double vodka soda and nearly bought a limited-edition silkscreen that was going for eight hundred dollars. I still kick myself today that I didn't.

Working for an agency instead of a bar, we got to glimpse the interiors of other people's lives. I tended bar in homes to which I would never otherwise be invited: penthouses A and B of a real estate developer on Fourteenth Street, in a building where David Bowie lived below; vast spaces on the Upper East Side, glittered with alabaster fixtures and sconces; a loft space in the Village with a marble double helix staircase on one end and translucent glass elevators on the other, both leading up to an immaculate terrace containing an outdoor bar and a rooftop pool that hung into the night sky; a Chelsea garden of such extraordinary lushness and landscaping that it felt like we had stepped foot onto a Brazilian movie set; a theater opening where some ferret-faced mogul had bought Dom Perignon by the jeroboam, so that it took a few of us to hold an uncorked bottle steady to pour into crystal flutes arrayed on silver trays. I had walked these city streets innumerable times and could never have imagined what was happening behind closed doors.

Confronted with a fantastic world of wealth and status, far beyond anything I could have ever dreamed into being, I felt keenly both my longing for—and my distance from—stature. Even authors who won the Pulitzer couldn't afford a penthouse. Why was I the one serving Grey Goose martinis instead of knocking them back? Why was it that I could only go so far in this life and no further? Like my father, Sam the Super, was I ultimately fated to hypnotize myself?

Partly in reaction, I redoubled my efforts to get into publishing or teaching and sent my résumé out at fever pitch. I got a job for six months working at Forbes Special Interest Publications Group, copyediting and fact-checking for magazines such as *Invention & Technology* and *British Living*. During my day, I would have to call up a restaurant owner in North London to verify if Madonna really had, in fact, ordered a mango-radicchio caprese with basil vinaigrette when she was last there. Many of the articles that would eventually be published in the magazine arrived on my desk as poorly worded litanies of non sequiturs that I would have to wrangle into readable form. We freelancers were all on expiring contracts, replaceable, and were never mentioned in the masthead or given a byline.

Then I caught a break when I landed a job working for a literary agent. How do I describe infamous über-agent John Brockman, who was part impresario, part visionary, and part crocodile? He has recurred in more recent news as having been sexual predator Jeffrey Epstein's intellectual enabler, which doesn't shock me. I can see him at his desk, in his signature wide-brimmed Borsalino hat and Armani suit, taking calls with his feet up while his assistant nervously checked to be sure if his carpaccio salad was pink enough. As he would probably be the first to admit, Brockman possesses the kind of steely brilliance that lacks empathy or patience. As a boss, he was a megalomaniac nonpareil who ran the office in his own unmistakable way.

First, he strove to create a truly paperless office environment, and so he was an early adopter of PDFs and of reading manuscripts on email. He loved to lampoon publishers, many of whom had given his authors the massive advances that allowed him to drive his Mercedes out to his Connecticut home each weekend. By the time I began working for his agency, his list consisted primarily of serious intellectual nonfiction, folks like Stephen Pinker, Jared Diamond, and Naomi Wolf. Brockman had famously posited the emergence of a "third culture," updating C. P. Snow's idea of the great divide between the two predominant intellectual cultures: that of art and letters, and that of the sciences. In his vision, scientists have become our most crucial public intellectuals, and their articulations of serious science writing as accessible to the general reader are the future of relevant discourse. Brockman loved to quote his old friend Stewart Brand on this matter: "Science is the only news."

I was the new foreign rights associate and given a desk in an open office space, next to his assistant, and looking into his office on the top floor of a building on East Fifty-Ninth Street, right at the edge of Central Park. It was my job to assemble press packets for authors and to help with the contracts for their foreign-language rights. Brockman believed not only in a paperless office but also in radical transparency, and everyone was encouraged to read everyone else's email. All of Brockman's own mail would be opened and circulated in a folder that each person in the office had to initial after reading. It was a highly instructive way to learn about the inner workings of the literary agency, though disconcerting to see Brockman's credit card statement for the month, in which the amount he had spent on electronic equipment might exceed my annual wage. And Brockman could be a real bully. He would routinely lambast his personal assistant—a shy, bespectacled German American—for not taking his calls properly or not reminding him of an appointment. Luckily, I was mostly out of the line of fire.

This seemed like my long-nurtured New York dream finally made manifest. I was elbow-to-elbow with cultural dealmakers, invited to Knopf's holiday party, and taking calls from people like Richard Dawkins and Steve Jobs. Brockman's big sellers at that time were Brian Greene, the director of Columbia's Institute for Strings, Cosmology, and Astroparticle Physics, who coupled his boyish good looks with the ability to write clearly about quantum mechanics; and Daniel Goleman, inventor of the concept of emotional intelligence, who has more than five million copies of his books in print worldwide. We were told to treat those two and Jared Diamond, who had recently won a Pulitzer Prize, differently than Brockman's other clients. He demanded to take their call no matter what he was doing, but he'd eschew others lower down the food chain with a wave of his hand. As a result, I got to have extended conversations with folks such as Tracy Quan, who wrote *Diary of a Manhattan Call Girl*, and Nassim Taleb, the Lebanese American essayist who has written about randomness, uncertainty, and those rare, unpredictable events that he called "black swans," which have a catastrophic impact on society even while being explained in hindsight as if they might have been predicted.

I sometimes fantasized about becoming an agent, negotiating my own deals, and signing my own clients. I sold the Lithuanian rights to one of our books at the Frankfurt Book Fair, but when I excitedly told Brockman, he laughed, informing me that advances from Eastern European countries weren't worth the paper on which the contracts were printed. In fairness, he did use a particularly heavy stock.

The dream, it turned out, was grimmer than I had hoped. I grew browbeaten, eking out my share of the rent while Parker pointed out how much I was charging on my credit cards. I decided to accept an offer to teach at Queens College some weeknights after finishing my day with Brockman. It was part of their LEAP, or Labor Education & Advancement Project, and my class consisted of twelve mothers and grandmothers of color and one ridiculously buff firefighter named Tyrone.

All these years living in NYC and I had barely visited Queens, so being exposed to another borough was divine, if not for the insanely long time it took me to get to campus. I had to take the R train to Forest Hills (learning firsthand why the N/R line got the moniker the Never and Rarely) before taking a bus, then walking two avenue blocks to campus. Nearly a two-hour commute, door to door. Later, it would take me nearly that long to travel from New Haven to Grand Central.

I didn't know Forest Hills, but I did know Flushing, having been a few times with my parents to the Hindu Temple Society of North America Ganesh Temple. Built on the site of a former Russian Orthodox Church, it is one of the oldest extant Hindu temples in the country. Now, the temple has undergone a massive renovation, with tons of granite flown in from India and a new towering gopuram, but when I used to go, it was a well-worn anomaly in a neighborhood that might have been plucked from a street in Delhi. You'd see men wearing saffron dhotis and women in brightly hued *salwar kameezs* and could buy Indian groceries at Patel Brothers. Adjacent to New York's second-largest Chinatown, where shop-windows were crowded with barrels of dried seahorses and a dozen varieties of ginseng as large as my fist, this outer borough stretch of little India was known affectionately as Brown Town. On my way to college, I was glad to glimpse faces that resembled my own.

The LEAP program brought me in contact with some of the most interest-ing students I would ever teach, paraprofessionals who worked in hospitals or for the city. I held class in a rickety classroom with out-of-date furniture and particu-larly hard chairs that might rival Stefan Zwicky's concrete armchair for comfort. The class was meant to take on the specter of labor, so, in addition to teaching writing skills, we read thinkers such as Marx and Engels, Guy Debord, and How-ard Zinn. I can still hear the lilting voice of the Caribbean grandmother reading John Locke to the class with perfect elocution.

I had always felt Brown, but never queried what that meant. I suppose I assumed a tacit kinship with African and Hispanic Americans. But, in class, I learned my people were not part of their struggle. "My people" owned gas sta-tions and motels, were doctors or engineers, and won spelling bees and science fairs. They had never worked on a plantation or been the target of slurs that embody the trauma of this period and reenact its history.

"That's why you up front teaching and we back here learning, Professor!" Tyrone, the firefighter, never had a problem boiling down a subject to its pithy essence, nor did he feel particularly uncomfortable being surrounded by so many women. His words reminded me of the prevalence of the model minority myth, which construed Asian Americans as the most successful immigrant population by mobilizing them against others. This was, in large part, because of the idea that they were intelligent, hardworking, and—most importantly—*quiet*; they did not speak back to authority, break any laws, or raise a ruckus.

"Tyrone, all Asians aren't quiet and studious. And all Asians are not crazy rich, trust me. Did you ever hear of the Khmericans in Long Beach or the Laotians in Sacramento? Some of the poorest immigrant populations in America."

"You ever pick cotton? You ever call someone *massah*?"

"No, but if I had been Japanese American, I might have been forced to live in a concentration camp during World War II."

"All I'm saying is that you may be colored, but you not Black."

"Fair enough. My family might have been immigrants, but they chose to come to the US and had the means to do so, which speaks to a certain privilege. I won't deny it."

We often had such spirited and engaging discussions, and, on the last day of class, in homage to the room and my frequent complaints about the furnishings, they brought me a framed poster of the history of chairs from the Museum of Modern Art.

I loved that class.

Another solace was discovering the Asian American Writers Workshop, which had its offices at St. Mark's Place and Second Avenue. I still remember the Gap store it was under, the narrow staircase leading down to a doorway plastered with stickers, and the warm rush of entering a place with the unimaginable specter of shelves crammed with so many books by Asian American authors. Finding that space convinced me that I might find a community of writers as well.

I have never felt as much at home before or since that time in New York. I carry a somatic memory of spending an afternoon in Battery City Park and buying some kosher bialys, which I carried, still warm, in a brown paper bag. The sun was shining, and I was healthy, my body without an ache, my mind not racked with anxiety. I walked across the Brooklyn Bridge with a throng of joggers and bikers. Midway through, I stopped to take in the view, and the most blissful feeling engulfed me. I could see through the trusses, Manhattan on one side, Brooklyn on the other, the Statue of Liberty raising her torch. Parker loved me for being myself, and I had plenty of friends. There was nothing more I craved in the world. In the panoramic view, my buzzing ambition dimmed. My sense of alienation disappeared. I was alive with wonderment in the wind, looking down at the rippling water, standing on Hart Crane's bridge in the greatest city in the world.

It was the feeling of finally belonging, safe in my own skin, and held aloft by those who believed in me and my work. If I had been plucked by a tornado from my life at that instant, I would have wanted for nothing.

Then came the day that changed history forever.

9/11.

On the morning of Tuesday, September 11, I was headed to work at the literary agency. I got off the train at Columbus Circle to walk along the base of Central Park as I usually did, glad to glimpse the carriage horses and smell the roasting peanuts before sinking in front of a screen for the rest of the day. On this morning, I remember seeing a disproportionate number of people dawdling on the corner. Across the street from where I worked was the CBS Studios Plaza of the General Motors Building, and a crowd had gathered to crane their neck at a giant outdoor television screen.

"What's going on?" I addressed a man in a suit planted in my path, literally blocking my way forward.

"Think it's a prop plane. Lost its engines and must have clipped the World Trade Center. They're showing some footage."

I looked up at the cloud of billowing smoke filling the screen, then down Fifth Avenue, where already the beginning of the massive dust cloud the impact had engendered was beginning to bloom. I experienced the strange dislocation of being in two places at once. What followed next needs no recap, no blow by blow, but as I stood transfixed, a rubbernecker, the second hijacked airliner crashed into the south tower of the World Trade Center.

Seeing smoke from what was happening that very moment downtown re-broadcast on a giant screen in midtown was like the nightmare of Jean Baudrillard's *Simulacra and Simulation* come alive to consume us all. It didn't seem real. It seemed beyond hyperreal. The man in a suit shouted a string of invectives in the air. Another woman next to me fell to her knees, weeping and gnashing her hair. Some people started sprinting toward Central Park. I looked down the avenue and then back up at the screen. One cloud made of pixels. The other made of burning flesh.

I had no words. I could not look. I could not look away.

When I finally went up to work, the agency was huddled around a small hand-held television. Brockman had the receiver of the phone from his desk in one hand and a cell phone in the other. Every few seconds, one of them would ring, and he would bellow into it like calling to someone down a well. We spent that early morning in disbelief listening to Diane Sawyer and Charlie Gibson on *Good Morning America*. Terrorist attack. The planes had been intentionally flown into the towers. Osama Bin Laden was involved. The more I found out, the more I wanted to go down to the financial district to get in touch with my friends who lived and worked down there, but Brockman had other ideas. He motioned us all back to work. We all looked at him incredulously, but he insisted.

"Back to work," he urged. "You stop working now, and the terrorists will have won. Act like nothing happened. The world needs books on science *now* more than ever."

But there could be no work done that day.

Parker worked in Chelsea and had come uptown to go home with me. I had to go down to inform her that I wasn't allowed to leave yet. I held her close in the office waiting room, both of us in shock. Finally, in the early afternoon, Brockman relented and allowed us all to take a half day. Mass transit had shut down all over the city, so Parker and I walked across the Williamsburg Bridge. A random man was picking up strangers and giving them a ride down to the Brooklyn Promenade. We jumped into the flatbed of his pickup truck.

The remainder of that afternoon is simultaneously a blur and a series of stop-motion images. It was the closest I might ever come to war. People streamed by me in gas masks, holding hands, and crying. I hugged anyone within touching distance. Parker and I stood holding hands on the cantilevered platform looking across the East River. There was the bridge I had just recently walked across. The sky filled with dust, ash, and what seemed like millions of sheets of paper, cascading in the air like gigantic snowflakes. Squinting, I saw what might have been chunks of pulverized building fragmenting, or else the shape of people plummeting to their death. It felt as if someone was continuously jabbing an ice-pick into my temples. I wanted to sob in dismay but had no tears, just a dry mouth. We stood there in silence for far too long and only made it back home long after the sun had set.

There was a brief halcyon period in the weeks after 9/11—perhaps six weeks of grace—when New Yorkers pulled together like never before. We left poems for the firefighters, held open subway doors, and let strangers stall us on the street with a smile. We donated to charity and filled the cups of the homeless with loose change. We tried to love one another, in spite of being so inundated with human-ity that it took a conscious effort to do so. In time, though, as it always does, the post-traumatic glow of compassion began to wear off.

Christopher Lasch writes in his book *The Culture of Narcissism*, "every society reproduces its culture—its norms, its underlying assumptions, its modes of orga-nizing experience—in the individual, in the form of personality." How ironic that, in light of this enormous tragedy, I personally felt let down because, at the very moment that I had felt in my bones a true New Yorker, everything suddenly fell apart.

In terms of the economy, publishing was one of the first industries to feel the pinch. Within months, I was laid off from the agency. Then began the discrimi-nation. Just when being Indian seemed passably cool, I was refused service at a gas station in New Jersey. I was spat at and cursed by a group of Black teens in Prospect Park. A cop near Ground Zero threatened to confiscate my phone if I took a photograph of the wreckage. I was told to go back "to where the fuck I came from" by a couple of blonde sorority sisters from NYU. In a diner, when Bill O'Reilly proclaimed on TV that Muslims should be banned from entering the country, everyone looked over at me.

I wasn't Muslim or Arab, Sunni or Shia. I was a New Yorker—devastated and shaken to the core as much as the mayor. But I was also an Indian American who flinched reflexively at how fear allowed for hate-mongering. Sikh or Hindu, Sufi or Zoroastrian, it didn't matter. Brown bodies somehow emanated anti-American sentiment. As President George W. Bush put it, "We're fighting evil-doers . . . fighting people that hate our values, they can't stand what America stands for. And they really don't like the fact that we exist." *Who* didn't like the fact that *who* existed?

When Parker got a job working at a private college in Connecticut, I hesitated for only a minute. I loved the city, but it had burnt me out. I had grown tired of standing for the hundredth time with an elbow ground into my back and my face buried in the scruff of an unwashed hacky sacker on a stalled rush-hour subway train, or waiting in the rain for three hours just to be denied a ticket to Shakespeare in the Park. I had begun to be weighed down by the masses, besieged by the enormous fatigue of someone who has had to battle hordes to accomplish the simplest task for far too long. I was ready for a new horizon.

I was ready to follow the woman who would become the mother of my children into the next phase of our life together. In retrospect, whoever I would eventually turn into must have been intimately connected to whatever I had experienced back in New York. Our deepest selves connect to the trauma we experience. A part of myself died when we left the city, and, in the coming light of a sedate life in a small town, the memory of my time in the Empire State would only grow.

Like Evelyn Waugh, I might have mistaken the neurosis in the air back then as energy, or, like Joan Didion, been convinced that something extraordinary would happen any minute, any day, any month. All I know, looking back, is that I had been truly alive in the city: an enzyme ready to catalyze experience into art; a flaneur in the frenetically changing urban space; a self-styled, alt-rock, lit geek, no-name, Frank O'Hara or James Baldwin wannabe; an urbane and confused immigrant son with too much ambition and too little money, craving the kind of success ratified by publicity; someone for whom, for a brief instant in time, anything and everything could be—and was in fact—possible. As that greatest and most tragic of New York poets, Hart Crane, once wrote, "It has taken a great deal of energy, which has not been so difficult to summon as the necessary patience to wait, simply wait much of the time—until my instincts assured me that I had assembled my materials in proper order for a final welding into their natural form."

I would not know what my materials would be, nor how to begin to assemble them. Recent events had changed the world around me, reminding me that I could still be construed as a threat for nothing more than the color of my skin, and that danger could come from anywhere. Whatever final welding into form my fate would eventually take, I just knew that when we left the city I had grown to love, I had a rotten taste in my mouth.

KAAR (*Monsoon*)

Dear Parker,

I know you're not going to love this book, nor my impulse to parade out some sort of public apology when it probably should have remained private, and this gesture risks trampling on the intimacy we once shared. But you're an integral part of my story, and, as the mother of my children, will always be in my life. I know my days would have gone very differently had I been able to wrestle with some of these demons before we got married. In turning away from you, I spurned the divine plan of my life. Once, upon a mountaintop, I had a vision of the unfolding of our days together. It was a cracking open of my cosmic egg, and, to be honest, I've never quite seen the world the same after that.

Remember that joke our old friends had that, without me, you would have less to laugh about and that, without you, I wouldn't have a roof over my head. Truer for me than for you, I imagine. We both did a lot of crying near the end, until a certain numbness set in. I carry with me, as we all do, a template of how to love that was passed on to me by my parents, who, in turn, grew up in a culture where romance was secondary to duty. You were the first person to truly *see* me, and would not overlook what I might have been deceiving myself about, even if I didn't always like what the mirror of your love reflected back at me.

I remember meeting you in Venice after someone had stolen my wallet on the train, leaving me just enough lira to buy you a single long-stemmed rose, wishing desperately that you would be there waiting for me. And you were. You always were. We had courted through letters, and I can still taste our furtive first kiss in a train car on the way to Prague. I remember the shivery music from the *pipa* at our wedding and the raucous party we threw afterward at our house to celebrate. You were my best friend, before my girlfriend, before becoming my wife. I was so relieved to find that you were always who you seemed to be. No pretense or subterfuge—so unlike those divas I had dated, desirous of drama, way too into themselves to think of someone else. We used to stay up for hours talking on the phone, and, in time, we'd visit the world: from the Taj Mahal to the Giza pyramids. I should have been satisfied, but I share the restless mind of a vagrant, the lusty appetites of our reptilian forebearers, the recklessness of a gambler, and carry with me the conditioning from a culture of arranged marriages.

Still, we have our two precious little girls to show for what was always truly good between us. What was real. I'm sure that, in many ways, your life has grown easier without me, an Indian son who needed to be taught how to use a vacuum cleaner, a reprobate poet whose own deceits were so deeply embedded that they became second nature, a partner who was inconsiderate, intemperate, and sometimes rageful. But I also know that your life has grown harder while you've single-parented for long stretches while I've been away.

Words are flimsy and cannot fully capture my gratitude for you being such a good mother and honest person. I wish I had done many things differently, and our relationship is no exception. During our last days together, there was too much damage between us and inside me to imagine repair, but now I can imagine rediscovering our enduring friendship. I know that it's presumptuous to expect the healing between us to accelerate, but I long for it.

Love,
Ravi

Chapter Seven

Hold Your Mud

Three weeks into my time, and I've adjusted somewhat. I've been moved from the gymnasium floor to one side of Dorm #4 of the Hartford Correctional Center, which sleeps sixty men on thirty bunk beds. The space that three bunks make together is your cube, and it constitutes the area to which you are relegated for most of the day. During "count," you remain motionless on your bunk until a full head count has been taken and then cleared. The COs mainly stay in an area called the "Bubble," which has telephones, request forms, toilet paper, monitors for the cameras always running, and the intercom system by which they make announcements and issue threats.

I am assigned a bunk atop a gruffly bearded, Black twenty-year-old called Weezy. Most of the time, we sleep. As Weezy tells me, "Any time asleep is free time. You sleep away your bid, you golden." There's a lethargic, even leisurely, air in the dorms. Weezy tells stories to the cube about messing with the COs, like the time he dipped toilet paper in coffee grounds and left it by the COs' door because it looked just like a turd. It's the same sort of insouciance and shit talk that you might find at summer camp, the derelict element of boys being boys. When the stories end, the conversation always shifts back to the perpetual question: Who's the best rapper in the world? The new jacks front Tech N9ne, Gucci Mane, Drizzy, and Chief Keef, while the OGs (Original Gangstas) come with Eric B. & Rakim, Biggie, and Tupac. Peanut, who bunks next to Weezy and me, "doesn't care who you talking about" because, for him, it's J. Cole or nothing.

"Come on, 'Born Sinner!' It don't get smoother than that! *You made me versatile, well-rounded like cursive know you chose me for a purpose, I put my soul in these verses.* Oooh lord, he didn't just do it like that, did he?"

Peanut is a big man, pushing three hundred pounds, yet he is surprisingly nimble, and the memory of J. Cole has him bouncing on his lower bunk with a grin that lights up the dorm. He has a $200,000 cash bond, so will likely move to the blocks when they open up. He has a solid alibi and pretty much knows the real guilty party, but when I ask why he hasn't told the prosecutor, he looks at me like I'm crazy.

"Snitch, bro, you serious? Ain't no snitch bitch, better believe that. Imma hold my mud."

So the memory of the sweet sounds of J. Cole in the HCC dorms it is.

In the evening, the conversation turns more nostalgic, reminiscent about love or food—the first meal that might be eaten when each man's bid was done. Lavish detail is paid to the conjuration of red snapper, butterfish, ackee, steaming okra, cooking out on an early summer evening, Red Stripes under the moonlight listening to reggae. Peanut would eat southern fried chicken, collard greens, buttermilk biscuits with his mother's gravy, an entire watermelon.

"How about that pizza place in New Haven, Frank Pepe's?" I venture. "Ever been there?"

"Shit, Professor has been all up and down this state, ain't that right?"

I nod and quip, but I don't tell them that I've been, not just up and down the state, but around the globe; and I don't tell them that, if all goes according to plan, I will be in Hong Kong teaching graduate students in a few weeks. Instead, I simply imagine the first place I would dine after a month of eating chicken slop, mystery sausage, elbow macaroni slathered in unsalted sauce, and the fish patty that constitutes the "vegetarian" meal option.

I have lost weight, for sure, and I'm always hungry. Breakfast is served before six, lunch at ten thirty, and dinner at four, so that by the time evening rec time rolls around, everyone is ravenous, trying not to think about how long it would be until breakfast. Jailhouse cooking is as inventive as a challenge on *Top Chef*. The men steal whatever they can from the chow hall, pieces of bread or fruit to make pruno—a kind of bootleg liquor—or else meatballs, peanut butter, boiled vegetables, and ground hamburger meat, so that in the evening they can cook up a dazzling array of dishes. The most common is mofongo, Puerto Rican soul food, but made without mashed plantain mixed with *chicharrónes*. Instead, potato chips and crackers are crushed into powder and mixed with water to make a fine paste. This gets spread into an opened garbage bag and then rolled flat with a cylindrical deodorant container. Meanwhile, your homey mixes up soups, rice, mackerel, chopped sausages, Mrs. Dash seasoning, cheesy beans, and whatever else is floating around to spread on top of the chip paste, cover with the top of the bag, and twist into an enormous sausage that can be sliced to accommodate your whole cube. If you're feeling bold, you can even make a stinger: a convection oven made from a cardboard box, some garbage bags, saltwater, and an extension cord being held open by a broken piece of a nail clipper to retain the charge. The mofongo bag will shrivel as it cooks in the saltwater.

I put forth to the crew that, when I get out, I would like to have nothing more than some paper-thin *masala dosa*, and an entire South Indian thali, rice, *sambar*, *rasam*, *kootu*, *vadas*, curd, crispy *papads*, and some salt *lassi* to wash it down. I'm explaining the properties of the perfect dosa—crispy and light yet supportive of its filling—when I'm interrupted.

"Yo, you got roti there, right?" asks Gerald, who has asked me on many occasions about all things Indian. And so the conversation swings to Buss Up Shut Chicken and Potato Curry Roti, and the steel drums of the West Indian day parade, and what Gerald wouldn't do to be sitting out on his stoop with his girl. He's the daddy to her three kids—none of them even his—and she loves him so deeply for it.

When he mentions his children, I think of my own daughters, seven and three now—precocious creatures whom I haven't spoken to in weeks. Though I had been dead set against it, Parker insisted, and so we made the decision to tell the older one where I would be for six weeks. I framed it as a kind of teachable moment, explaining that even if we didn't agree with the rules, we had to follow them, and if we didn't, there would always be repercussions. I would be totally safe, I assured her, unsure myself of the truth of what I was claiming. Outwardly I smile when Gerald shows me the photographs of his own three little cuties, none of whom resemble him in complexion or body type.

Looking around Hartford Correctional, the racial dimension of mass incarceration is incontestable. The vast majority of inmates are Black or Hispanic—Puerto Rican, Dominican, Mexican, Haitian. There's someone from Iran, who won't speak to anyone. I'm the only one who originated from India. There are only a handful of White guys, probably six or seven in this dorm of sixty, and at least two of them are rumored to have serious weapons charges pending. Otherwise, it's all Brown and Black men, including a very strange guy with large, mournful eyes who swears he's from Bohemia and whom everyone curses at.

He has been incarcerated for obscenity and public indecency, having purportedly been seen handling himself in a public library. I don't push for details. He provides us with a vision of Bohemia instead—somewhere I have apparently mistaken for a kingdom that became part of the Czech Republic because, he assures me, it is actually an unknown island in the Caribbean. It's a place without electricity or modern commerce; you disembark and immediately enter the realm through two stone gates, and it's as if you have rediscovered the garden of Eden. There is alligator pear, *pop poi*, and *blim blim* growing wild, and a marketplace entirely based on the barter system. Later, I would hear that he might have flashed a child, and that is why everyone is so hard on him.

At morning rec time, we are awakened to the television tuned to some ungodly talk show and the sounds of men flapping bath slippers down to go wash up or shave. By then, the card and chess games have started, except in the poker cube that doesn't get going until much later. I go out to play basketball in the yard guarded by barbed wire. Some inmates refuse to go outside, claiming that the sight of the sun boxed into a rectangle is too much to handle, but I never forgo outdoor rec, if only for the Vitamin D and the exercise, the kiss of a momentary breeze. Beyond the gates, we can see the bottom halves of tires rotating past us, so I try to stay focused on the court. If I have realized one thing about myself while I've been in Dorm #4, it's that I'm much better at basketball than I thought I was. I go to work underneath the rim, clearing the boards and making a little fall away to the surprise and delight of my teammates and the chagrin of the others, especially a muscled and dreadlocked Black man called Dracula, who is the team captain by default.

"Shut down that Abu Dhabi motherfucker!" Dracula scowls. "I don't want to see him make another shot. Break his face if you need to, just shut him down."

"I got him, Dracula. Seriously I do." The sleepy-eyed Black twenty-year-old in for a domestic probably should have me. He has a springy first step and a passable finger roll. But he is breathing heavily and seems defeated by the sun. Weezy dribbles and dishes to Peanut, who should post up, given his girth, but always chooses to take wild jumpers instead. This time, though, he passes to me as I'm cutting in the lane with the kid on my back. I give him a pump fake, and he uncoils high into the air with his palms outstretched, ready to smack some rubber. When he's halfway back down, I go up myself and lay in an easy two. Dracula is not happy. From that moment on, he makes me one of his first two picks.

Indoor rec is always more trying. During the day, I sink into books as often as possible. The selection offered to inmates is always shifting, and each book has to go through the Publication Review Board, which determines whether or not the material is fit for consumption. Every few weeks, a memo appears on one of the corkboards telling the population which publications have been reviewed. The list encompasses periodicals as well—going so far as to list what exact pages in *Men's Health* or *Hip Hop Weekly* need to be removed for objectionable material. The April 15 issue of *The Nation* is allowed, but only if pages four and six are removed. None of the books that have been ordered for me from friends have arrived yet, so I'm scrounging for anything I can get my hands on. The PRB-approved list for today is limited to Amanda Knox's memoir; *Hell Razor Honeys 1* and 2; and Mark Leyner's *My Cousin, My Gastroenterologist*, so when I find a random pile of books discarded on top of the Plexiglas-encased television in the day room, I parcel them out like rare, delectable treats.

One of the books in the pile is by Chatral Rinpoche, who issues this challenge: "In its true state the mind is naked, immaculate, transparent, empty, timeless, uncreated, unimpeded; not realizable as a separate entity but as the unity of all things, yet not composed of them; undifferentiated, radiant, indivisible … to know whether this is true or not, look inside your own mind." Reading that, I sit concentrated on my breath, letting the waves of guilt and regret wash over me, abiding in and releasing it with each breath.

When my commissary money finally comes through, I buy shower shoes so that I no longer have to cadge them off someone else, along with some other essentials such as toothpaste and soap. It's a relief not to have to use that shard of state soap that burns like bleach.

Each week, I also order the maximum allowable number of soups, which are the basic unit of currency on the inside. The packs of Ramen noodles cost thirty-two cents apiece, or roughly three for a dollar, and so are perfect to value everything that you could possibly buy or trade for on the inside. Throughout the day, calls can be heard for some good or service being offered in soups: "honey bun, four soups"; "handmade drippers, two soups"; "pack of slim jims, three soups." Those deemed indigent, or who have had less than five dollars on their books for at least a month, are allowed the meager provisions given during orientation, which they could then trade for soup. Others perfect one hustle or another; they cut your hair or rent you a radio for a soup. In a real sense, the spirit of entrepreneurship and ingenuity is on full display.

Some run the medical hustle, traffic in the pills that they are meant to take but keep lodged in the roof of their mouth to dry out and sell. There's Wellbutrin, jailhouse coke when ground up and sniffed, and suboxone—or subs—for heroin addiction, which is coveted by some. Anytime there's an influx of new inmates, there's a sudden enthusiasm and rumor about anyone who may have swallowed a balloon. The correct way of doing this is told to me by a Hispanic guy called Tio. You take a plastic balloon and put that in a condom, then put that back in a balloon before you put your drugs in it. You need the three layers for the digestive acids because you might get sick and not be able to shit it out.

Today someone has brought some herb into our cube and, as I'm lying immersed with a book, Tio is suddenly kneeling near the back of my bunk, gesticulating for me not to draw attention to him. He is squatting by the electric outlet and produces a small pipe, rolled from a playing card that has the metal top to a pencil punctured into it. From somewhere in his pants, he brings out a Q-tip, which he coats in Vaseline and attaches a small nib of pencil lead to, then sticks it in the outlet. The makeshift match glows brightly as he nudges it to the lip of the pipe, inhaling deeply. He takes a long drag and doesn't even look to offer me one, then he springs up, producing from another unseen orifice a sock filled with baby powder, which he waves so that it mingles with the smell of weed. It smells pretty obvious to me, but he just grins and gives me a thumbs-up. He's crawled back to his bunk and has his headphones on before the CO even notices a thing.

My main interaction with the other inmates comes from chess. I used to play when I was younger, and I have picked it up again with an avidity that surprises me. There's one Black guy called OG, short for Original Gangsta, as any man over thirty invariably is called here, whom I play with multiple times a day and have only beaten thrice. I don't dare to ask him his name and haven't gotten a glimpse of his ID card, so he is OG to me as well. I enjoy our thoughtful, reflective games as well as his story, which is unfortunately common. His girlfriend and mother of his two children had a restraining order against him that they both tried to get dropped once they had reconciled, but the family court would not allow it. When he was over there visiting his kids, someone else called the cops because there was a fire next door. When they ID'd everyone, they found out about his restraining order and put him in jail. He thinks that if he waits a full thirty days, he'll get time served and they'll let him go, though he doesn't know for sure.

"Connecticut is a woman's state, tell you that, Professor. If you a crazy jealous chickenhead who want to take a brother down, you can do it easy. No fault, no way! Put a restraining order on him, and then find out where he at. Next thing you know, he be at the library, she be at the library. He at the coffee shop, her girlfriends tell her to go there as well, track him and then call the cops to say he violating his order just because he's dating someone else. Happen to a bunch of friends of mine." OG pauses, his brow furrowed in consternation. "My case even crazier because, my girl and I, we get along real good these days and just want to be parents. But I done lost my job now, being in here for thirty days, for what? For seeing my kids. Had a good job too, have my electrician's license, Local 35, been working with a contractor real steady, and now I got to start from scratch when I get out."

Since OG is a convicted felon, it is that much harder for him to reenter the workforce or have a protective order dropped. He shot at someone in self-defense and spent most of his twenties in Osborn, one of the other correctional facilities in the state. That's where he first learned how to play chess. But, since his release, he had been doing really well—all things considered.

Until now, that is. It is his first time here in six years, but he seems to know he'll be back again before long. We play chess during afternoon rec and, invariably, he beats me. I try to move my knights out first, build a pawn defense, try a bishop sacrifice, and, almost every single time, he outfoxes me in games that take a half hour or more—not because we are moving slowly but because there's such an intensity of grappling. Or so it seems to me, when, in fact, he could be toying with me. I don't think so, though. He compliments my strategy when I bait him into exchanging a knight for a rook and press my advantage until attaining a hard-earned checkmate. But, mainly, our games end with me trudging back to my cube dejected.

Playing with OG has improved my game, and I start to win soups from those who see me lose time after time and call me out as a potential easy mark. I have some tight matches with Tatu, named for his resemblance in height and visage to the character from *Fantasy Island* ("ze plane! ze plane!"). He talks a big game and has surprisingly chiseled forearms for someone pushing fifty with eight grandkids. At times he seems to be quite harmless and avuncular, but then he suddenly verges into talking about his life as a pimp. How he was slinging crack away from his main woman down in Virginia Beach, tricking with his shorty on the side and his jump off, and a whole different side emerges.

"It's always the jump off you got to worry about," Tatu tells me, racking his brain on whether or not to castle. "You think you have her on the down-low, but she can go loco on you. I had one who call the cops on me, tell them about where I hid my burners, how much cane I sling, everything. Just because she want me for herself."

He's a good chess player, but I win three soups off him before we're through.

The one I relish playing the most is Domo, a big, good-looking, slightly gap-toothed Dominican, the eldest son of a family that owns a few car dealerships and auto body shops around Windsor Locks. He calls me Indio, so, in turn, he's Domo from the DR. Domo is a fun-loving kind of guy. He is the first-generation immigrant son of Dominicans who have found the American dream. They began with a small auto shop in Bristol and moved on to buy a wrecker, then a car dealership, and they now own three auto body shops and two dealerships between them. The first time Domo was in trouble for hot-wiring construction equipment and having a real-life demolition derby in an abandoned Hartford lot, his mother paid a straight cash bond to keep him out. Then there was that unfortunate drunk driving episode when he spun out his car, got the ride drifting, and then hit a tree in the front yard of the chief prosecutor of the New Britain court. Talk about bad luck.

"Her husband is a state trooper," he tells me, "and he comes out in his robe, no badge or anything, and flips out, wrestles me to the ground when I'm staggering out of the car. He has me on the ground with his boot on my neck when the paramedics arrive. That's got to be a lawsuit, right?" I have decided to agree with everyone who thinks they can win money from the state or beat the charges they are accused of, simply because it will buoy them up, so I nod in assent.

"My lawyer got me through all of this, but the last one, Indio," Domo continues, "man, he royally effed up. He made me cop-out on a weapons charge even though I didn't have a piece on me. See, I was just in Taco Bell in Berlin when this *cholo* started jawing at me. It was late at night when all those muscle cars and pimped-out pickups line all up and down the Turnpike. This guy thinks he smooth, he drives a tricked-out Toyota with rims and tints, but I drive a BMW X5—you catch what I'm throwing? I don't need no nitro valves in my shit to make it fly. He still running his mouth and following me, and I see his gang all circled around my car like they want to throw down, and I think I see someone flash some steel. I'm not sure what I saw, but I put my finger under my hoodie like I'm packing and run past them yelling mad crazy shit, scare the fuck out of them and jump in my ride, peel out fast, then come back around with that 4.4 liter engine humming. Their eyes popped out white now. They cowering, and I just squeal by and leave them in the dust like a bunch of losers, but one of them has to call the cops. They pull me over a mile down the road. They got nothing on me: no gun, no video, no booze. But my lawyer tells me that, because of this five-year cap he put on my ass last time, they're going to drop all the other charges—interference, threatening, all of that—but that I just need to cop a single weapons charge. So I do. But there was no gun! It was my finger. And that shit's a felony!"

He looks so pained that I refrain from once again confirming that, yes, without a gun it is unlikely that he would have been found guilty, and that he likely got a bum rap—if he is indeed telling me the truth. Instead, I challenge him to another game of chess.

My practice with OG pays off, because I beat Domo like a tabla. Straight up, double or nothing, soups or no soups, I beat him nearly as much as OG beats me. But he's cool with it because we have a side business together selling coffee balls, so neither of us is suffering. Coffee remains the most craved-for drug in jail, and there are those who can spend hours trying to cadge a splash. If you can afford a bag of Colombian freeze-dried crystals, some Sweet Mate, and some creamer, you can parse that out into enough coffee balls to pay for the raw material three times over. If you're able to control the supply, coffee can be your come off.

I've been somehow introduced to the upper echelon of black-market commerce because I've been able to garner an oversize garbage bag that Domo has torn with the side of a bolt and filled with all the makings of a coffee ball, the elemental unit equivalent to one soup. You can make a ball of anything: a cheese ball, a peanut butter ball, a lotion ball, a shampoo ball—all of them for sale. If you know the right person, someone who does laundry and who moves from the blocks to the dorms, you can find someone who wants to buy or sell what you are looking for. I manage to leverage my soups and coffee balls into a cheap radio, and now Domo accuses me of dream driving at night, my eyes closed to groove to *Late Night Love*, instead of staying up bullshitting, watching them play jokes on the new guy with the Gene Shalit mustache, or playing spades.

Spades is my card game of choice. The cards we play with are Connecticut Cold Case cards, which never cease to disconcert me. All fifty-two cards in the deck have an unsolved homicide on them, with the name and photograph of the victim. There's Dionn Brown, aka "Queens or Q," a twenty-two-year-old male who was shot and killed in a parking lot at Church Street and East Street in New Britain. Now he's the queen of spades. There's Black George "Junebug" Fawcett (seven of diamonds) and White Dennis "Seaweed" Kelp (nine of diamonds), both of whom have cash rewards for any information leading to the apprehension of their murderers. There's the seven of clubs, seventy-three-year-old Joseph Kulikowski, found stabbed to death in Bridgeport, and the ace of spades, Tynell "Blue" Hardwick, shot and killed in Norwich, whom some of the inmates seem to know. They call his name when the card wins them a hand: *Get money, Blue!* Joey Juice, another new transfer, knew Antonio "Tont" Perry, killed at age twenty in 2006, so, whenever the four of spades is played, he insists on a moment of silence. It's odd enough to see these victims transmuted into suits on a deck of playing cards, but even more bizarre that some lives are valued more than others so explicitly. I wonder how successful this anonymous tip line is, or if the "no snitching" policy supersedes even the promise of a cash reward.

Somehow, I doubt that the campaign is very effective. Ultimately, the Department of Corrections is an Orwellian misnomer: the DOC ensures that criminality is alive and well. The addicts here need rehabilitation clinics and counseling; the young men here need to finish school. I constantly hear about the impossibility of reintegrating convicted felons into society, the obstacles put in each person's pathway by probation and parole—from restrictions on movement and travel that preclude one from holding a job, to the unholy mandates of a restraining order that make it impossible to be a father. Before I arrived here myself, I may have blamed these prisoners for getting themselves into their predicament, but now I'm not so sure. Even though HCC is a county jail, not a permanent address for the sentenced, I am nonetheless unable to find any possibility of rehabilitation, no matter how hard I look. I know a school exists, though when I volunteer my services to tutor there, I am told my name will be kept on file and never hear anything again. The on-premises library has been removed because too many inmates were doing legal research on their cases.

I manage to fill my days, but nowhere do I see the Department of Corrections doing what it promises to do: fulfilling the mandate that I see hanging pinned on a corkboard, a notice to the inmate population signed by DOC Commissioner Leo Arone in 2010: "As you are aware, the Department of Corrections is charged with providing a safe, secure and humane environment while providing opportunities that support successful community reintegration. In closing, we have an obligation to provide a safe environment to all concerned. We shall do everything within our control to fulfill this environment."

Bullshit. Besides screening a video about STDs upon arrival and telling us that mental health counselors are available upon request, the Connecticut DOC takes no further interest in the lives of its prisoners. What I see day to day is the enforced inculcation of laziness, which requires that inmates sit on their bunks for half of their waking hours, gambling or provoking others, which are some of the easiest ways to pass the time. After being cooped up for so long, it is clear that the first thing some of these guys are going to do when they get out is go on a huge binge. These men, often identified and stigmatized as problematic from a very young age, have not been given even the most rudimentary tools to reintegrate into society. Indeed, idle conversation among them often turns into how to commit better crimes, because every shot at legitimately making an existence has proven a virtual impossibility for those with a criminal record. The fact that most of these men have committed a felony or misdemeanor means that, even though they—we—will do our time, and even though we might have truly repented and changed, we will never quite be forgiven in American society. Too many people are forced to eke out their existence on the margins, moving into and out of a state of incarceration that is implicitly sanctioned and explicitly paid for by society.

So, instead, we ball. We bait bishops. We run money early and often. We tell comic stories, inflecting with machismo and swagger the hour when we might be cradling a loved one. We do push-ups in the dayroom and curl water bags for our biceps. We put apples and bread down our pants. We wait for our turn at the Securus telephones, where our calls are recorded and monitored. We wait on letters and visits with the ardor of a man at sea waiting for land. We barter soups and try to survive. We are not being corrected but feel the sting of rejection, our lives typified into a litany of charges on a piece of paper in the bail commissioner's hand. Some of us will bond out, and others will be transferred up the way, where the leisure apparently multiplies, where there are handball courts and full-contact visits and salad bars. If we are lucky, we will learn that even those of us on the outside are all doing time, that our own habits can constitute a kind of prison, and that, even enclosed within four walls, our mind has the extraordinary capacity to be free.

In the evening, we have to remain on our bunks until the count clears and every man is accounted for by the COs. I might wallow that long hour away, or write in my journal, sometimes transcribing quotations from the books I had borrowed, like those of Milarepa taken from a dog-eared Buddhist prayer book. *I am indifferent to the experiences of good and bad. With mind free and effortless, I rest in happiness and joy. When subject and object are realized as a single sphere, happiness and sorrow mingle as one. Whatever circumstances I encounter, I am free in the blissful realm of self-awakening wisdom.*

Alone with myself, in a place I never dreamed I would be, I realize that I am not the perfect son, not an unfailing husband, not a role model professor, not the most fully realized father, much as I endeavor. I'm not my name, or my family history, or my social class. I'm not just a subversive poet who somehow ended up in jail. Rather, I'm a being who, irreducibly, at base is simply a pulse of pure potential and cosmic energy, entering and leaving my body. I am the lives I am touching briefly, that have accepted me—and I them—as roommates for a time. I am not judged by them and thereby can suspend my own judgment of myself, halt the recitation of missteps that unreels obsessively in my head. On my bunk with these men for this brief instant in time, playing chess, cards, and basketball, sharing stories along with our interpretation of certain statutes and photos of our family, I find myself no more or less human than anyone around me. At last, I can simply breathe.

Chapter Eight

Nomenclature

In the early days of my stint in jail, I grew immune to the labels the other inmates called me: Abu Dhabi, India, Apu, Kumar, Bin Laden, 7-Eleven, Terrorist, Professor—all interchangeable, uttered casually and unironically. Sticks and stones, right? Paradoxically, rather than growing insulted, having a nickname actually made me feel more accepted by the men around me, all of whom had nicknames. Often they were a kind of ethnic shorthand, which would have rankled on the outside, but strangely created community inside. However, I had learned early in life the lesson of detachment from any given name, so I was unbothered. After all, I share my name with India's most famous musician!

On NPR, Alan Greenblatt published a piece titled "Identity Crisis: Your Name Is Famous but You Aren't," which begins, "Chris Brown is a 30-year-old white guy from Alabama who can't sing or dance to save his life, but he has gotten sick of all the Rihanna jokes." The article goes on to detail the mild nuisance that sharing a famous name has for a number of Americans. There's a Meg Ryan, who always gets, "Tom Hanks is waiting for you in the lobby"; a Michael Jackson, who is greeted with, "Yeah, and I'm Madonna"; and a Carla Bruni, who confesses to the incalculable number of times she's had a man ask her with a wink how she likes being French royalty.

My favorite example has to be the gangsta-rap loving character in the movie *Office Space*, who refuses to change his name from Michael Bolton because, well, he's not the one who sucks. That exasperation seems relatively mild, of course, compared to those who share a name with a mass murderer, a porn star, or someone on a terrorist watch list (especially when they are trying to board an international flight).

Did my name account in part for my obsessive shape-shifting, for the gaping void I felt at the core of whatever my true identity might be? Was I fated to steal myself back from the pandit sitar player, or die trying? Names might carry family histories, follow trends, or just smack of cosmic coincidence, although, like all of us, when I was still an embryo floating in Amma's womb, I was free and nameless. Even though there had been a name already picked out for me—someone else's more famous name, as it would turn out—I was undefined in utero, just a conjoining of chromosomes, a growing pulse of pure potential.

In South India, I would have remained in that nameless state for the first eleven days of my life on earth, at which point a *namkaran* could be performed. One of the sixteen *samskaras*, or purification rites, this formal ceremony (which derives from the Sanskrit root "*nam*" or name, and "*karan*," or create) is the moment when the father disperses grains of rice on a bronze thali, or dish, then traces out the child's chosen name using a golden stick. It's the moment for him to whisper that name four times into his offspring's right ear and thereby officially socially sanction the newly emergent life.

During my time as a young boy in Madras, our family would take walks at dusk, past the colonial-era dak bungalows and stuccoed lime buildings fixed with facades to resemble stone. Sometimes we would walk as far out as Marina Beach, where there were kites flying high in the air, *jalebi* and *pakora* wallahs jostling for your attention, and knots of people everywhere. In some stretches, a proliferation of plastic bags and soda cans made passage nearly impassable. Still, there was the Bay of Bengal stretching to the horizon. Amma would write our names, or ॐ, in the part of the sand where the water had not touched and, in mere moments, the gray froth would wash it away.

It was during one of these long walks that Rajni and I stopped with Amma at the storefront of that Nādi astrologer through whose corrugated tin door one could see newspapers stacked floor to ceiling, in what was surely a severe fire hazard. I can still feel my boy's hand in the rough shriveled claw of the astrologer as she flipped my palm backward and forward as efficiently as if she were frying dough. She asked Amma for my birth date and peered closely at my thumbprints before consulting a set of long, brown, rectangular palm leaves bound by string and covered in minute scribbles. It was there that she foretold my rise and eventual fall into misfortune.

When you are born in South India, you are assigned a nakshatra, or lunar mansion, according to the position of the constellations. Instead of the dozen signs of the Greek zodiac, Indians have twenty-seven (or twenty-eight) star signs: from *bharani*, the gift-bearer; *mula*, the root; to *hasta*, the hand. Being born in January, a Capricorn, my nakshatra is *tiruvōnam*, represented by three bright stars: Alpha-Aquilae, Beta-Aquilae, and Gamma-Aquilae. Often, you will see this star sign symbolized as an ear, a trident, and a set of uneven footsteps. It is the birth star of Saraswati, the goddess of knowledge. Vishnu, the preserver among the Hindu trinity, is its main presiding deity. By its illuminating and cryptic lights, the lines on my palm were etched.

I don't believe in astrology, but I don't necessarily disbelieve it either. The map of my hand has proven true, though perhaps I was simply bound for notoriety from the moment Appa whispered my name into my infant ear. Laura Wattenberg, creator of BabyNameWizard.com, advises expecting parents against burdening their newborn with a famous moniker, suggesting, "even before you're born, someone has stolen part of your identity. Everybody who hears your name thinks of somebody else." Unfortunately, Amma and Appa never heard this advice, and though this happens less frequently these days, at least once a week during the first forty years of my life, someone would remark on my name. After all, Ravi Shankar is one of the few Indians of whom any non-Indian has ever heard, because he was a sitar master who played at Woodstock and served as an ambassador for Indian culture in the West. For good measure, he also had one famous daughter, Grammy-winning jazz-pop singer Norah Jones, out of wedlock, and another, Anoushka, who would go on to become his protégé.

What's it like to share a name with India's most famous musician? It's a curse and boon, being rendered forever both anonymous and unforgettable. It means being subjected to bad George Harrison puns and air sitar solos. The irony is that my parents are not even music lovers. Save for John Denver and Hindu bhajans, Amma has no keenness for song, and Appa, in his stern disavowal of all forms of sensuality, finds even Kenny G's jazz saxophone riffs a little too profane. I was only named Ravi because I was born during Pongal, which is the Tamil harvest festival that celebrates what my name means in Sanskrit: the sun.

Ever since I was in suspenders and knee socks (a fashion statement I only wish was figurative), I have recognized that, no matter what I might accomplish in this lifetime, I will always be eclipsed to some degree by this elder statesman whose name has become synonymous with his instrument. Ravi Shankar, the musician, was born Robindro Shaunkor Chowdhury (really, Pandit? You couldn't, like a Brazilian soccer star, have stuck to Robindro?) in Varanasi, India, in 1920. More than Les Paul or Jimi Hendrix, Yo-Yo Ma or Jascha Heifetz, when you say *sitar*, you immediately conjure the great Pandit. Unfortunate for me, then, to live my life as the secondary Ravi.

Actually, I'm no more than the world's *third* most famous Ravi Shankar because in addition to the late musical genius, there is also Sri Sri Ravi Shankar, whose work spans the role of humanitarian ambassador, meditation instructor, spiritual teacher, and peace advocate. According to his website biography, he was a precocious child who could recite parts of the Bhagavad Gita by age four and graduated with degrees in physics and Vedic literature by age seventeen. His Art of Living self-development courses are offered in more than 150 countries. Touché Sri Sri.

Now, if you've ever seen a sitar in real life, the most impressive thing about it might be its size. About four feet in length, it's not exactly the kind of instrument that you can strap to your shoulder and wail away on. It has a large, gourd-shaped body made from teak or Indian mahogany, a long and hollow wooden neck, two bridges, and around twenty curved and scalloped frets. Most challengingly, the Indian sitar usually has seventeen metal strings (and can have upward of twenty-three). These include melody, drone, and sympathetic strings, which are used to play and accentuate the rhythm, giving ragas their signature shivery, reverberating buzz.

While you pluck the instrument with a wire plectrum called a *mizrab* with one finger, you might use another finger to strum an overtone. Adding to this complexity is the fact that the instrumentation and musical notation for the instrument are totally different than in Western music. There are no chords or harmony, but rather talas (rhythmic cycles) and *rasas* (moods), making the sitar one of the most difficult instruments to play, let alone to master.

Thankfully for me, I was never asked to live up to my namesake on this most daunting of instruments, though I was for a brief time first-chair cello in my middle school orchestra. (First and *only* chair, that is—one out of one.) I had wanted to play the drums in the jazz band, feeling intuitively that I might make up for what I lacked in pitch and melody with rhythm, but whatever Appa felt about Kenny G's saxophone only went doubly for the lusty and primal drum. I placated him by choosing the cello with its deep and honeyed mellifluousness, not foreseeing the social suicide my choice would engender.

I didn't realize at the time what relative privilege even having access to classical music training in a public school entailed, as so many schools around the country have begun to systematically defund the arts. Instead, I lamented how most of the other members of the orchestra were wealthy enough to have a practice instrument that they left at home and a performance instrument that they stored at school. However, I had just the one rented cello, massive in its zippered nylon case, which I lugged to and from school. If any potential new friends had thought about sitting next to the lone Indian boy on the school bus before, their choice was made easier. After about a month in the orchestra, I wished desperately to ditch or hide the oversized albatross, but it turns out that's hard to do with a companion the width of a 1950s refrigerator.

Being the only cellist in the orchestra, I groused over the bright and nasal tones of the viola and violin, resonant as a baby hippo being strangled by a boa constrictor. Always off-key and behind the measure, I never *felt* the music and, instead, memorized fingerings the way one would multiplication tables. I cringe to imagine what further acoustic violence I might have wrought with the far greater number of strings on the sitar.

In kindergarten, where I was only enrolled for a month before being skipped ahead, my teacher, Mr. Fatuma, a mildly patchouli-scented man whose shoulder-length gray hair was tied off in a ponytail, remarked upon my name daily with amazement. He read to us each morning with a beatific smile, which I now fear might have signaled that he was stoned the whole time. One day, noticing me reading a chapter book during nap time, he motioned me over and walked me over to a classroom full of first-graders. This was one of those primordial dislocations that would have a profound effect on me well into my later years. From then on, I was fated to be younger than all of my peers—a skinny, brainy Indian who wanted nothing more than to be a regular, all-American White boy. What is more, having inherited this toxic ancestral idea of the uniqueness of my genes, I now had proof. I was marked: a TamBrahmAm who had skipped kindergarten.

As I grew up in Manassas, a city that still had many houses that flew the Confederate flag, I would hear from a wide variety of people—librarians, school bus drivers, grocery clerks, and new neighbors—how I shared my name with the only other Indian whom they had ever heard of. Somehow, however, perhaps out of sheer stubbornness, I didn't listen to my namesake's music until high school. By then, I was a bona fide mongrel with no real cultural home. My bifurcating sense of self had metastasized, and I had begun to compartmentalize completely: model Hindu and strict vegetarian at home, skateboarding punk who sneaked out to McDonald's for cheeseburgers and cigarettes in high school.

That summer between tenth and eleventh grade, I was loitering with a couple of buddies, exploring one of the new homes being built in the neighborhood. We used to love these transitional sites as they had all the hallmarks of a suburban adolescent's jungle gym. They were complete with rafters to swing on, rolls of pink insulation to use as punching bags, and pallets on which to lay pieces of drywall to make killer launch ramps. We would duck into these homes out of the humidity of the Virginia heat and run amok.

One of my friends was a wiry boy with a missing front tooth who would later serve time in a juvenile detention center for setting off pipe bombs in a salvage yard, which only added to his cultural capital. He was the best skater among us, and also something of a musical aficionado. Everywhere he went, he carried his ghetto blaster, pumping out jams at the bus stop or in the unfinished basements we would carve our boards around. Usually, we listened to terrible stuff, bands whose percussion sections sounded like revved-up dentist's drills, music like DRI (the Dirty Rotten Imbeciles), Testament, Anthrax, and the Butthole Surfers. But, on this particular day, Jason waved a cassette tape in our faces.

"Time you fools got schooled in the classics."

"What's that?" I asked, trying and failing for an umpteenth time to ollie more than a half inch off the ground.

"Here's a clue," he muttered prophetically, then turned to stick a lewd and mottled tongue between two fingers. "Ring any bells?"

No one answered.

"You Betties dumber than you look."

"Whatever, dude. Blast it, if you got it," said Jonathan Upperman, the son of the county's superintendent. He was busy grinding the nose of his deck against what would someday become someone's kitchen countertop. Jason fiddled with his portable stereo and stepped back triumphantly.

I see a red door and I want it painted black. No colors anymore I want them to turn black. I see the girls walk by dressed in their summer clothes. I have to turn my head until my darkness goes . . .

"Who the hell is that?" asked Jonathan. "Journey? The Rascals?"

"You really are dense," Jason, the only one of us who had flunked a grade, chortled. "Ever watch *Full Metal Jacket*? That's the Rolling Stones! You know, Mick Jagger and Keith Richards? You know . . . those lips." He flickered his tongue out again like a rattler. "Used to make some righteous shit before they went soft."

"I like that guitar lick," I ventured hesitantly, as much of a poseur in the terminology of rock music as I was in skating.

"That's not a *gee-tar*, that's a, how you call it, a *see-tar*," Jason informed us. "You should know, Shankar. That snake-charming sound comes from the towel heads in your part of the world."

It turns out that the Stones' lead guitarist, Brian Jones, had picked up the sitar from George Harrison, who had used the instrument in the Beatles' "Norwegian Wood (This Bird Has Flown)." The Beatles apocryphally discovered the instrument at an LSD-fueled party at Zsa Zsa Gabor's LA mansion in 1965, thus inspiring them to discover Indian classical music, meet Maharishi Mahesh Yogi, and embrace transcendental meditation, turning on and tuning in a generation of hippies. In time, Pandit Shankar would play the Monterrey Pop Festival and, yes,

Woodstock. However, he was innately conservative and apparently so shocked by what he saw in the drug-addled, mud-rolling youths, and so enraged at seeing Jimi Hendrix destroy his guitar that he nearly walked off stage in protest.

But he didn't. He stayed and played, and his performance at Woodstock cemented his reputation in the West as "the godfather of world music." He might have been bothered that a form of music that he considered sacred was being used as the gateway to superficial hedonism, but he was nonetheless shrewd enough to realize what performing with American and British rock legends would do for his career, and for exposing the world to Indian classical traditions. Without the Beatles and Woodstock, Shankar might have simply been another Gauhar Jan, Ustad Amir Khan, or Shivkumar Sharma, giants of Hindustani music who are little known outside India. With them, his time-bending ragas came to embody a certain apotheosis of the psychedelic movement during the heyday of sixties counterculture, ushering a yogic influx into the consciousness of the flower power generation.

I can think of dozens of times since childhood that someone has related to me some tale about being in an arena in Detroit, a festival in Helsinki, or a high school gymnasium in San Jose, sitting or lying face-down in the haze of pot smoke on a rolled-up peacoat, wafting away on the otherworldly reverberations of the mystical sitar, in a concert they would never forget. Plus, though he is deified, the Pandit was no saint, and while he might have rejected hippie culture, he certainly didn't mind the codicil of free love that led him to numerous extramarital liaisons.

It sounds depressing, but it was also empowering to realize that I would never be Ravi Shankar, even as I surely was. My name had already been taken and, therefore, I could do whatever I liked and be whomever I dreamed. Overdetermined by family, this fact made me utterly and irrevocably free. If it was always going to be a mild letdown or vicarious thrill for someone to meet me, if they were going to prejudge me even before they actually got to know me, then I'd be a creature beyond their wildest imaginings.

Over the years, sharing a name with a famous person has had both positive and negative aspects. If I were keeping score, in the former column would be moments such as when, as a poor graduate student in New York City, I was hand-delivered a gold-embossed invitation to attend Roberto Calasso's book launch at the Pierpont Morgan Library in midtown Manhattan. When I arrived at one of the inner chambers of the Italian Renaissance-style palazzo, there was Dom Perignon being served in flutes by tuxedo-wearing staff, silver trays garlanded with lobster canapés, deviled quail eggs speckled generously with Tobiko caviar, and risotto croquettes drizzled with truffle oil. Gorging myself, I had to admit that a case of mistaken identity was not always so bad.

In the latter column are the number of times that the light of enthusiasm suddenly dimmed into disappointment when someone realized that *I* am not *he*. Possibly the most egregious example of this was when I was performing at the Carrboro Poetry Festival in North Carolina, an area self-styled as the "Paris of the Piedmont," and had agreed to do another reading at a local library. When I was being introduced by the self-effacing librarian and began to take my place in front of the podium to read from my latest book, an elderly gentleman in a fedora and rheumy eyes stood up and shook his cane menacingly at me.

"That's not Ravi Shankar!" he shouted, as if I had perpetrated the crime of body snatching. Loudly clattering aside his folding chair, he dramatically but glacially made his way to the exit, muttering epithets under his breath. Emboldened by their comrade outing me as a fake, the rest of the dozen or so blue hairs proceeded to follow suit, some of them looking at me with pity and silently tut-tutting, while others glared at me as if I had cheated them out of the price of admission (free). Because they were mainly senior citizens, and a couple of them were in wheelchairs and walkers, the mass exodus happened in agonizing slow motion. When they were gone, I was left onstage with the sheepish librarian and just one other person in the audience, a drowsy teenager bottled up with earbuds, likely oblivious that there was even a poetry reading scheduled to happen.

I've often been asked why I don't just change my name. There are blogs that offer advice on how to market yourself if you share a famous name, tips that run the gamut from switching to a middle name (as long as it's not "Norbert" or "Hortense"), using just initials, using all three names, adopting a nom de plume, or even legally changing your name. After years of feigning delight and chuckling along to someone's idea that they are the first to have made the connection between myself and the sitar, I suppose I've gotten used to it. And you won't find me grousing too much if someone buys my books because they think they are his. Plus, as my own reputation gets dragged through the mud, I'm glad for the anonymity his name provides—that I'm buried deeper down in Google search results than I might have been.

Nonetheless, perhaps hoping to close some existential loop in my own life, for a period, I became obsessed with meeting my more famous doppelgänger. I saw him in concert a number of times: once for Amma's birthday in Virginia; once in New York, where he had composed a piece with Philip Glass; and once in Boston, where I was supposed to interview him, but he fell ill at the last minute. Another time, I met his daughter and protégé Anoushka at a concert she gave at Connecticut College. She was twenty years old back then, just making her way into the world of music, and I joined a small group in the student center where she answered questions and spoke about what she was going to play at the concert. Wearing a sweatshirt and jeans, barefoot and shy, not yet the frequent resident of the pages of English and Indian tabloids she would eventually become, she could have easily passed for one of the students to whom she was speaking.

I never did meet her father, though I did, in time, come to appreciate his music. For me, there comes a moment when listening to a raga when the music simply takes over, when the mind, with its litany of anxieties and ticker-tape parade of desires, ceases to clamor—not quieting exactly in the mode of meditation but more in the sense of being overtaken by the music, caught up in a pure sound that evolves outside time. Ten minutes might have passed, or an hour, or a century. Experiencing a raga allows me to hear the world anew as if listening to it for the very first time. The Pandit himself has said, "Music is like worshipping, and through music you worship God . . . I believe in the age-old saying 'Nada Brama'—Sound is God."

Even more than the ragas, however, what I like best about my namesake is his willingness to experiment, to take chances, to master the tradition but then to break from it. He was a true groundbreaker and pioneer: writing numerous film and TV scores; collaborating with George Harrison on one of the first-ever benefit concerts, the Concert for Bangladesh; playing the first sitar-violin duet with world-renowned violinist Yehuda Menuhin; collaborating with the founder of compositional minimalism, Philip Glass, on electronic music; creating a new breed of musical theater that combined dance and drama with the old Rajasthani motifs of maharajas and courtly life; and exploring new technological musical innovations such as the synthesizer and the emulator, and merging them with classical Indian instruments and dance.

Looking reverentially—and bitterly—at the trajectory of his life and work as I lay prostrate on my bunk before count, I see a viable model of how to be an artist in the world—never settling but always pushing the imagination forward. Pandit Shankar, my namesake and burden, the man who inadvertently made me feel second best, a replica of myself, nonetheless represents a perfect fusion between the old and the new, between the staunch classicist and the progressive experimenter. His roving, unbounded, insatiable, and transnational creative curiosity, steeped in ritual and discipline but pointed outward toward play, is a position I aspire to every time I sit down to write, even in jail surrounded by men who seem not to know him or his legacy.

When he finally passed away, on December 12, 2012, at the age of ninety-two, I wrote a brief elegy for him, "Ravi Shankar on Ravi Shankar" in the *New York Times*, and in so doing, made my peace with him. I've decided to be glad that I have borrowed my name from him, to be allowed to use it for a while before passing it on to the next Ravi Shankar. The chords of my own raga will be fundamentally different from his. They will be textured with the subjugated and the marginalized, with pride's relationship to shame and compassion, with the illusion and actuality of uniqueness, and with the negligible, if crucial, distance between the most heralded and most loathed among us: the ones traveling the world as superstars and the ones languishing alone in jail. My own raga will be less about mastery and more about error, less about the sound of God and more about learning how to hear my fellow humans.

Chapter Nine

Chaos Theory

It's hard to hear yourself think inside. Sound, as variation in pressure, often can't be measured in decibels. You expect men who are housed in a chicken coup, without access to personal space, the chance for growth, or proper medical care not to re-offend? Norway is known for its humane, even enviable, prisons and has one of the lowest recidivism rates in the world at 20 percent. The United States has one of the highest, with more than 75 percent of its prisoners rearrested within five years. When most prisoners reenter society, they haven't been rehabilitated or had their dysfunction addressed. Paradoxically, they leave with more rage and mental strife than before they entered.

According to sociologist Nick de Viggiani, "Prison social environments play an important role in the health of prisoners." That seems self-evident, but what I didn't realize until my incarceration was the complex shapes those social formations might take. At the top are the warden and deputy wardens, whom one rarely sees. They might stroll through the dorms once a week. The lieutenants and commanders patrolled more frequently, but mainly to break up trouble. We dealt with the COs, an ethnically diverse group of men and women. Some of them worked double or even triple shifts, and, just as it's hard to generalize about the inmates, it's hard to generalize about the COs.

Navarro, a Peruvian gentleman with a sleek aquiline nose, looks like he stepped straight from the opera house, and he says "please" and "thank you" even to prisoners. Saunders, the Jamaican, has little-big-man's complex, even in his combat boots, and so can be counted on to take any question or comment as a provocation. Jakwoski, a strapping blonde, is a great favorite among the inmates. She's a biker with tattoos running up and down her arms, and she ran with the Hell's Angels in the 1990s. She doesn't condescend when she speaks to the men but has an air of tough love. Stevens, on the other hand, looks like Clint Eastwood in *Gran Turino* and enjoys nothing more than reprimanding the inmates.

Like an irritated father, he scolds us for loitering in the tier, for not having our tans tucked in, or for making shoelaces out of our state issue sheets, which, he assures us, is destruction of property and a Class A violation. When he's on shift, he will get on the intercom theatrically, calling inmates to line up for their meds, which seem to range from selective serotonin reuptake inhibitors (SSRIs) to methadone to treat heroin addiction, by booming, "Screws and schizos, come get your Skittles!"

Many of the COs could be the mirror images of the inmates they police. They come from the same neighborhoods, have some of the same ink on their arms, and speak the same idiomatic language. They wear what are dubbed "superhero belts," with face masks, whistles, blue latex gloves, pepper spray, walkie-talkies, and jangling keys. They spend most of their time inside the Bubble, jawing with one another and trying to avoid the dorms unless they have to take count. Thankfully, only a small handful possess the mindless brutality that is genuinely terrifying. Nonetheless, I try to avoid them, but sometimes it's impossible.

The men I'm in constant contact with are my cube mates, the inmates who occupy the bunks in and around me. They will cycle through, as the prison administration constantly has us moving bunks and moving dorms. I would never work out whether this was done deliberately, to prevent friendships, or just part of the random ebb and flow of the population.

One of my cube mates is called Smurf. Contrary to his nickname, he is a good-looking, well-proportioned Black man with cheekbones. When I first meet him, he quizzes me.

"How old I look?"

"Mid-thirties?" Seems plausible.

"Ha! No, young brother, I'm not. Add a decade and a half! Proves what I been saying all along, why you wet up. The black bag with embalming fluid in it. Formaldehyde, nail polish, all that good shit. They a preservative. More nutritious than essential oils. That's why I look so good, baby. I got the hook up they use for King Motherfucking Tut."

The "black bag," or "wet," refers to PCP—what was known as angel dust in the 1970s—and Smurf remains unrepentant about his drug use. Almost every one of his stories begins with him heading out looking to score. His daily life is an adventure centered around how to stay high on no budget, and these last few months at HCC are the longest he's stayed sober.

"I wetted up and then ended up on the street butt naked, seeing double, ready to swing on *morenos* if they jumped up from behind cars. Had to be strapped down by three of my cousins.

"I make my own batch with Black Flag, tranquilizers, embalming fluid, and a sprig of fresh mint. Stick it in my girl's freezer, get it gluey enough to sprinkle on a joint."

Smurf has a whiff of putrescence clinging to him, which makes me doubt he is lying. Another "lick," which is what drug addicts at HCC are called, is Junkie John. A skinny, wide-eyed White guy, he gravitates to me, claiming we share an indiscernible mutual refinement.

"You a cut above these other losers, I can tell. I have the instinct. I come from good people. Solid middle-class family. Not like these broken-home cockroaches." Junkie John has an intense indrawn face like a woodpecker's and even makes a sound like one—*wicky-wicky-wick-wick-querrr*—while listening to music on the cheap translucent Sony radio that he assures me is one of the best deals from the commissary. "Just twenty-five dollars for batteries, unit, and headphones, and you got yourself insulation to seal yourself from the verbal jerkoffs. Lay back and float away.

"What these animals roar, it's not for guys like you and me. When I go up the way, I'm going to splurge on a TV because then—*whoosh!*—plug in the head-phones and you're gone. Do a bid flat out on your back. But in here, in county, all I need is a radio, and I'm all set."

Junkie John has just been on the run for sixteen months, his longest run ever. Now he is afraid that he might get hit with persistent offender status, which would automatically triple the length of his sentence. He looks at me dolefully.

"They might give me five years, maybe less with good time, I'm not sure. I can't go back to my parents this time, though. I have to ride it out." He is one of the few inmates who speaks freely about his guilt and appears clear-eyed about his predicament, which is some serious jail time considering he has already done two three-year bids for drugs, trafficking, and something that he insists was not *exactly* pimping out prostitutes. This last run, he was desperate, living a truly fringe existence fueled by getting high and shoplifting. He racked up a dozen "failure to appears." Sixteen months, living as a hustler junkie, having outrun bounty hunters and cops numerous times.

"Closest thing to a nine-to-five job ever. Up each morning with oversize jeans, pockets cut out, bottoms tucked into the cuffs of my socks. Pop on a T-shirt and an overcoat. Ready to roll. If my girl's car broke, I'll take the bus to Rite or Wal-greens or Super Stop & Shop. Get there right after it opens, full hour before secu-rity gets in. Head straight for the deodorant aisle. *Shoomp, shoomp, shoomp, shoomp!* Down my pants leg. Next, Red Bulls, razors, batteries, packs of gum, vitamins, I fill my jeans like a piñata. Jacket fat as Santa Claus. One quick circuit, then out the door."

"What would you do with all that stuff?"

"I roll back to Hartford on the bus and head straight to the bodegas. Spanish *mamacita* pays two dollars a can for the big Red Bulls. She turns around and sells it for five dollars. *No hay problema.* It's legit. Got books in the backroom. Proof I cleared seventy grand one year, easy."

The first time I can remember breaking the law, I was ten years old. I stole Boba Fett, the jaunty jetpack-strapped Mandalorian bounty hunter from *Star Wars*. I stole him from my ophthalmologist's son after we spent the afternoon warring action figures in his backyard, using all his toys. I possessed only two *Star Wars* figures myself, and they were both droids, gifted me by Amma after months of begging.

My friend, on the other hand, had what could only be described as a squadron. He had the Millennium Falcon and the Death Star, plus dozens and dozens of action figures. He had so many that we could cherry bomb some of their articulated limbs off. While we played, I noticed he had not one, not two, but five Boba Fetts! Greed begins in such a somatic way, and the unfairness of our discrepancy radiated in my gut until it was time to leave. Under the guise of needing to use the bathroom, I snuck back upstairs to stick him down my pants.

Saying good-bye while feeling Boba Fett lodged in my crotch was the precursor to what a shoplifter would feel, walking past the threshold of a department store, having plucked off a RF tag like a tick to flick away in a changing room. How the adrenaline courses through your veins and your heart thuds. How pure the clap of the dopamine rush when the cool air slaps your hot neck as you head unmolested into a parking lot.

In high school, I would steal small things because they were easy to rationalize. I didn't get an allowance and lacked what my friends had. I was fighting capitalism with a low-grade dereliction. I was disfiguring my identity of nerdy Indian. Buoyed by punk and alt-rock, I would sneak out of the house to see Fugazi play at Saint Stephen's Church, or Nirvana play the 9:30 Club in Washington, DC. Sometimes my friends and I would dine and ditch during these trips, scattering out the back doors of crowded diners, never considering how shitty it would be for the waiter.

One of my high school friends was an avowed Communist. He would discuss *Das Kapital* as we strolled Georgetown, hoping to see the salesgirl with the purple hair and nose piercing at Commander Salamander. *Workers of the world unite!*

I still remember the anarchic joy I felt when he taught me how to make a free phone call by poking into the receiver of a pay phone with a paper clip, or how to master the art of using a piece of double-sided tape to make a dollar bill spit out two quarters and a free soda from a Coke machine. I romanticized being an existential bandit, stranded with my last dollar yet wily enough to survive.

A pack of us at the science and technology high school would go out on our lunch break to Visionworks, a large optical box store, and while the one with the thickest glasses would pepper the doctor with questions about retinoblastomas and microphthalmias, the rest of us would fill our pockets with sunglasses. We were blinder than we imagined, and polarized lenses wouldn't help.

One summer in college, living with some friends in an apartment share, taking summer classes and working in facilities management at the business school, I concocted what seemed like the perfect crime. You could buy anything you wanted at a department store, then show up a few days later with the receipt in hand and just pick up the same item from the shelf and return it for cash or credit. I didn't do it often, but when I did, I would thrum with adrenaline to get away with it.

What was I thinking? It was unthinking in one sense, a reflexive response to ennui, but there was also a sly pride in how such skills could be acquired and improved. I liked being able to do what others could not see, to palm a chess piece, or set a deck of cards right in the middle of a card game: magician's traits.

Maybe then it was karmic that I have ended up in jail. More than for driving on a suspended license, it was actually for an accumulation of generational debts and small acts of duplicity. After all, I'm Appa's son, and he's the most mysterious man I know. He's a private misanthrope, yet a public officer of the Optimist Club, an international civic organization dedicated to helping communities through service and whose creed is "bringing out the best in kids." He incarnates frugality, yet he has certain collections, like an array of pewter pencil sharpeners shaped like antique rolltop desks, sewing machines, clothing irons, coffee grinders, farm-house kitchen scales, and miniature cannons from the Revolutionary War. I once saw them in a Colonial Williamsburg gift shop for fifty dollars apiece.

He won't buy cereal without a coupon and yet has an assortment of fine cuff links, Tic Tacs, and bottomless bottles of vitamins in his car trunk. He even had a room in the basement that he forbade us from entering, his Ali Baba cave, that I used to break into with a penknife and find a mother lode of magic supplies, packs of gum, and hotel shampoos. When Appa found out I had infiltrated his room, he changed the locks, plastering on the back of the door a picture of an oversize Beefeater royal guard in tunic, knee breeches, and stockings, his bulldog scowl framed by a round-brimmed Tudor bonnet and a white neck ruff, his stocky arms holding a rifle with bayonet. How much of a man is in his genes?

One day, Junkie John tells me about his own family while describing the hungry-and-homeless hustle he had going during the summertime. "If I could have kept that going, I would never have boosted like I did. Could have been a method actor. All I needed was a piece of cardboard and a Sharpie. Write some heartwarming message about being a vet or homeless or God-have-mercy-on-my-soul BS. Then I'd camp out off the exit ramp at a place like Kohl's or Hecht's."

He stops to ponder for a moment.

"Never Macy's or Nordstorm—their patrons are too stuck up. I'd stand there with my shirt off"—he points to his sallow, sunken chest—"and one look at me and they'd know I hadn't eaten for a week. Never mind it's because I'm a junkie. I'd show them skeleton man, even put some real hunger pangs into my eyes. Broke their hearts every time. I had housewives giving me cold cuts, bread, bananas, gift cards, water bottles, you name it. Some lady took me out to lunch. A businessman bought me a bike, so I wouldn't have to walk from home.

"People are unbelievable. They see what they want to see in you. I would have stayed all summer but got hit with a town ordinance by the cops. Two months later, I'm back with my crazy ex, boosting more than ever."

He has nothing to show for it now, of course. As soon as he was done in Hartford, he would walk the few blocks to Clay Hill or Frog Hollow to cop some smack to shoot in his arm and some crack to put in his pipe. Like Smurf, he is unrepentant when he describes his drug use. Drugs make him feel alive, give him a purpose; they allow him to play the numbers, bone his girl, nod in and out of delirious ecstasy. He needs the crack to get wired and the smack to sleep.

That's what a lick is. Nothing else matters but getting high.

"I'm a no-good lick, Ravi," John says to me. "I'm someone who had it all. Come from good stock. Solid people. You're from Saybrook way, you know what I'm talking about. My mother was in insurance. My brother was an investment banker. We vacationed on the Cape. I'm not like these guys in here. You're not like them either. We don't belong here."

He leans in conspiratorially as we walk up and down the length of the dorm.

"These other guys, the ones who you hear talking lick-this and lick-that, well screw them. They wouldn't have a penny for diapers, let alone rims for their rides, if it wasn't for us licks. We keep them in business. Buy their products. Yes, that's right. Without us, they're nothing. So how dare they come in here, in here"—his voice rises to a squeal as he points around the dayroom—"walk into my fucking home, disrespecting me like I'm some kind of derelict, no good, soup-for-brains, dirty, sniveling junkie crackhead. Because without me, they're nothing! I'm middle class, Ravi. Hyannis Port. Cape Cod. Even been to South Africa. Had a girl out there." John pauses his monologue and looks at me. I find the vulnerability in his eyes disarming.

"You know why they call us licks, don't you? Because we're so desperate, we'd lick up the last little bit of anything, some coke off a mirror, some dust from a bag, some aerosol spray foam, lick it right off the floor to get that last little high. Touch something too beautiful for this world. So what? Who are they? Talking about their baby mamas and their sweet rides that they got because of *us*. At least we know who we are."

"John, you can kick that habit. You're a smart guy. Come clean."

"A lick knows what a lick knows. Just like a dick is what a dick is. Thanks anyway, *Professeur*." He uses a phony French accent and turns away from me.

Entertaining as he is, I'm thankful that Junkie John is not my cube mate. I have, however, gained two other cubies: Leonard, a White, fat, bearded neoconservative lawnmower repairman; and Chaos, born Kendrick Krause.

Chaos grew up in and out of foster care. Now he's a baldheaded Black man with a prominently missing tooth. Also undeniably a lick. He's the sort of guy you'd instinctively shimmy away from on the sidewalk, and you'd be right to do so, because he's a self-avowed, vicious crackhead.

Licks are at the bottom of the prison social system; the only factions lower are the rapists and the pedophiles. Chaos was a kleptomaniac junkie and drug dealer, which constituted a sort of lower middle class in prison. The ones at the top of the pecking order were the ones in for homicide or money laundering. Upon meeting me, Chaos starts up immediately.

"I'd stab your mom in the back for a dollar. Remember that about me. Don't say I didn't warn you."

I have no trouble believing him, for I've seen him drop kick the board during a chess game. Chaos happens to be the best chess player I've seen since OG. He plays with blazing speed, and when he's playing Tio, they both slam their pieces down in a ritual dance that dazzles the eye. It's only after the opening has been set that he slows down to consider his moves, but, even then, he places pieces in synaptic bursts. He has lost only one game since he's been in here, and that time, he flipped the board and pinned the kid he was playing by the throat.

Maybe that's the reason OG refuses to play him.

"He's the kind of guy who'd borrow your chessboard and then bark at you later because one of your own pieces gone when he had it last," OG tells me. "No thanks. Not for me." This makes me sad, for I desperately want to see Chaos and

OG go at it, their contrasting styles like an irresistible force against an unmovable object. Unfortunately, the discussion is a nonstarter.

Chaos doesn't have a lot of friends because he is a straight-up hustler. He gets up before everyone so that he's first in line for breakfast, scarfs down his tray, and then gets back into the end of the line with the stragglers for a second serving, right under the eye of the watchful CO. He trades items for people, always taking a cut for himself. He has junkie buddies all up and down the correctional facilities—even brags that he once had a laptop and a burner phone brought into him when he was at Gates.

"Back there," he brags, "I charged one soup a minute to use that thing."

If you engage in a conversation with him, it's likely that you will be taken for something. Sometimes, however, it can't be avoided.

"How the fuck a guy like you end up in here?"

"DUI," I tell him. "Driving on a suspended license. Probation violation."

"You a Paki? Stay home with the little missus, Paki. Can't have you coming in here fraternizing with my kind. Who gonna own up them motels and gas stations if not for you, Paki?"

"My parents are Indian. I was born in DC. And I'm a teacher. Let you know if I get lucky enough to own anything."

"Don't be rolling up on Park Street, Paki, don't let me catch you there trying to buy some rock, you hear me?" He chuckles. "Keep your swerving ass back home. Now let me grab some soup off you."

His patter and devious ways don't engender a lot of goodwill from his fellow inmates, who often complain about him behind his back. Like many of these men, he has spent the great majority of his adult life inside these kinds of facilities. He is also prone to spontaneous rages and will explode at someone's ignorance, or even at his own. He is on some serious medication and is always first in line when Stevens calls the men to fetch their Skittles.

Because I haven't hardened my heart adequately, I make the mistake of lending Chaos my radio one day, and now he comes over each morning to borrow "just a splash" of coffee to start his day. Leonard and Chaos don't get along. I like Lenny, though, as he's a real salt of the earth type. He's in here for repeatedly hunting and fishing without a license. He runs a small appliance and lawnmower repair shop in Granby. He lost the hearing in his right ear in Vietnam and, at the end of his tour of duty, his wife dumped him. Now he's alone and embittered.

Lenny suffers from (what in retrospect were surprisingly prescient) apocalyptic visions of the future involving superviruses and climate-triggered earthquakes. He also esteems Ronald Reagan as a personal hero, which makes me avoid politics with him. Instead, we sit and play rummy, hand after hand, while he worries about his arthritic father and his Deadhead son. Lenny doesn't blame anyone but himself for his troubles, unlike many of the others he sees and scorns. He is particularly galled by Chaos, who loafs around, borrows everything, and would steal and lie right to his face.

"You know, once you start, that he's not going to stop with the begging, don't you?" Leonard asks, playing kings.

I grimace and nod.

"You're too nice. You don't see me giving out buttski."

The next day, Chaos sees me winning at chess against Domo and starts to comment.

"You smooth, Professor. Don't think I don't see you. You got your own hustle going. Can't fool me. Selling coffee balls and winning at cards. You gonna do all right in here. But you don't belong with us garbage. Real talk.

"You know why they call me Chaos? Because disaster follows me. I tore up my mom real bad coming out of her pussy, so she left me on the church steps. My grandmom raised me and I stole her earmuffs soon as I could walk. Pawned off her jewelry. She loved me, but I got arrested too many times."

Chaos has grown very emotional in his telling. He's tough but completely thin-skinned. His face is a living mirror for everything he's going through, from hunger pangs to devious plotting, from rage to utter chess focus. Now his face has transformed into an anguish that wraps itself around me by making his grief into that of a little boy's.

Somehow Chaos's contorted face makes me miss and fear for my own daughters. I find that he's loosened a plank in the wall I have constructed to keep myself uncontaminated by these men. I'm sorry that the world has done this to people like him. I try to tell Chaos, but he shakes me off.

"Chaos. Garbage. That's what it means. That's what got me locked up the first time, and that's what got me locked up the last. All the times in between, well when I show up, it just goes bananas. Got the nickname Chaos during a Fourth of July cookout. Cracker tried to big-time me. So I tied a bunch of fireworks to his propane grill. When it lit off, the whole sky glowed a hundred different colors. Colors between the colors. Then a shooting. After that, everyone called me Chaos. Unpredictable. Disorder. Disaster. I'm a demon."

And when he looks up at me, I believe him. I see a fiend flashing hate in his eyes, and his visage has been transformed into one of those Tibetan masks, like leering Mahakala, the personal tutelary of Kublai Khan. He glares venom.

"But I'm really garbage. Swear to you. True talk. I'll steal a ring off a dead man's finger and pawn it for a dime bag. I'll sell black bags and bricks of coke and dirty needles to little kids in school zones. I blaze a police chief down just for looking at my girl. No hesitation. I don't want to be this way, but can't help it, swear to God. I raised myself, and I'm a piece of filth."

Chaos goes silent then, his animated face as placid as the surface of a lake that has stopped rippling in the wind. I find myself soaked by the torrent of his words, as if I have been standing in a storm without an umbrella.

Lenny doesn't buy his act, though.

Ever since his toothpaste went missing, he has suspected Chaos. I am on the bunk on top of him, and Chaos is on the bunk next to us. Domo and Tio are a few bunks over. We lie there immersed in our thoughts until we can use the phone again.

The wait to get on a phone in this dorm is deadly, and each day begins with men clipping their ID cards to the phone's receiver cord to indicate their place in line. Even though Chaos often claims not to have a dime to his name, he is constantly speaking to someone, often using up more than one call at a time, which also severely grates on Lenny. A devout Catholic, Lenny attributes all the bad behavior in jail to the hypocrisy of those jailhouse pastors, of which there are many, who preach the holiness of Jesus and then steal your soups. He thinks Chaos is one of those two-faced operators, although I have never heard him mention anything the slightest bit holy.

Lenny only has two people he calls: his father, who is suffering from Alzheimer's and dementia; and his son, who he's actually ambivalent about speaking to at the moment since the "piss-wad" wrote him an intemperate letter blaming him for his own problems. But his daily call to his dad is a must. He's afraid the old man will pass away while he's in here and that he will never forgive himself. He has been waiting for the phones for at least a half hour, and he keeps looking over at Chaos jabbering away unconcerned. I can sense that he is beginning to heat up, because Lenny is grumbling under his breath. To distract him, I offer to play cards.

Lenny refuses.

Just when it seems like it must surely be time for Chaos to get off the phone, he does the unexpected. Instead of turning to hand over the phone to Lenny, who has been waiting, he gesticulates wildly until a squat brother with a nasty leg wound that gapes as pink as the inside of a guava ambles over. Chaos hands him the phone, whispering something frantically in his ear. The wounded brother's eyes shine with misgiving as he picks up the phone to dial.

Lenny is about to go ape. I can see him transforming. He's not the kind of guy to stick a finger in someone's chest and say, "Yo, you're hogging up the phone lines, wait your turn."

Instead, he turns to me, his face reddening.

"Did you see that?"

I nod sheepishly.

"Did you see that! That toothless fool, K-ass or whatever the hell he calls himself, has no money. He's always begging someone for something. But he's on the phone all day. He saw me waiting, but he gives it to someone else? And rec is about to end. I'm not going to get to talk to my old man today. Damn it!"

Lenny punches the wall with a closed fist.

Right on cue, a disembodied voice on the intercom calls the end of rec.

"Count time, gentlemen, on your bunks. Put down the phones and the card games, return to your bunks."

When Chaos returns to the cube, Lenny glares at him, but he seems not to notice. I stay uninvolved. I quickly dig the radio out from under my mattress and stick the headphones in my ears, an instant before he's in front of my bunk, looking up at me.

"Oh, you using the radio now?"

"Yes, sorry, Chaos." I shrug.

He looks disappointed, then peers down at Leonard.

"Hey, old man, let me have some cheese and crackers."

That does it.

"Cheese?!" Lenny explodes. "Crackers?!"

His beard is peppered with spittle as he attempts to catch his breath up to his voice.

"Are you serious, you selfish crackhead monkey? Don't ever come around me asking for stuff again. Stay in your part of the cage."

Chaos stares. Inwardly, I cringe.

When he speaks next, it is with the purest derision and rancor.

"What you call me, old man? If I ever hear you talk to me like that again, we going to bang out right here. You lucky I let you keep your teeth now, you punk ass, bitch ass, faggoty ass, honky fucking redneck trailer trash cracker. You lucky you laying down now, or I'd knock you the fuck out."

Chaos has started shaking, his brow a contortion of animalistic ire. I know that he once had a year added to his bid for attacking a correctional officer, so this is not mere braggadocio. I imagine the violence of which he is capable, so I'm scared for Lenny. I need to intervene.

"Look, Chaos. He's sorry. He was waiting to use the phone to call his old man, and you gave it away to someone else. He didn't mean what he said."

Chaos trembles with fury like a leaf in the wind. His ropy muscles are coiled around his lean body. He looks ready to pounce.

"Listen, why don't you listen to some music. Just relax for a second. I'm done with this now."

Chaos stops shaking and looks at me. I hand him my radio.

"I'll get you that battery, straight up," he says, looking at me in the face, his mood swinging 180 degrees. But I can see that hot tears have formed in the corner of his eyes. He takes the radio and swivels back around to face Lenny, spitting.

"But we not done, old man. Believe that."

Then he's off to his own bunk, leaving behind the after-odor of premonition and aggressive endorphins.

Lenny's face has turned pallid. He has his sheets pulled up around his shoulders.

"I can't be here." He is half mumbling to me, half to himself. "I can't be in this place any longer. I want to go home."

That night, long after third shift has taken count, and the loud swapping of insults has waned away to snores, I awaken to use the bathroom. Like in one massive sleepover, I move past the lumpy, jittery, withdrawn, or exercise-hardened bodies of men sleeping on their bunks in the dim light. When I return, I can't get back to sleep. My mind wanders, I think of my family. My little girls. Amma and Appa. Parker, who was likely in the process of filing for a divorce. Julie, whom I love, but who has expressed misgivings about her ability to trust me. The few friends who remained in contact with me. The others from whom I've heard less and less. How many days did I have left? I try to crunch numbers when suddenly I see a shape start to shift and move in the dark.

It's Chaos. He's getting up from his bunk and coming over. He's standing three feet from me. I don't breathe a sound. Then he crouches, staring at Lenny's sleeping body. He doesn't move any closer. He doesn't go back to his bunk. He just stares, transfixed on Leonard's arms with crude tattoos and scars on them, his grizzled graying beard, his slight potbelly.

Very plainly, Chaos has the look of a homicidal maniac. He doesn't move, but even in the dark, I can see his gaze steadily intensifying from evil eye to death curse. I'm scared looking at him, convinced that Lenny must feel the irradiating hatred of those eyes.

But he doesn't. He moves in his sleep and mutters, snores, and scratches but doesn't wake up. Suddenly Chaos's face is an inch from Leonard's, so close he could be about to kiss him. He keeps it like that, breathing in Leonard's face for a long, protracted moment, eyes bulging from the sockets.

Then, as if nothing had happened, he retreats to his bed and falls asleep.

I need to get out of here too.

The next day I see Chaos sitting by himself in the dayroom during rec. He has a pad of paper and a pencil and is doodling. His face sags, like a balloon that has lost some of its air.

"You cool, Chaos?" I sit next to him.

He nods, not looking up.

"What you drawing?" He looks up then.

"Not drawing. Writing. Well, wishing I could write my daughter's name is all."

"What's her name?"

"Aliyah. But I want to write my name too. My real name."

"You never wrote your name before?"

"Told you, I never finished school. Never really started. Missed so many days, I lost count. But don't need to know how to write to buy a strap and sell crack. But my little girl . . ." A beatific smile passes over his lips. "She so pretty. Her mom White, actually, which is why, when I hear that racism that your boy be talking, it makes me bug out. She caught all kinds of hate for being with me. Got kicked out her own family. They wouldn't even let her go to church. But she the only girl I ever loved. I treated her real good. Aliyah is my only daughter."

"Like the butterfly spawn of Muhammed Ali and Yahtzee?" I venture.

"What you say?"

"Never mind. Aliyah, right?" I take the pad of paper from him. "A-L-I-Y-A-H." I form large block letters. And your real name is Kendrick, right?" I form the letters of his name underneath his daughter's, then write out the entire alphabet in upper and lower case before handing him back the pad. "We can practice more after count if you want."

That evening is the first one in the nearly two weeks that I have known him that Chaos does not pester me with any requests. I sit on Lenny's bunk, playing rummy. He's lamenting, as he usually does, bygone days, when he was happier, riding his Harley, mostly sober, maybe a beer here and there, but building his house and raising his ex's three kids as if they were his own. Now they're all gone. All he has left in the world is his idiot stoner son and his dying father. He can't see either of them because he's stuck in here, losing money on his lawn-mower business.

"I want to be a tax benefit, not a tax burden. Always done right by the law, but the law ain't always done right by me. I should be collecting disability. I can't near move this hip. But they have me locked up, for what? For trying to get my meds because I was injured serving this country, that's what."

I have promised him that, when I get out, I will call his son and try to reason with him to get together his bond money. I have eight days left in this stint of six weeks, and I am trying not to think too much about that since it will just make things drag on longer. That evening, after a meal of soggy toast and hard-boiled eggs, I see Chaos smoothing out a handkerchief. When he sees me, he beckons me over to his cube.

"Professor, check this out. Don't tell anyone." Under his mattress is a pipe that he's wrought from a playing card and some kind of crushed-up pill. "Want to hit this?" It's clenbuterol and an upper, ground together in a granular paste. I defer and watch as he puts his index finger in the powdery mix and runs it discerningly along his gums.

"Okay, we'll hit it later. This is what I really wanted to show you." He unfolds the checkered handkerchief. Upon it, sketched in wobbly but unmistakable letters, are the names Kendrick and Aliyah. Around the two names, tulips and stars twirl and enmesh.

"You wrote that?" I'm amazed and impressed.

"I'm going to send this to her," he tells me. "Just as soon as I can steal me a state envelope." And in that one sentence, he has encapsulated himself. The yin and yang of Chaos. Someone capable of such ruthless and despicable behavior one moment and such sweet gentleness the next. He's elemental, a jouncing contradiction embodying the warring impulses in us all. He's clearly been let down by the institutions meant to prop up his mental well-being and social integration. He's had no stability in his life, no family. Quite frankly, I'm worried about his balance and fear he may eventually harm himself or someone else. Even though I'm not even sure that he really wants help, being in here has done nothing to address those underlying issues.

All the people I meet at HCC—Lenny, Junkie John, Smurf, Chaos, and many of the others—need counseling, not incarceration. Love, not disdain. Without a more compassionate system, it is a virtual certainty that they will tumble heedlessly back down the path of self-destruction and find themselves locked up again. The statistics bear out this promise. As much as I hate being here, each day I wake up in jail, I find myself moved by some aspect of humanity I share with these men. Small variations in the initial conditions of their lives have led them— and me—to this place, but it's not the last word, nor eternal damnation. It's actually not an ending at all.

Amma and Ammamma in Bangalore, India, 2010

Three generations of Shankars: C. H. Krishnan (Thatha), Ravi, and Samara, 2009, just before Thatha's passing away in 2010

Ravi at the *Drunken Boat* launch at Hygienic Gallery, New London, Connecticut, 2010 (reprinted with permission of Doug Anderson)

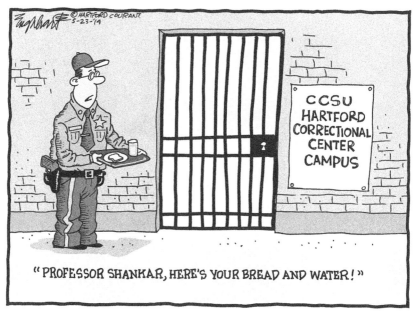

Cartoon published in the *Hartford Courant,* May 22, 2014 (reprinted with permission of Bob Englehart)

Ravi and Rahini at the Virginia Festival of the Book celebrating the launch of *What Else Could It Be*, Charlottesville, Virginia, 2016

Ravi with Salman Rushdie at the Matwaala Poetry Festival, New York City, 2019

Portrait of Ravi Shankar painted by Michael Peery in his studio, New London, Connecticut, 2014

Ravi serving as Writer-in-Residence at Sun Yat Sen University in Guangzhou, China, 2016

Ravi and Julie at Sea Level
Oyster Bar in Salem,
Massachusetts, 2017

Launch of *The Golden Shovel: New Poems Honoring Gwendolyn Brooks* at the Bowery Poetry Club, New York City, 2017 (reprinted with permission of Dominique Sindayiganza)

Ravi and Anupam Kher, Indian actor and the former chairman of the Film and
Television Institute of India, at the Indo-American Arts Council Literary Festival, 2019

Ravi, Samara, and Talia at the Sri Satyanarayana Swamy Temple, Middletown, Connecticut, 2015

Ravi and Talia lunching in Brussels, Belgium, after a visit with English novelist James Scudamore and family, 2019

Ravi and Ashwani Bhat at the Festival of Saint Anthony (who, local legend has it, stole into hell to bring back fire à la Prometheus) Galtellì, Sardinia, Italy, during the New York Writers Workshop, 2020 (reprinted with permission of Forrest Gander)

KULIR (*Autumn*)

Dear brothers,

Male intimacy is a timorous creature, too rarely sighted and more often hidden behind bluster and banter—a performance that cuts us off from our most vulnerable selves. From the crib, we are taught to be stoic and to repress our hurts, to concentrate, in the words of Coach Joe Ehrmann, on the 3 Bs: the ballfield, the billfold, and the bedroom. He's given a TED Talk on the prevalence and harm of the advice so many young boys receive to "be a man." Implicit in that imperative is an acculturated and toxic ideal of masculinity, complete with aggression, greed, misogyny, the suppression of emotion—and ultimately, in too many cases, suicide. It's part of what results in violence and cuts us off from forging deeper connections with one another.

When I think back to some of the closest male friendships I had in high school and college, there was always some element of competition, shoulder slap, and shit talk that masked our silent insecurities. We all made fun of each other as a socially sanctioned way of showing affection, even if it was anxious and base and bullying at its root. Certainly, I'm not immune from having acted in such a fashion myself.

In my head, I've written and revised letters to each of you individually and collectively dozens of times. Each time, I can tease out a new strand of the complexity of my feelings for our bond, both lasting and broken. I mourn the former roommate with whom I traveled through Europe and the dentists and Canadian stonemasons who were on my soccer team. I miss the friend at whose wedding I was best man and the rotating game of poker with the neighborhood dads. I don't begrudge the unanswered email, or being dropped from the family holiday card list, but being ghosted by a blood brother cuts nearly as deep as death.

Since I never found it in Appa, I've been searching for a good male role model ever since I grew fuzz on my upper lip, and I am thankful for the surrogate fathers and sidekicks that I have had and have been over the years. In

Tamil, there's a proverb that loosely translates as friends walk in when everyone else walks out, and so I won't miss those brohemes who disappeared when my own disrepute was but a glimmer in futurity, though others I will mourn forever. It's true that sometimes I dream of being more stoic. Sometimes, I admit, I wish I had been born White.

I could never quite be one of the guys, because, well, I never was quite one of you. For most of you, being racially profiled would never rise beyond a theoretical conjecture (with a taint of criminality). But I descended from a land of six seasons, yet never have fit perfectly in any of them, and my America has always been different than yours. Growing up a Shankar, too Indian for my American friends and too American for my Indian ones, I was overly sensitive to what I perceived masculinity to be. Later I didn't always act with integrity because of some absurd sense of oneupsmanship that I felt would define me as a man. The truth is that I broke down in tears when I stopped speaking to some of you, and that I still harbor the hope that others of us might eventually mend our differences and break bread once again. And regardless of what happens, I'm so glad that, through knowing you, I have learned better what it means— and what it doesn't mean—to be a good man.

Your pal

Chapter Ten

At Long Last, Whiplash

Everyone has warned me that the last week of this first bid will drag by, but I can't imagine how much so until I reach that seven-day countdown. From that point on, the minutes liquefy to wax, and the more I try not to think about how much time I have left, the more I do. I am going to court on the same day as Domo, and he is a nervous wreck, playing out the different scenarios in his head. He alternately claims he is either going to fire his lawyer, win a settlement from the state, or walk free back to his girl's house. Each time he just wants me to agree with his conclusion, which I'm happy to do.

Chaos promises he is going to score me some drug I've never heard of before as a parting gift, and Lenny's rummy game has taken a charitable turn for the worse as I beat him three, then five, then seven games in a row. The COs are nastier, the heat stickier, and they turn off the fans intermittently in the middle of the steaming nights because someone has yelled out "Turn up!" or "Lick my balls, piggy!" or "I'm a real boy," a popular refrain in the dorm that I would later find out is a quote from *Pinocchio*. I still can't make out if that was supposed to be insulting or just silly. In any event, I can't believe I've survived this long, though, in the relative scheme of sentencing, I've barely done any time at all.

One of the highlights of this final week is that the NBA Finals are happening, and one of the more decent COs has allowed us to watch the games in the dayroom well past the time when rec is supposed to be over. It's the Miami Heat versus the San Antonio Spurs. When Connecticut's own Ray Allen hits an implausible three-pointer from the corner of the key to send the game into overtime and the Heat to a fantastic game six victory, the entire dorm explodes in jubilation. It's one of the most memorable sporting events I will ever watch.

During this last week, I also hear Obama's name a lot, which strikes me as strange in such an apolitical environment. When I hear from somewhere, "Nice job, Obama! You dumb as a brick wall," at first, I think it's akin to using the Lord's name in vain. But, during rec one afternoon, I find out differently. Whoopy and I are playing spades against a Black guy called Joey Juice and a University of Hartford student from Nigeria. The latter has ended up here because his roommate was found blasting reggae, and when campus security searched their dorm room, they found twenty pounds of weed and an unregistered shotgun in his safe. He fears deportation.

When we argue about what "going Boston" really means, Joey Juice hollers.

"Yo, Obama! Come help lay down the law of the land!"

Suddenly a short guy materializes next to our card game, and to my amazement, I see that he is stubble-headed and White. His skin is the color of gray crushed quartz. He wears a lopsided grin and clutches a beanie cap, and I realize I've encountered him before. He has shared coffee with me on a few unsolicited occasions, and we've even exchanged fist bumps, though I never knew his name. *He's* Obama?

"You need to grab all thirteen books to go Boston. And if you're set twice in a row, that's game," he proclaims and then disappears.

When we line up for chow, I make a point of standing behind him. While we wait, I again work on memorizing the gang names on the wall, all of them prohibited in HCC. They sound like an occult incantation: Hell's Angels, Outlaws, Pagans, Ching-A-Lings, 10th St., DDP, Black Guerillas, Vice Lords, Mexican Mafia, La Familia, Florencia 13, Latin Disciples, Bandidos, Texas Syndicate, Sureños, Norteños, New World Order, Trinitarios, Mongols, Ashcan Boyz, G27, Fresno Bulldogs, Tiny Rascals, 5 Percent Nation.

We are the world gone *Grand Theft Auto.*

The Tiny Rascal Gang is a Long Beach, California-based Cambodian street gang, although I can't help but picture them riding around on pimped-out tricycles with spiked wheels and bandanas that double as bibs. Then there's the Ashcan Boyz, evoking for me that early twentieth-century art movement known for realist portrayals of poor urban neighborhoods. I imagine a bunch of gangbangers hawking counterfeit paintings—triptychs of street kids, alcoholics, indecorous animals, crowded tenements, boisterous theaters, and bloodied boxers to sell on the black market from the back of a van. Then I find out it's a typo for the "Asian Boyz," started by Filipino American Marvin "Shy Boy" Mercado, and a gang known for its violent acts of extortion, robbery, burglary, theft, and murder.

Still, even with its errata, the list provides me with fodder to engage Obama with a question.

"Hey, Obama, you think the Ching-A-Lings are Asian?"

He turns around and the grin is still hanging. I can tell by the way he'd enjoyed refereeing our card game that he likes to be asked questions.

"Nah, dude. Motorcycle gang. Puerto Rican graybeard dopeheads from the South Bronx."

"So why are you called Obama, anyway?"

My real question bubbles up immediately.

"You don't know? Didn't you see me on the news?" His voice swells with pride.

"Not that I remember."

"I like to do some hunting, skeet shooting. Do target practice in the Bloomfield woods behind my house. But just with a pellet gun. Shoot out cans, photos of ex-girlfriends, that kind of thing. One small problem. The last day I was out there shooting, I didn't realize that President Obama, the real one, would be passing in his motorcade right in front of my house.

"Secret Service did a sweep, and, when they found me hunched in the woods with a pellet gun and a scope, they weren't too happy. But I didn't even hear them coming. They lit me up with red crosshairs. On my own damn private property. What do I care if POTUS drive by? In the back of my own house, with a pellet gun that you can buy at Walmart? This a free country? Unfortunately, Secret Service didn't see it that way. Guess it didn't help any that POTUS was on his way to speak to the Sandy Hook families later that day." He pauses. "Or that I was being a smartass when they nailed me."

"Explains why they call you Obama."

"But I have a plan. I'm charged with breach of peace and threatening in the second degree, plus interfering with an officer. I'm sitting on a $15,000 bond, but I won't pay it. Because I had my civil liberties and constitutional rights trampled on, I'll wait it out—time served—then get out and sue the federal government. Won't have to work another day in my life." I reflect on the fact that half the inmates at HCC feel like they can sue the state when they get out. The thought that it's a hope to cling to when you feel utterly impotent flashes through my head. Then I remember that I had won a settlement from the NYPD in the not-too-distant past.

"Well, it's like you said, Obama. We are the change that we seek." I quote a line from President Obama's Super Tuesday speech, made when he had won the Democratic nomination in 2008. That world feels far away.

During my stay, any surface with writing on it has become my best friend, and I've clung to texts that float by like life rafts, convinced the words might contain some wisdom to help my survival. I've read much of the Bible, followed by a ragged copy of Charles Darwin's *On the Origin of Species*. I scribbled down on the back of my inmate handbook a typology of soldiers listed by Leo Tolstoy in "How Much Land Does a Man Need?" because it reminded me so much of the correctional officers I've encountered here. I've read and reread the bureaucratic abstractions of the administrative forms. I even found a copy of *Twilight* and drank it in a fizzy gulp, happy enough for its sugary vampiric froth to distract me from my predicament. During this month and a half, I will read anything in here to pass the time. Julie's letters sparkle with both her sadness and her belief in me, which I can scarcely believe. Anyone else would have walked away long ago. Another friend has mailed me some books and one of them is Jane Hamilton's *A Map of the World*, and I feel like the book has been written specifically for me.

The novel is lyrical, well crafted, and deals with the predicament of a woman falsely accused of molesting a student and jailed in a small community. The book begins:

> I used to think if you fell from grace it was more likely than not the result of one stupendous error, or else an unfortunate accident. I hadn't learned that it can happen so gradually you don't lose your stomach or hurt yourself in the landing. You don't necessarily sense the motion. I've found it takes at least two and generally three things to alter the course of a life: you slip around the truth once, and then again, and one more time, and there you are, feeling for a moment, that it was sudden, your arrival at the bottom of the heap.

Here I am at the bottom of the heap. Away from my family, gambling packets of Ramen noodles with men called Whoopy and Peanut, I find it hard not to succumb to rage. I hate credit cards and Subaru Foresters. I loathe the cops. I am persecuted by the media. But when I turn that beam inward, I realize that it's my own habits I have to undo. My riskiness and sneakiness had caught up to me.

I lie on my bunk, listening to the dorm life humming around me. As if it were a truffle, I want to savor each bite of Hamilton's novel, so I'm taking my time with it, periodically putting it down to soak in the social interactions around me. There's Lenny playing solitaire, and Chaos talking seemingly to himself about his creep, a word he uses to refer to his girlfriends. When he sees me looking at him, he glints a toothless grin below me, spittle bubbling at his cracked lips.

"She done me dirty, Professor. Heard she running around with my boy now. She a fine ass Spanish chick too. Thick. Pure badonkadonk. She a straight ho though, through and through. That's why I creeped with her in the first place."

By the time I'm ready to finish *A Map of the World*, another day has blessedly passed by. I find another passage in the novel that speaks so perfectly to my situation that it feels uncanny:

> It is marvelous how few details there are in jail; it is a feat, that in a world so various men can pare a place down to hard steel and dull, unforgiving concrete, a few thin blue blankets. . . . We could never get away from our own smell, or anyone else's smell, or the noise of the TV or the noise of angry talk. So that after a short time we began to hold like fury to ourselves, because our very distinctness seemed endangered.

I feel this force toward homogeneity pushing down on us all, in part because of the martial aspects of jail life: the lines we are meant to stand in with our tan uniforms tucked in and the unvarying and inhumane schedule of visitation, medicine, and recreation. No hope of rehabilitation. No decent care. No clear plan to be reintegrated into society. It's an institutional attempt to pulverize monotony into the minds of those who likely will explode in a violent binge upon their release as a result of this drab, contrived discipline and punishment. I believe our descendants will one day look at our current system of incarceration with as much bemused horror as we look at the rack and the heretic's fork today.

I dip back into the novel, finding other passages that echo my experience, especially on the prevalence of storytelling. Jail seems to be one of the few places on earth where there is still a thriving oral tradition. I think about Chaos and Junkie John, dramatizing their misdeeds with color and flair. I recall the meticulously detailed conversation of an outlaw called Travis, who bragged about being wanted on federal charges for forgery, extortion, and wire fraud, and gave detailed lessons on how to wash a bill with engine solvent so you can change its denomination. Even someone as conservative as Leonard would talk about his predicaments unendingly.

Each time a story is told in here, it gets embellished; the teller makes himself out more and more to be the victim or the hero, and the narrative gets reshaped in the telling so the narrator can feel better about it, or at least achieve some measure of illusory control. With each telling, the tale will accumulate grievances— all the cruelty of the woman who left him; the overt police brutality; how Vietnam War vets are treated; or how Obama, the real one, is no good—and will strive to transcend its prosaic origins from the workings of lust, greed, or rage, into something more epic, or at least understandable. Each iteration of its telling helps us critique the business of justice through its own embellishments.

At HCC, I find that my own bullshit detector, that finely honed piece of psychological equipment developed over the years, is not functioning so well. I can usually determine upon first meeting someone how much they mean what they say and what their true intentions are, but, in here, I find I'm unable to distinguish ulterior motives from truth, or relative guilt from innocence. I'm not sure if the Hispanic dude with the three tears tattooed on his cheekbone actually did twenty-five for a triple homicide. I'm not sure if someone as volatile as Chaos could actually sustain a girlfriend and a family. I can't say for certain whether Obama really was just shooting soup cans in his backyard when he was arrested.

After finishing *A Map of the World*, I save a copy of Paul Hawken's *The Ecology of Commerce* from being used in an impromptu futsal game, trading off *Twilight*, which someone shouts for immediately. Hawken presents a vision of humanistic economics as a corrective to capitalism veering out of control. "If Hawaiians had 138 different ways to describe falling rain," he writes, "we can assume that rain had a profound importance in their lives. Business, on the other hand, only has two words for profit—gross and net." Later in the same book, he writes,

> Some think humans are predatory by nature. I cast my vote with those who feel humans can take the shape of their cultures and that shifts in culture can occur in rare moments with remarkable speed and vigor. Good design can release humankind from its neurotic relationship to absurd acts of destruction and aim it towards a destiny that is far more "realistic" and enduring. The urge to create beauty is an untapped power, and it exists in commerce as well as society.

Looking around the dorm, I meditate on beauty and commerce. Here are men, jettisoned as criminal, hunched over a pad to draw a unicorn with colored pencils, or partitioning their living space into more comfortable quarters by turning emptied toilet paper rolls into eyeglass holders, or saltine boxes into cupboards, or twisting strips of garbage bags into a laundry line on which to dry their socks. Good design applies, not just to merchandise but to our social institutions as well. How much better would this jail function if these men were able to improve themselves by building workplace skills or speaking to a psychological counselor? Why is the ratio something like twenty COs for every one mental health worker? How does good design interface with rehabilitation?

Then, waiting it into being, I have one night and one wake-up to go. The cube has a new infusion of arrivals, and rumor has it that the gymnasium floor is more crowded than it has ever been. I begin giving away my possessions. I give Junkie John some bagels and cheesy beans. I give Whoopy my playing cards. I give Tatu, much to his displeasure—for he wanted something more—my coffee cup. I give Leonard the rest of my pad of paper and my pen. I give Obama my Softee "3N1" conditioning shampoo. I give Chaos my chessboard and my radio, and I'm afraid that he might kiss me. The only things I keep are my notebooks, the letters I've received, and the commissary envelopes, which have actual postage on them so that I can use them on the outside. Domo won't accept anything from me because to do so would be an admission that he might have to come back here after court.

"You must be clowning, Indio," he booms when I try to offer him my shower shoes. "I'm soaring with you. We free birds. Flap our wings and flying free. No coming back for you and me."

Ever discerning, Chaos notices that Domo has refused my shoes and comes around with a hangdog look of desperation on his face in the hope I will give them to him instead.

"Yo, Professor, I'll take them shoes."

I'm sure he will.

"Plus, remember I'm getting you a going-away present. Don't forget about us when you're out of here."

I smile.

"How could I ever forget you, Chaos?"

"No, I'm serious. Real talk. You the only one here who can tell our stories."

Chaos has moved from his bunk to sit on Lenny's pillow. To sit where someone lays their head is cause to fight, so I am thankful that Lenny is away at medical.

"People be listening to you. I been opening my mouth all my life, but no one ever hear me. But you different. You can tell the world how we caged up like animals. How them Cos don't do jack. How we can't get on with our lives, even after we done our time."

His face shines with torment, his gap-toothed mouth drawn into a half scowl, half despair.

"I done told you, I ain't nothing but a piece of trash, but my daughter ain't. Aliyah beautiful. She half-White. She got a chance. But only if this world change, you hear? I'm a piece of garbage. I'm going to get out of here and keep slinging that rock. Still rip your granny's earrings out her ear for a quick fix. Don't know no other way. I tried to go straight, work construction. I worked real hard, until my fingers bled blisters. But once they find out about my record, I'm done every time. And I end up back in here."

Chaos has started to tear up.

"Promise me, Professor." He blinks hard. "Promise me you'll tell our stories."

"I promise, Kendrick."

He puts out his fist to be bumped.

When I meet his eye again, the amazing protean capacity of his visage is on full display because there's no longer a lingering trace of sorrow, but rather the intensity of a crow's sly hunger, and he's hopped up onto his feet.

"Now watch me work." Chaos drifts through the cubes like a ghost, slipping over into the high side, the other half of the dorm where he is not supposed to be.

Domo and I stay up that last night laughing, sharing stories of girls and stupid pranks we've pulled, talking about food and music, making plans to meet up in Hartford, though I doubt either of us really thinks that is going to happen. Lenny usually lies at night with his T-shirt over his face and, when the noise level increases, curses at everyone under his breath. Tonight, he stays up to join the conversation.

"I'll miss you," Lenny says earnestly. "Hope I won't get killed with you gone."

He looks truly despondent. I pat his shoulder, promise him that I'll reach his son when I get out (the phone number he would provide me would be a nonworking number), and that he'll be out, seeing his father, before he knows it. I swap names and inmate numbers with a few other guys in the dorm and then finally drift off. I'm too agitated to sleep, and, by the time wake-up comes at five thirty, I have already showered, and I'm waiting in the day room with my few remaining possessions bundled in a garbage bag. I shaved the night before with a terrible one-blade razor in cold water, and my chin has scabbed over. I wait with Domo and a couple of other guys for the call.

"Courts! Pack your stuff. Let's go!"

We follow a group of men to the door, where we are escorted by a CO down the hall, through two metal detectors, past medical, to the area I entered HCC a month and a half ago. We are asked to pass up our IDs if we want our court clothes, and we tag our bags with markers and masking tape. I will be going to Middletown, and Domo to New Britain, so we will each wait in another cell. We pound fists and wish each other the best. We'll never see each other again.

Then, as if dreaming in a black mirror, I am removing my tans and stuffing them in a box, replacing them with the button-up shirt and wool pants I wore when I arrived. I'm being ankle-shackled and handcuffed to a row of men and asked to enter the ice cream truck. My journey resumes, in reverse. As the sunrise glints through the pointillist window, illuminating dots of green and blue, I am struck by how vivid the colors are, even seen through the back of the van, and how my vision has become monochromatic, used to seeing prison tans and gray walls.

The rest of the day blurs. I wait in the bullpen, the area where you wait to be called into court for what seems like an extraordinarily long time. I go in front of the same judge who was on the bench when I first arrived, and I see my attorney for the first time in weeks. My bond is lowered again so that I am back on "Promise to Appear" status. My attorney has continued the case for one month so that I can teach summer school, and he's promised me that he will talk to the prosecutor and that, with any luck, I may not have to serve the remainder of this pretrial confinement. At this point, I don't even care. I'm just glad to be out of jail.

When I'm finally allowed to leave the court, I do so on wobbly legs, like a hibernating bear that has just emerged from its cave. Parker had to work, and I've asked Julie to stay away because I don't want her to be seen by anyone, so no one is there to greet me save Rajni, who has traveled all the way from North Carolina. She's grown into a dedicated professor of education and an impassioned social justice activist, and I'm gladdened beyond belief to see her. Her support has been unwavering. However, although she keeps asking me, I find I can't tell my sister much of what I've experienced. I'm stunned wordless. Instead, I ask her to take me to Taco Bell to have my first meal on the outside.

When I see my daughters, they seem like different creatures. It's been only six weeks, but they have grown in some imperceptible way. I find I can't kiss and hug them enough. Half the town knows where I have been, and I suffer on behalf of them for that fact. I gather them to me and find it hard to let go, especially because our reunion will be short-lived.

A few days after departing the Hartford Correctional Center, I'm on a flight to Hong Kong, en route to teach my graduate students. The vicissitudes of life boggle the mind. Days ago, the only patch of sky I had was framed by barbed wire in the rec yard. Now, I'm watching the city I had been detained in recede to a postage stamp, then disappear beneath the clouds. Bon voyage, Hartford.

High in the air, I carry my secrets with me.

None of my fellow faculty members know where I have been, and I don't plan to volunteer the information. I'm hoping I can get through this entire pretrial confinement, however long it will last, under most people's radar. Still, when I look in the mirror, I can see the experience has been etched under my eyes, and I'm afraid there's still a whiff of the prison yard about me. Largely, though, as in Pieter Bruegel's *Landscape with the Fall of Icarus*, I would find most people either didn't know or simply didn't care. As in W. H. Auden's poem about that painting, they had somewhere else to get to and sailed calmly by. Even some of my closest friends haven't reached out to me in eons, and I feel, having been away for a month and a half, I've been barely missed.

I've changed in other ways as well. I'm more present in the moment. The interminable texture of jail, with its deprivations, lack of variations, and punitive deferrals, has colored the world around me full of personality and kinetic grace. I feel childlike, more alert to my own surroundings. On the way to the airport, I find myself unable to ignore the homeless man standing on the highway exit ramp or the other one at the gas station struggling to count out his change to buy a pack of Newports and a scratch-off lottery ticket. They feel a part of me, somehow.

The first thing I do when I arrive at my hotel room in Hong Kong is to draw a hot bath. No shower shoes needed. The thick towel—really, everything in the room—feels like a luxury. I sink into the water and feel a layer of skin slough away. That week in Hong Kong, I interview Pulitzer Prize–winning poet Rae Armantrout in front of a packed auditorium, eat a superb Szechuan meal, and explore Lamma Island with new colleagues who are rapidly becoming good friends. My students, who come from mainland China, Singapore, Vietnam, India, Australia, and the Philippines, are full of invention and polyglot curiosity. They remind me what it was like to be a graduate student, and I FaceTime with Julie from across the world, grateful for this reprieve.

One evening, just days away from being at HCC, I sip lychee martinis in a herringbone suit and eat Asian tapas at Ozone, the sumptuous lounge at the top floor of the Ritz-Carlton. Below me is a breathtaking view of Victoria Harbor, one of the world's busiest port facilities. Cargo cranes loom above the floating drydocks and moored container ships. Panamaxes and bulk carriers are a floating city in and of themselves, laden with multicolored industrial containers, making their dreamy way past the glittering skyline of skyscrapers. As I await the cocktail waitress in a strapless black dress bringing around a plate of sushi, I can see the Star Ferry crossing between Central and Tsim Sha Tsui on the Kowloon side of the harbor. For a long breathless minute, I don't know where or who I am.

Chapter Eleven

The Spectacle of Captivity

There's a famous parable by the Taoist Zhuangzi in which a man dreams he is a butterfly, then awakens unsure if he is a man dreaming he is a butterfly, or a butterfly dreaming he is a man. In a similar fashion, I would pass the next year of my life unsure if I was a professor dreaming he was a prisoner, or a prisoner dreaming he was a professor.

When I return to Connecticut from Hong Kong, I have a message on my voicemail from my attorney. He's sorry to inform me that I will have to finish off the entirety of my ninety-day sentence to satisfy the state. The good news is that he's managed to break it up so that it does not interfere with my teaching schedule. I have to go back in for ten days, then parse the remainder of the sentence out over my winter, spring, and summer breaks.

Thankfully, I'm still flying under the radar for this latest arrangement. The media has not picked up on it, plus it is not a conviction anyway, but a pretrial detention. Obviously, this is dismaying, but I'm ecstatic to be teaching again, and my classes are full—the notoriety from my previous brushes with the law creating a buzz within the student body. When I return, however, some of my colleagues are standoffish, or worse, but it's good to be back where I'm most comfortable. At home, I'm glad to be a full-time father again, although Parker and I barely speak. My life remains segmented, and, while my students are headed to the shore for the Thanksgiving holiday, or up north for Christmas, I return to Hartford Correctional. You would think that, having done time before, I would get used to it, but each time I'm asked to lift my balls and spread my ass cheeks, I feel the same level of humiliation, the same palpable dread at my loss of freedom.

I have been eligible for promotion for a few years, so that autumn, I put together my application to become a full professor. I fill a few cardboard boxes with binders full of every article I've ever published. I tabulate my teacher evaluations and update my CV. In spite of what's happened outside the ivory tower, considering what is taken into account for promotion (research; teaching; and university, department, and community service), my promotion is incontrovertible. The department, the dean, the university's promotion and tenure committee, the provost, and the president all sign off on the recommendation, and, though I have to wait until the spring for it to become official, I have been decreed a full professor of English.

I should celebrate, but saying it's awkward in my department would be like calling the Civil War a minor domestic dispute. The bearded chair, a Shakespearean, gives my classes out to adjuncts. The medievalist whose solstice parties I had been going to for years looks right through me. I get an email with sentences in bold, italics, and all caps from the nonfiction writer, whose hiring committee I had sat on, proclaiming that the consequences of my actions on the university, the department, the writing program, and academia in general have been utterly demoralizing but, more critically to her, PERSONALLY DISTRESSING! Going through a crisis is a litmus test to let you know exactly what people think of you, what their truest feelings are. It's akin to finding out you have cancer, leaving friends to ignore you, or to overcompensate with pity. My transgressions, writ large, have made any proximity to me a liability.

Thankfully, other people step up in a big way. Friends I would have considered peripheral reach out to me without prejudice, asking for my side of the story. Rajni calls with a reminder to keep a gratitude journal. Julie texts me: "Firstly, I love you. *Now and always.* You have altered my life, touched me like no other. I know you know that, feel it in the shudders that ripple through me variously, with the wrenching that is grief, the unbridled arch that is desire. When we are together, we are one." Parker, even though we've frayed beyond repair, hasn't kicked me out. I still have a few strong male friendships, such as with Andy Thibault, an inimitable character who has worked as a private investigator, a professional boxing judge, and a muckraking journalist at various points in his life. Andy is the type of guy who will answer his phone with a growl, "Yo, what's up, douchebag?" and could have been typecast from a Raymond Chandler novel. He also has a huge heart and works tirelessly for social justice in his own special way.

As the fall and spring semester pass, I visit Hartford Correctional Center three more times until, at the beginning of summer, I'm left with two final bids to finish off the ninety days and "satisfy the state." Whenever I hear that phrase, I think of a fanged goddess who has to be propitiated with human sacrifice.

Having survived over two months, what's another couple of weeks? I've become a jailhouse hustler by the end anyway, selling coffee balls and winning far more chess and card games than I have lost. I have deluded myself into thinking I know how to jail.

After grading my last portfolios for the spring semester, I arrive at HCC wearing three T-shirts, two pairs of boxers, and three pairs of socks. I look like the marshmallow man. I have put money on my books, so I don't bring anything else—no wallet, no phone, no keys, nothing I would have to drive back to Hartford to retrieve. When I walk into dorm number three, shouldering my bedroll, I'm smacked by the stench I had been subconsciously trying to forget.

Rec time has just finished up, and there is a dreadlocked incarcerated man sweeping the empty rolls of toilet paper, wadded napkins, hairballs, and empty soup sleeves into a heap. My bunk is in the middle of the dorm, and, to my dismay, I'm assigned the top again, directly underneath a grate that has mold growing on it.

I look around at my cube mates. One is an obese Black man with a scraggly beard and a bandanna tied around his head. Above him is a younger Black man with an old-school high-top fade. Across from him, there's a man who looks half-Hispanic and half-Black, with stringy braids and tattoos covering every visible inch of his arms and hands. Below that guy is an athletic-looking Black guy, asleep in a shroud of sheets. My own bunkie sports a tribal tattoo on his forehead and a T-shirt so yellowed by time or misuse that it appears to have been dredged from a swamp.

"Yo, Abdul, the sand-kisser."

I look up to see my tattooed Afro-Hispanic cubie looking at me.

"See, proved it. Made him look!" he announces triumphantly to the rest of the cube.

"You isn't staying here, is you?" He squints at me.

"Afraid so."

"Oh, hell no!" the older Black guy with the bandanna sits up to interject. "No fucking way we having some Arab up in here. You best ask the CO to move you, because we going to pack you up otherwise."

High-top fade joins in.

"Yeah, tell him about the last dude up on his bunk. Tell him, Big Country."

Big Country must be the corpulent Islamophobe in the bandanna.

"That faggot? He made a pass at me, and I pounded his face. You know cameras can't reach back here, right? He in seg now, fingering his own asshole."

I make a mental note: both racist and homophobic.

"Just trying to do my time, man."

I try to sound reasonable but hard, and spring up to my bunk.

"Big Country and Tookie see about that." High-top fade laughs.

Fourth day in, there's a fight in the back cube. I come in from chow to see a short Puerto Rican dude called Ñeta attached like a pit bull to the waist of a tall, stacked Black man they call Brooklyn because he has the area code "718" tattooed on his calf. Ñeta has his legs wrapped around Brooklyn's hips the way a lover would, and he's wailing punches at his face. Brooklyn is much stronger, but it's clear the smaller man is getting the better of the larger man, which pleases the entire dorm, especially the Hispanic guys.

By the time I elbow in to have a look, a team of COs has begun to run down the tier, screaming for everyone to return to their bunks. There must be fifteen of them, men jangling keys and exhaling hard breaths, cordoning off the area around the back cube. Even the doctor from medical and a couple of the mental health counselors have run over, and they have all gathered in a thick knot of congestion.

Suddenly, amid the sounds of the scuffle, my vision begins to waver. I'm sitting on my bunk trying to figure out what's going on, but I feel like someone has shoved a stick of cinnamon gum up my nostrils. I'm finding it difficult to breathe. I hear Brooklyn screaming out in a falsetto, and as if on cue, my own eyes start to burn.

The watery scene unfolds around me: first, Ñeta is being pushed out by two COs, his hands cuffed behind his back, his nose gushing blood. Then the rest of the brigade behind him, some wearing masks and some coughing into their hands. Then two burly COs, one Russian, the other Jamaican, have Brooklyn held roughly under the arms. He's squirming in distress, his eyes wrinkled into prunes, and he's frothing and flailing out.

"Suck it!" he yells. "All of you!"

As he's being dragged away, and I'm finding it more and more difficult to breathe, I realize that Brooklyn has been pepper-sprayed.

Pepper spray, with the unadulterated ingredient that gives chili pepper its spice, is a lachrymatory agent, meaning that it causes the eyes to tear up and can even cause temporary blindness. What I didn't realize is how powerfully it affects a given radius of space because, in short order, it became nearly impossible for any of us to breathe or see. The COs yell at us to line up out in the rec yard by number until the dorms air out.

We stand in the sun for more than two hours, still coughing and blinking the tears out of our eyes and trying to breathe the blaze from our lungs. Everyone is excitedly reliving the violence. I think of Brooklyn's muscular body, undulating like an eel on a fishhook. Finally, we are allowed back in the dorm.

Later that day, playing basketball, I find I've become the last pick again. Determined to prove myself anew, early in the game, I take a bounce pass along the baseline and go up hard for a layup. Big Country is waiting, and he swats me right

in the head. It feels like I've been devastated with a two-by-four. I crumple immediately to the ground, and as I'm sprawled out, someone else stomps on my hand.
Everyone is laughing. By the time I limp to the sideline, I find I can't bend my
middle finger. Grimacing, I sit with the junkies and the loners, seeing for the first
time the old basketballs, bleached and swollen cyst white in the sun, caught in the
teeth of the barbed wire that runs the perimeter of the fence that keeps us
enclosed.

Hours later, I realize I have a real problem. I still can't bend my finger, and it
hurts like hell. I've asked the COs to get me to medical, but their diagnosis is that
it is just jammed and I should sleep it off. But the next morning, my middle finger
radiates like a radio tower broadcasting one loud signal—*pain, pain, pain*—and I
can't take it any longer. I demand to be seen. As a result, I'm ignored for much of
the rest of the day.

After dinner, I'm finally called into medical, and escorted by a CO. We move
past a familiar hallway, where I've been attending Jumu'ah, the Muslim service.
I've decided to change my religion to Islam this penultimate bid. By the time I
finished my bid at HCC, I would have an introduction to the liturgy of all the
world's great religions.

We continue onward to a part of the jail I hadn't seen before. I sit on a steel
bench next to a man who is sitting holding his stomach. I don't engage him, but
before long he is showing me his intestinal hernia that hangs out of his waistband
like a cartoon Wiener schnitzel, except that it is his actual stomach. I can barely
stand to look at it. He tells me that he has been trying to get it treated for weeks,
but they won't send him to UConn unless something ruptures, at which point it
would be too late.

By the time I am called in by Dr. LaPlante, the resident physician, it must be
close to lights out. She takes one look at my finger and scoffs.

"Looks like it's jammed. Give you a prescription for Motrin that medical will
bring down later. Stop wasting our time."

She turns to leave.

"I really don't think it's jammed," I plead to her back. "I've had jammed fingers
before, and this feels much worse. I can't straighten it, and it's been almost forty-
eight hours."

"Well, we can take an X-ray, but you'll have to sit here for a few hours and miss
your dinner. In the end, it won't change the prescription."

Unlike a regular ER, there is a dearth of medical equipment here. For anything
serious, inmates are handcuffed to a gurney and taken to the UConn Medical

Center. In this space, there are no more than stacked folders and pens, doors with reinforced windows, and the cuff of a blood pressure monitor hanging like a doll's noose. Given the agony in my finger, I'm willing to wait.

When I'm finally X-rayed, and the film comes back, Dr. LaPlante concedes, "Well, it does look like you have a preexistent fracture. Likely re-aggravated it. From the X-ray, it appears to be an old injury."

"Never had any trouble with my hand."

"Looks like an old break. We could have splinted it if you had come in earlier. Now the best we can do is a bandage and some Motrin." Seeing the dismay on my face, she asks, "Who told you to play basketball?"

I trudge back to the dorm, my middle finger still hooked like the number seven, the top joint perpendicular to the finger. As soon as I get out, I will see an orthopedic specialist. Right now, I can't even shut my right hand into a fist.

When I get to the dorm, the half-Hispanice, half-Black guy with the tattoos, Tookie, is sprawled out comfortably on my bunk. He sees me, and instead of getting up immediately, he dawdles in conversation with Big Country.

"Yo," I confront him. "What are you doing up there?"

"Sorry, Bin Laden. Just checking you not making bombs up here." He leaps off the bunk and shimmies past me. Big Country cracks up when he sees my hand.

"Don't you know your kind can't ball? No camel polo out here, son."

While, in my previous bids, I've integrated with the guys around me, this time, I'm the newbie, the one who is teased. When I try to sleep, Tookie tickles my ear with a Q-tip or puts toilet paper over my nostrils in the hope that it will bob in my snores. I've become the butt of their jokes. I haven't been bullied this much since middle school. My cube mates spend all night shit-talking and catcalling, then they sleep during the day, so that when I'm opening my bin to get my soap during afternoon rec, they moan and snap at me to keep it down.

One afternoon, I notice a pair of my underwear has fallen from my bedroll onto the floor. Before I can snatch it, Big Country has noticed and is doing an exaggerated double take at the foot of my bunk.

"What the hell is this?"

"It's someone's dirty draws!" volunteers the ever-insightful Tookie.

"Whose nasty ass is these?"

I stay quiet.

"They belong to Ali Baba. Saw he was wearing tighty-whities." The voice comes from nowhere. Then I see that it is the sleepy, athletic, usually silent guy in the cube who has spoken up, who I think of as Town Fair Tire. He always seemed decent enough to me, employed as a cashier making eight dollars an hour, but is in here for not paying his child support.

Tookie howls in disgust.

"Them shits is *crawling*. Oh my fucking God, those dirty draws *is crawling!*"

I'm not sure what I'm more surprised by, that Town Fair Tire has joined the fray or that he has noticed my underwear. When preparing for jail, I brought my worst stuff—my oldest, rattiest T-shirts and underwear, the kinds of things I would only use for yard work. But by this point I've noticed the others rocking Joe Boxers and Ralph Laurens. I've seen Big Country on his knees, as if in prayer, using a toothbrush to ensure the toe of his sneakers stays unscuffed. I realize that most of them have worn their best clothes into jail. It's a status thing.

Tookie has wound a garbage bag into a bendy rope and he's pushing my briefs around the floor like it's a dog on a leash. Everyone in the cube yowls with laughter. Tookie talks to my underwear.

"Good boy. Do your business in the woods? Shit stain on you and everything?"

Red-eared, I grab the underwear from him and tuck it under my bed. Big Country is writhing with hilarity.

"Oh shit, oh shit, did you see that? Walking it like a dog. Tookie crazy! You can't afford new draws, son?"

I'm peeved and try to protest.

"How about hygiene?" Town Fair Tire asks.

"Tell us what that mean, Professor," asks Tookie disingenuously.

"You should really throw them out."

I'm shocked that Town Fair Tire has begun to lecture me. In terms of group psychology, I guess it makes sense to side with the bullies so that the target is on someone other than yourself. Still, it makes me smart. Dealing with Big Country and Tookie is bad enough, but, for some reason, having *him* sound off is just too much.

"What you mean, Town Fair Tire?" I call him the name I've given him in my mind. "What do they pay you there? Eight bucks an hour? I make that in ten minutes. And you think I'm cheap, when you're in here for what? Child support? Because you're a bum who can't even take care of your kids?" I spit the words.

When the silence descends on the cube, I realize I've gone too far.

Big Country whistles.

"Whoa, you going to take that shit?"

"Harsh, Bin Laden. Harsh."

I feel bad, but it's too late. Town Fair Tire has closed his eyes. When he opens them, they're bugged out, and he addresses me with fury in his voice.

"True talk, you ever talk about my kids again, I'll cap your ass. You don't know me. You lucky I don't want to catch a ticket, or I would mess you up. You better never say boo to me again. Swear to god."

I'll admit it. I'm scared. What am I doing? I *don't* know anything about him. Don't know what kind of father he is, but I do know that he's one of the guys in here who actually has a job. I feel ashamed at having lashed out at him, but his incursion had been too much. I have to stand my ground or be walked all over. But, considering I can't make a fist at the moment because of my broken finger, I need to be smarter.

When rec is called, I jump down off the bunk before anyone else and head straight for the bathroom. I bury my underpants in the trash can, under a smattering of paper towel waddings. When I return to the cube, my possessions have been flung everywhere. My T-shirts. My sheets. My pen. The inmate request forms on whose backs I had been keeping a journal. I stoop to pick up everything, and no one in my cube is laughing now.

"Who did this?" I ask, but everyone looks away.

"Wasn't me." Tookie grins. "But, just saying, looks like those draws of yours done walked off on their own two legs."

I look over at Town Fair Tire, and I know he's the one. He's back in his sheet with his face turned away from me, but I can tell. I should challenge him to a fight if I cared about my rep in here, but I don't, so I go up on my bunk to read, my ears burning. I realize now how vulnerable I actually am. I'm not one of them, and that false sense of belonging I had from doing the past bids doesn't mean squat in here.

I bide my time after that and keep completely to myself. Obviously, I can't play basketball anymore, but I don't even feel like playing cards. I withdraw into myself. I listen to the banter around me, jotting down colorful bits of conversation. *I used to middle for him. Got him shook half-crook. She a straight dripper. When we molly together, we freak the back seat. Then I had to go clap him, blam!*

Halfway through this penultimate bid, I get a visitor. It's my friend Andy.

Typical of his style, even though he is on my visitation list, he does not come to see me through the normal route of lining up and speaking with me on a phone through a glass partition. Instead, he has finagled his way into the jail as an investigator for my attorney, which means he can meet with me in a private room, and we can have a conversation without being monitored or recorded. He has visited me a few times before, but when I see him today, I can tell that something is wrong.

"Yo, T-bone." I greet him with a hug. "Why so glum? I'm the one in here."

"Well, you might feel like you got kicked in the balls when I'm done telling you."

"What?"

"Kevin Rennie got ahold of your whereabouts."

Kevin Rennie? The name rings a bell. He's that former Republican state legislator who writes for the *Hartford Courant*, his slanted political commentary masquerading as a conscience for the people. Rennie has already blogged about me numerous times, claiming that I'm "the CCSU poet with a taste for run-ins with the law . . . not humbled by events." In each article, as further proof of my fecklessness, he also somehow manages to work in the fact that I run a literary journal called *Drunken Boat*. I had intended to send him a copy of Arthur Rimbaud's *Le Bateau ivre* but decided it wouldn't be worth the postage.

"What do you mean? I've been doing this for a year. Nothing has changed."

"You just got promoted? Lead story in the Sunday *Hartford Courant*."

In keeping with Puritan tradition, Connecticut is one of a handful of states that will publish the names of individuals and the towns in which they live on the basis of pure allegation. It's a place where police reports can be quoted as fact, and the eventual adjudication or dismissal of charges is generally not newsworthy; neither is the fact that Blacks and Hispanics are arrested at a rate nearly ten times their White counterparts in the state.

When I return to the dorm after Andy's visit, I'm shaken. I have spent the last year mending my relationships and reintegrating myself into the community, so knowing this scab will be ripped off anew is utterly demoralizing. I stagger back to my bunk to stew.

"Yo, Professor? What's Gucci?" It's a Muslim called Carl, another contradiction in terms. He's someone who follows a chart that lists all the times that salat needs to be performed, and prays five times a day, yet who spits gangbanger slang. He's been teaching me the different names for a gun—hammer, ratchet, biscuit, slammy, burner—and other phrases such as "getting brain" for getting a blow job; "I got that White girl, that Christina Aguilera," for scoring cocaine; and a "smutty" and a "slore" for a "sloppy, slutty whore." Carl's looking at a five-year bid for a knife fight that violated his parole.

"You look like you feeling some kind of way."

"I think I'm going to be in the news again."

I'm dazed, powerless, nauseous.

"Shit, mean you famous, bro."

"Infamous, more like it."

"Don't sweat it. Give this to you off the muscle."

He tosses me a soup.

"How do you mean off the muscle?"

"Off the strength. Like good looking out. Shirt off my back, because I'm a nice guy. Off the muscle. Means you don't need to pay me back."

That evening, while I'm heading to the bathroom in borrowed shower shoes, I'm stopped by an excited Hispanic dude, who grabs my arm.

"Yo, yo—you the professor, right? Shit, I just seen you on the news!"

"What?" My heart sinks farther. I thought it was just going to be the newspapers, but TV as well? This can't be good. I wander over to Carl's tube, as he has invested in a TV. When I arrive, he's waiting for me with a dangling earbud.

"Here you are, Professor. Put this in your ear. You be up again soon. You the lead story on the evening news. You know how they cycle through it. You didn't tell me about your credit card scam. Look like you was sniffing pills."

I put the headphone in and, sure enough, after a few commercials, my mugshot fills the small screen. There I am, looking bugged out, deer-in-onrushing-headlights, thankfully in a button-up shirt and not a jumpsuit, but being introduced to the concerned audience with my inmate number. What an odd, dreamlike sensation to see your own face on television, especially when you've been looking for validation, even fame, all your life. To have it come in this context, as a persona non grata, is utterly crushing.

There I am alongside the headline flashing, "Breaking News! Professor arrested and promoted while in prison." A reporter interviews random students at Central, ones I haven't taught, to ask them how they feel about me. Carl switches channels, and there I am again, and again. On NBC, ABC, CBS, and FOX-CT news, each time an inaccurate litany of charges against me being recited.

"Mastermind of a credit card scheme . . ."

"Arrested for the third time in a year . . ."

"Driving under suspension and criminal impersonation . . ."

"The Board of Regents should be embarrassed . . ."

There is a state senator, Kevin Witkos of Canton, ringing in with his opinion that he is "shocked and appalled" by my promotion, issuing a statement that says, among other things, "it's simple logic. When you go directly to jail, you do not get to pass go, you do not get to collect that $200. That applies to real life too. Our state should not be funding a pay raise and extending a benefits package to someone who has violated the law repeatedly."

I never would have imagined that I would have any sympathy for the phrase "fake news," but much of what is being reported is false. This is not a recent arrest, nor have I been convicted of anything, but rather I am dealing with the after-effects of a legal issue nearly two years old. I was promoted months ago on the basis of my merits, and I'm not even in prison now. I'm in county jail on a pretrial detention.

This wall-to-wall coverage is excruciating. Kevin Rennie's op-ed piece, when I finally read it, asks, "Why can't marauding poets be more like Emily Dickinson and stay at home?" When I awaken the next day, mortified and chagrined, wishing that it had all been a bad dream, I find that I have become an overnight jailhouse celebrity. In line for chow, I am being clapped on the back and congratulated by inmates who haven't paid the slightest attention to me before. My cubies are constantly supplying me with information gleaned from the news, telling me that the Board of Regents is going to reconsider my promotion, and that even the governor is getting involved in my case.

Even the COs call me into the Bubble and want to shake my hand. They ask me about my job, about how to get a college degree. After that first news broadcast, I don't go hungry another night that I'm in the dorm. Every night, someone has a scoop of cheesy beans for me, or a free soup, and I suddenly morph into the jailhouse lawyer/pastor/teacher/psychiatrist. I can't even walk to the bathroom without being showered with felicitations. Even Big Country and Tookie stop messing with me.

For three days running, I am the lead story on the local evening news. True enough, the Board of Regents has launched an investigation into my situation and has convened a special meeting to reconsider my promotion. The president of CCSU has been forced to apologize to the board, saying he was unaware that I was incarcerated at the time of my promotion. The misconstrued facts of my story are being posted everywhere, from personal blogs to local news websites, always with an undercurrent of outrage. How dare this professor whose salary is being paid by taxpayers be allowed not just to keep his job but to advance within it? Can he be deported? And what about our children, the minds of our poor impressionable children?

Where am I? Humiliated outside, fêted within the jail walls. The drumbeat of the media is savage and unrelenting. I find I've even been turned into a political cartoon. Bob Englehart, the *Hartford Courant*'s longtime cartoonist, has drawn a jail cell labeled "CCSU Hartford Correctional Center Campus." A CO holds a tray out for me above a caption that reads, "Professor Shankar, here's your bread and water!" Not particularly funny, but it would run in Chicago, Baltimore, Orlando, and even reach as far as India.

Within days, I start receiving mail as well. One is a letter from a reporter from WFSB Channel 3 Eyewitness News, who asks to interview me regarding the controversy surrounding my promotion. Cameras are not allowed in the facility, so she would just be present with a notebook and pencil to get my side of the story, but I would first have to fill out and sign a DOC form, "Inmate Consent to Interview," on behalf of myself and my heirs. It's to make certain that I would receive no consideration for consenting to the interview and that I released the State of Connecticut from any claims that might accrue as its result. I would love to speak with her, but my attorney has forbidden me from speaking to anyone.

I also get a letter from Elder Jimmie Eason from East Hartford, with the message "God Put You on My Heart" scrawled in large block letters across the back of the envelope. The letter begins, "Dear Friend: I read about you in the newspaper and I am concerned about your plight." Elder Jimmie goes on to counsel me against sex, tobacco, obesity, alcohol, and homosexuality, telling me about how he himself was in jail many times, a drug addict and an escapee from a chain gang, before he got the Good News of the Gospel of Jesus Christ in his heart. Jimmie writes:

> I tell you of these things because I was guilty of most of them. I had knives put to my throat, guns put to my head. I was run over by a car, set on fire, and was confined for nine months. I almost drowned twice, tried to commit suicide, was beaten with a golf club, had my teeth knocked out and beaten up many times. I tried to run my girlfriend off the road, tried to choke people, stole cars, even tampered with a car to try to hurt someone. I almost got my finger cut off. My car almost fell on me while being jacked up. I almost got stomped by a horse. I almost got electrocuted. I almost lost my life over a dice and a card game. I almost got blown up by a pressure tank. I drove somebody else's car over a cliff with a load of people from being drunk. I almost got hung with a rope around my neck. I almost got killed by a bear. I was trapped inside my house during a flood. I almost got killed trying to hold on to a moving dump truck. I almost got my foot cut off. I almost got killed with an axe by it falling off the handle. I have been cut up by barbed wire. I had tar spilled on me and lost all my skin. I split my foot with an axe while cutting wood. When I was born I was sick. I've had poison ivy all over my body. I have lost many friends from all kinds of death. I lost my baby sister who was stillborn. I was told I was the best dresser in the city and won prizes for being the best dancer in Hartford. I am positive I was one of the best liars in the world.

Next time I am in East Hartford, I plan to visit this man.

With what's brewing outside, HCC becomes a sanctuary. I feel like the most notorious man in Connecticut, and I'm scared of what awaits me when I get out. If my plight is such big news, why has it gone unreported until now? A few days later, I see on the news that the Board of Regents has allowed my promotion to stand. A spokesman for the BOR says the board is planning to focus on reviewing the procedure followed for promotion and tenure, but that it is highly unlikely that their decision with respect to me would not stand. I'm in Carl's cube, peering at his small television, when the news is announced. The entire dorm erupts in cheers and shouts.

"Professor! They going to let you keep your promotion!" Carl gives me a hug, and I'm high-fiving other inmates as they gather around the cube, raising the roof and pumping their fists in the air. *Woot, woot!* The joy that emanates from them is infectious, and I do an impromptu shuffle-step, feeling like I have won a victory for all of us, although it is really only for myself.

When I return to court, the cameras are waiting. I am being released to teach summer school for a month and then have eight days left to complete my sentence. A news camera zooms in on me as I take the stand, still in ankle shackles. My bond is lowered, and I'm again given a Promise to Appear. I'm desperate to say anything to counter the steady stream of negative coverage, but, again, I've been advised not to speak.

After my paperwork is processed, I emerge, blinking in the midday heat, accompanied by my attorney. I exit the doors of the courthouse in Middletown, and sure enough, like in the movies, there are four or five reporters with cameras and microphones waiting for me. The reporters thrust their microphones in my face as they start shouting questions.

"Mr. Shankar, how do you feel about being allowed to keep your teaching job?"

"Did you enjoy your time in jail?"

"What do you want to tell the taxpayers who might be watching?"

The questions come at me from all sides, and all I say is, "No comment at this time, thank you," as I push past the reporters. One of the cameramen chases me down the road, and he resembles nothing as much as a gigantic puppy dog, trying to angle in front of me to get the best shot. I feel simultaneously awful and oddly invigorated, a minor celebrity for all the wrong reasons, getting some small taste of what it might feel like to walk the red carpet. I hoped Oscar Wilde had it right when he said that the only thing worse than being talked about is not being talked about.

When I return home to Chester, there is a white van parked across the street. Over the next few days, I will see other camera trucks and vans, and even a news helicopter hovering overhead. Parker tells me that reporters have knocked on the front door and have staked out the bus stop where my elementary school daughter disembarks. I'm furious. Are my misdeeds—my misdemeanors—so worthy of this level of attention?

Now I understand why my fellow inmates were so excited by the nonstop media coverage I was receiving: for most of them, many of whom had been accused of far more serious offenses, there had been no fanfare and no attention. Society had dropped them in a cell and thrown away the key. No one cared. Even homicides in Hartford barely received any attention. So while I would have imagined they would feel resentful, when the inmates saw the media coverage of my case, it helped validate their own lives by dint of my proximity. I understood then the power and allure of celebrity.

That entire week, I hide in the house, trying not to talk to anyone, afraid even to walk downtown. I've never felt so exposed and humiliated. News reports about my incarceration have spread like wildfire on Facebook and Twitter. Writers I don't know, lacking tenured jobs of their own, are glad to pile on. I even attract the attention of *Inside Higher Ed*. I feel compelled, though I'm not sure why, to write a public mea culpa on Facebook, which doubtlessly only calls even more attention to my predicament. A scarlet letter has been digitally branded on my forehead.

Meanwhile, Kevin Rennie continues to have a field day. His latest hit piece, titled "Memo to CCSU: Your Penitentiary Poet Returns to Court Thursday," reads in part, "Cossetted Central Connecticut State University poet and professor Ravi Shankar returns to criminal court Thursday on a host of unsettling charges. The state's incurious Board of Regents last month promoted the recidivist to a full professorship while he was waiting in the hoosegow in an unusual arrangement that allowed Shankar to go in and out of incarceration as his schedule permitted. Some of Shankar's pending matters have appeared on the docket 28 times. This is not typical treatment of a chronic defendant."

The recidivist in the hoosegow? A friend points out to me that it is an election year, and that the Board of Regents has been appointed by Democrat governor Dannel P. Malloy (who, when asked about my situation, said he found it "a little strange"). A Republican like Rennie can use the fact of my promotion as a shorthand way to besmirch the policies of his Democratic opponents. He doesn't even have to do any research into my professional career, teaching or publication, because, in the game of political football, I'm just the pigskin.

And I still have to do my final bid. My attorney has told me that I will be sentenced to ninety days for the probation violation and the driving under suspension, and that the charge of criminal impersonation will be changed to interference, which sounds less roguish. My probation would be terminated, and most of my sentence would be commuted for time served. I just owed the state these eight more days. A final irony is that my End of Sentence (EOS) date would be

July 4, Independence Day. Because that is a federal holiday, it means that I just might get out a day earlier than I should.

I stand in front of the judge in a courtroom full of Brown and Black people awaiting their own sentences. I've rehearsed this moment. Nearly three years since that fateful soccer game, I am finally one week away from paying off my debt to society. When I am read the charges of driving under suspension and interference, I plead no contest under the Alford doctrine. The judge looks down his nose at me.

"Mr. Shankar, do you have anything you'd like to address to the court?"

"I do, Your Honor." My attorney prods me in the ribs, but I persist anyway. "I'd like to take this opportunity to apologize for the impact my actions have had on my friends, family, and colleagues. I believe the human soul has an astonishing capacity to turn the worst curse into the highest blessing, and, while I regret what I have done and lament the punishment I've had to endure, I will not soon forget the men I met or the lessons I've learned about the American criminal justice system. I will use these lessons to help me grow."

"Thank you. Now, Marshals." For the fifth and final time, I am handcuffed and led away from the courtroom into a small cell, where I wait until I am transported, once again, to HCC.

By this point, I've become a regular at the jail, so when I arrive, I'm warmly greeted.

"Look who's here. Big Bang Theory's back again," jokes one of the COs.

As extraordinary as it might have been that my sentence was split up in this way, each reentrance traumatizes me anew, and having had to deal with this punishment in such a fragmentary fashion over the last year has only made it more, not less, difficult for me to move forward.

I'm placed back in dorm number three, and, selfishly, I'm glad to see Carl is still there. He is drawing when I see him and has covered the pages of his notebook with nonfigurative vegetal patterns and intricate elaborations of interlaced circles and squares, arabesques of polygons that seem almost cosmic. He is also reading the Quran, and when I go over to see him, he greets me with a fist bump and this passage: *Do they not consider the camels—how they are created? And the heaven, how it has been raised high? And the mountains, how they have been set firm? And at the earth, how it has been spread out? God is He Who is the Absolute Truth and Ever-Constant, and He gives life to the dead, and He has full power over everything.*

Does God have a purpose for each of us in here? I can't say for sure. I do know that many minor quotidian miracles surround our waking each morning, even in jail. From the gravitational force that keeps us pinned to this orbiting planet, to the shimmering translucent wings of the dragonfly that alights briefly in the rec yard, there's always mystery and splendor enough if we remind ourselves to look for it.

As I move toward my cube, I try to take it all in a final time: to memorize the cinderblock walls, the Hispanic guys rolling out mofongo, the banter of the Black guys playing cards. I am determined never to return. Walking slowly, lost in reverie, I trip over someone hunched on the ground. When he opens his mouth, he sounds vaguely familiar. Then I place his patter. It's Jay, the drug addict I met during my very first bid.

"Jay?" I'm amazed. "You been here this whole time?"

"Naw, bro. Been in and out like five times since we hung out last summer."

Hung out. His words puncture me. How sad that, for so many, this is an extension of their lives on the street. Each evening when the new inmates are brought in, it's like a prolonged family reunion—folks hugging and fist-bumping, talking about their cousin and their baby moms, and what the latest charge they caught might be. In some respects, being in jail is preferable to being out on the streets because you have "three hots and a cot," shelter and meals guaranteed, even if you are treated worse than an animal. It's with horror, but also a sense of sanctuary, that I realize that I've become one of them. I am recognized, and I see familiar faces.

My bunkie's name is Lord Intelligent, which he swears is what it says on his birth certificate. I can call him Tel for short. Like an immersion journalist on his last tour of duty, I am trying to hear and to see everything at once. There's also a young overweight boy who looks like he can't be more than fourteen in our cube, and he is being goaded by some of the more hardened inmates to reenact his attempt to rob a German couple of their iPhones in Hartford.

"Do it again, Biggie!" Tel demands.

And then this baby face would-be robber runs from the back of the cube, drawing his face into a mask of wrath and jamming an index finger underneath his shirt to shout, "Give me your shit, or I'll bust your melon top!"

The entire cube erupts in laughter each time, though not me. I feel nothing but sadness. I no longer have the stomach for any of it and pull the sheets over my head in my bunk.

The next day, wandering the cubes again, looking for a card game or a story, I stumble into Jay again. He is an entertaining raconteur, and I quiz him on the reasons he has been at HCC so frequently.

"Why? Drugs, bro."

"But can't you get a program?"

"Been there, done that. They got no beds anyway. All I do in here is kick the drugs. The withdrawal is unbearable. Medical won't do squat for me. I got a tight fist squeezing my chest tighter all the time."

Jay appears to have grown wiser and more melancholy than I remember him.

"That was beautiful. You ever think about writing any of this down?"

"Been writing since the day I was born."

"Really? Show me what you're working on."

The next day, Jay hands me a page torn from a journal.

Early evening stepping off the city bus express to the airport where I often sleep in a sitting position. A bed is a luxury for a junkie babbler. Ooohh baby, when I met you that terribly cold winter, I just wanted to suck on you until I got through your hard candy shell right down to the sweet sap running wild down your thighs. But I'm a creepshow carnival ride. Damaged goods. Stagnant pond scum praying to God I can puncture through scar tissue to hit that hidden vein. I lay awake at night and you split the universe in two. All is not lost. I hunger for more than what I have ever known, I'm sick of standing in the human centipede of a medicine line. Let's do this together, hand in hand, through bridges and shadows, your ice cream thighs, your lollipop eyes. But I am alone, afraid of the night when sleep comes to everyone else while I lay awake, an apparition centuries old like the Colosseum's construction site dust making tomorrow's storm clouds. You are that lovely haunting lullaby that finally puts me to sleep and that golden morning glowing each time I wake.

"Jay! This is good. I mean, this has real potential." I'm serious. It's better than much of the work produced by my students.

"You can have it."

"You sure?"

"Got me hundreds of pages in notebooks, all filled front to back with writing and drawing. Keeps me alive."

That very night, Jay is moved to another dorm. Like many of these men, I will never see him again, though I will sometimes pray that he has found his way to get clean. If he does, it will be in spite of—not because of—the system. I wish I had gotten the chance to see what else he had in his notebook, and it makes me feel dejected to imagine all those words entombed forever.

The week drags by, in part because of an inmate who has been up all night coughing and in the morning is moved to quarantine. The rumor quickly spreads throughout the dorm that he has tuberculosis. When I ask the CO in charge, he looks uneasy before confirming it. None of us, including him, have been tested, and he doesn't even know if the disease in question is communicable (it is). For the next few days, we are in lockdown, which means we are allowed no movement, no phone calls, no television, and no visits. Our meals are brought directly to our bunks, and we can only get up to use the bathroom. Uncertainty, boredom, obliviousness, cruelty—these seem to be the tropes of the correctional handbook.

When this time passes, I spend as much time as I can with Carl. He tells me he has a brother who played in the NBA and now owns car dealerships all up and down the East Coast. He shows me the long gash he has running from his breast to his sternum, the result of a knife fight in the 1970s from which he lost so much blood, the doctors didn't think he was going to make it. He tells me about the five pillars of Islam—beginning with the *shahada*, the most important, the simple affirmation of singularity, that there is no God except Allah, and that Muhammad is his one and only messenger. Hajj, the pilgrimage to the Kaaba in Mecca, is the last pillar he has left, and he hopes, if he ever gets out of jail, to complete it. I write down his information and promise that I will write him a letter when I'm on the outside.

When July 3 finally arrives, I'm antsy and agitated. I've been told that I will be allowed to walk right out of the jail, but I don't know for sure, and the not knowing is killing me. A handful of us are meant to be released on this day, and I shuffle forward with them to reclaim my street clothes. I've been given my certification of discharge from all Connecticut confinements. It lists my inmate name and number, my docket number, and my offense, as well as instructions about how to restore my voting rights. I have been advised to keep this on my person for at least a week, just in case I'm picked up again and thought mistakenly to have escaped.

When the prisoners to be released finally queue up, we each stand on our own, without handcuffs or ankle shackles, lost behind our own eyes. We are marched out in unison to the sally port, where the prison vans, those infamous ice cream trucks, will be securely unloaded with new prisoners coming in later tonight. Then, the reinforced doors creak open. There in front of us is the alleyway greeting us like a mother's open arms. We're free!

The sun is bright, and we are hollering, whooping, and skipping as we walk. One of the inmates with the same EOS as me has just finished serving a twelve-year sentence for attempted burglary, and he has been telling us how foreign he imagines the world will be for him. The last time he was out in the world, there were no smartphones, no hybrid cars, and his baby girl was only three years old. Now she's a teenager with a baby girl of her own. He turns in slow circles with his arms outstretched, around and around, with his eyes shut tight.

Women and children wait for some of these men. There are hugs and high fives. One man lights up a cigar. I walk slowly, reflectively—breathing deeply, drinking in the colors, and reveling in each step. Not knowing when I might be released, no one is waiting for me. I will have to borrow someone's phone to get a ride. Just like every other time I have entered and been released at court, I walk around the perimeter of the facility where I have spent some of each season last year, seeing it from the outside for the very first time.

Gates within the gates, razor wire, the cracked asphalt edge of the yard where I played basketball and had my finger broken. I walk back around to the front doors of the Hartford Correctional Center, where my visitors would have come in to see me. There are the tinted windows behind which a CO presumably sits, and there, tacked to the wall, is a list of articles of clothing forbidden to be worn by visitors. These include halter tops, sports bras, and spaghetti straps. There is the Securus machine where someone can put money on an inmate's phone account. Connecticut's former governor Jodi Rell and a number of elected officials are investors in both this company and in Keefe Foods, the company that runs a virtual monopoly on prison commissary items throughout the state.

It's too depressing to linger here any longer. I walk out, past the car dealerships and the post office, the skyline of Hartford, once the insurance capital and, more recently, the murder capital of America, rising before me. I go into a Dunkin' Donuts and borrow a phone to call Julie, without whom it feels like I wouldn't still be alive. In spite of mounting cataclysm, we can still sense the other's mood across a room and make each other laugh, which are blessings beyond compare. I can't wait to intertwine my fingers in hers. Thankfully, I still have people in my life willing to give me a ride, who believe in my goodness. A writer friend of mine thinks that bad experiences don't make us any better; they just make us worse. Waiting for a ride back to the small town in Connecticut where I have been living, I can't say for certain whether or not I agree with him.

MunPani (*Winter*)

Dear Julie,

In our path, to quote Hafiz, the sky has strewn pearls from the necklace of the Pleiades. When I think of us, even in the wrack of all we have been through together, it's our first night that I conjure with an instantaneous quiver of recognition. The sky was the starriest pool I've ever stepped foot in, and, holding hands, we glowed phosphorescent in the moonlight, not knowing how our first touch might, despite all odds, eventually grow into an unorthodox life. You had shared half your hummus sandwich with me in a church pew earlier that afternoon, and I had eaten it, both of us starved for someone with whom to have those conversations that we had only had with ourselves for far too long.

It was not the first time I had been unfaithful, nor the first time I had fallen in love with a woman who was not my wife. That time, when I briefly left my marriage to sublet a flat in New Haven that smelled of wet dog and shoe polish, I'd had my heart broken. I've so thoroughly walled myself off from how devastated I was back then that it's hard for me even to conjure that relationship fully now, though I know I had been in love and that I had struggled hard not to be. So no, you are not to blame for the dissolution of my marriage, just as I am not to blame for the breakdown of yours.

It's hard to trundle the love between us into verbs, to sketch the lines of magnetism that have kept us coupled, even as we defy expectations, being years, ethnicities, and often cities apart. If you were me and I you, the world would tolerate us better. Still, there's no denying that on one another's arm, we light up a room and that we both share a way of seeing and making that's remarkable. That's not to brag, but to affirm, because such affirmation is needed given how many people, including our own families, have wanted to keep us apart, and given how much pain our pleasure has engendered.

If only everyone could see how you fit like a key in the latch of my shoulder and how, in another life, we lived overlooking the sea with a brood of raven-skinned, vibrant-eyed, lithe beauties darting between our legs. In this one, we survive incarceration, legacies of depression and abuse, intramedullary spinal cord tumors, the falling out of families, and homelessness in its many guises. Though coincident, such misfortunes aren't the karmic punishments for the choice we made to be together, but the necessary side effects of trying to get it all right and to stop pretending. Plus, did we ever *really* have a choice?

True love compels, and each time I put my mouth on yours, the firmament unfurls a little further. We are all exiles from another place, put on this planet to grope our way forward in the dark. To find someone who sees us in all our inglorious imperfection and loves us anyway is the rarest, most precious gift. My own days are proof of the flux of fate, and so, while our promises are written on the wind and I can't foresee the future, I do know that this connection between us was meant to be. No matter where on and beyond this earth we go, I won't stop loving you, which, I suppose, is one version of eternity.

Your beloved

Chapter Twelve

A Mantra to
Heal the Unhinged

There's a song by the brilliant Manchester band the Stone Roses that has a simple, catchy refrain: "I want to be adored." Don't we all? From a young age, I obsessed about what others thought of me. I looked back at myself from some distant vantage point in the future, not recognizing that, lost in those clouds of reverie, I was ignoring the very ground on which I stood. Once I'd had the hard light shone on me, however, my fault lines exposed to the world, I went from wanting to be adored to being publicly despised. In that moment, I wanted nothing more than to hide.

My pride got in the way. Forbidden to tell my side of the story for so long, one of the first things I do when I get out of jail is to write an op-ed. The *Hartford Courant* runs my piece "The Eight Things I Learned in Jail" in its Sunday edition. The salient points from my brief essay, which I would later find out inflamed the state's judges and prosecutors, include how probation is a setup, how rehabilitation is a myth, and how, empirically, the criminal justice system is not color blind.

Next, I speak to more lawyers and public relations advisors. "While you could have a decent case against Discover Card and Ticketmaster," one of them advises, "corporations so indemnify themselves in fine print that you are going to have a hard time winning a judgment. Even though you've recorded conversations of them admitting to a computer glitch, that's unlikely to be admissible evidence in court. Not to mention the statute of limitations on most credit card cases is one year. Plus, you actually repaid the debt in question! If you had wanted to sue, you shouldn't have paid a dime and should've let your credit score go straight to hell."

But surely I could challenge the erroneous reporting in the newspaper? "The challenges of a libel suit," another attorney tells me, "are that, even when you can prove the media has falsely represented someone who is not a public figure—you might be disqualified from that, given your work on radio and in publishing—you still need to prove malicious intent, which is nearly impossible. My advice? Just move on with your life and forget all of this happened. In a couple of years, everyone else will forget too."

How about my standing invitation to appear on the news? Andy Thibault has recommended a PR expert who lays it out for me. "Let's start with the worst-case scenario to prepare you. Say you go on the offensive in the media, then prepare to have your whole life exposed. Your problem is that you have a consumer narrative and a vehicular narrative. Now, even if you can get people on your side with respect to the independent intervening event, which is the credit card company's computer glitch, how do you explain the drunk driving?"

"Well, no Breathalyzer results, for one," I tell him, "and the fact that the other driver was passed out high on the side of the road, for another."

"Victim blaming? No good. No Breathalyzer? Even worse. Here's the problem: you're not Joe Blow but Ivory Tower. That's already one strike against you. Regular guy might think you got screwed in one case, but not the other. Plus, since you're so smart, he's going to think something doesn't add up. Why did you try to resell those tickets to a third party? Why weren't you forthcoming with the cops? Doesn't look good.

"Look at it this way. The public is a litter of pigs picking through a dump. They find something to eat, that's dinner. There might be the juiciest filet mignon sitting unwatched in an open restaurant window right next to them, but that's beside the point because they've already satisfied themselves rooting in the scraps. The public, you see, has already eaten."

Some friends tell me to take solace in the fact that I'm a poet, telling me that infamy could help me in the long run, and that no one wants to read poems written by a Boy Scout. Their commiseration sounds to me like the superstition that rain on your wedding day is good luck. Nonetheless, to make myself feel better, I embrace famous authors who have done time in jail, such as Oscar Wilde, convicted of "gross indecency" for being a homosexual and sentenced to two years of hard labor during which he wrote "De Profundis." I pin a quote from the essay to an index card above my desk: "To regret one's own experiences is to arrest one's own development. To deny one's own experiences is to put a lie into the lips of one's own life. It is no less than a denial of the soul."

I reread Jack London, who details his arrest and imprisonment on charges of vagrancy in Buffalo, New York, after he was found sleeping in the streets in the summer of 1894. He begins with outrage, but, by the end, the time he served ground down his protest. "I saw with my own eyes, there in that prison, things unbelievable and monstrous. . . . My indignation ebbed away, and into my being rushed the tides of fear. . . . I grew meek and lowly. . . . Each day I resolved more emphatically to make no rumpus when I got out . . . to fade away the landscape."

I discover Joan Henry, descended from two British prime ministers and cousin of philosopher Bertrand Russell, a woman who spent eight months in prison for passing bad checks, during which time she wrote *Who Lie in Gaol*, an exposé that shone a light on the horrible conditions of the women's prisons. "I came to the conclusion," she writes of her experiences, "that this kind of thing is less sadism than smugness of mind . . . [which] finds no difficulty in regarding a convicted person as unfit for normal consideration."

I write a poem about O. Henry, the short story writer who served three years in a federal penitentiary in Columbus, Ohio, for embezzling from a Texas bank. He fled to Honduras to escape prosecution, but when his wife was diagnosed with a terminal illness, he returned, only to be subsequently tried and convicted. As prisoner no. 30664, he worked as a pharmacist and began to write short stories, churning out hundreds before his death in 1910, a penniless alcoholic. In an ironic twist that might have come from one of his own short stories, the official administrative headquarters of the University of Texas system is now housed in O. Henry Hall.

I make a list in my notebook of others: Miguel de Cervantes, jailed for fiscal irregularities, who began *Don Quixote* during his incarceration; Fyodor Dostoevsky, sentenced to death by firing squad for circulating essays critical of the government, only to have his sentence commuted to four years' hard labor in Siberia; Daniel Defoe, who did time in London's Newgate prison and in the public pillory for political pamphleteering; crime fiction writer Chester Himes, who did seven and a half years for armed robbery; Ken Kesey, arrested for possession of marijuana, a charge he was unable to evade by faking his own suicide; Jean Genet, a self-confessed vagabond and petty criminal, who, from the age of fifteen, was in and out of Paris prisons for such acts as theft, use of false papers, and lewd acts; Issei Sagawa, the Japanese writer who admitted to murdering and cannibalizing a young Dutch student in Paris while studying at the Sorbonne; William Burroughs, who shot and killed his wife Joan Vollmer in an inebriated game of "William Tell," a crime for which he would astonishingly spend only thirteen days in jail before "skipping"; Saint Thomas More, inventor of the word "utopia," imprisoned in the Tower of London and then beheaded for refusing to sign the Act of Succession that would make King Henry VIII the Supreme Head of Church in England; Paul Verlaine, imprisoned at Prison de Mons in Belgium for shooting at his lover, Arthur Rimbaud; Jimmy Santiago Baca, who spent five years in prison for drug charges; and Etheridge Knight, who began writing poetry as an inmate at the Indiana State Prison, where he was serving an eight-year sentence for armed robbery.

None of it makes me feel much better, but still, I hum Knight's poems to myself in bed, turning his lines into a continuous lyric: "It is hard to make a poem in prison . . . Here is not even sadness for singing. Not even a beautiful rage rage." His repetition echoes my own ire, though I feel lucky to reenter my life as a tenured professor. I consider putting a shingle outside my office door that reads, "No one quite puts the 'con' in Connecticut like Professor Shankar." Colleagues who used to stop in during my office hours keep their distance. In Chester, our small town where I already stood out, I feel like I'm wearing a neon fedora, yet remain weirdly invisible. People stare around me but won't meet my eye. Their gaze burns my back when I walk by them.

No wonder, then, that with the onset of spring, I follow the path of those European settlers who couldn't fit into the narrow strictures of the Massachusetts Bay or Connecticut colonies. While it's been long overdue, Parker and I officially separate, and I move to Rhode Island with Julie. Providence, home of the country's first synagogue; a place founded on the principles of freedom of speech and freedom of religion. Roger Williams, its founder, might have been a religious zealot, but he was tolerant, and that air of acceptance and weirdness continues to characterize the state.

I move into a condo in Federal Hill. Julie helps me transform the space, changing the color of the walls from garish papaya to shades of sandstone. We pool our furniture and buy new pieces to capture an urban rustic aesthetic. Lots of grainy wood alongside wrought iron. Mirrors and artwork and streaming light. We make love in each room and, when the morning shines through the large windows, the place glows. It feels like a new beginning. From the chrysalis of my solitude, I feel fragile new wings beginning to emerge.

But, once a deviant . . .

Afflicted with the flu of Yankee thrift, I decide to build bookshelves for the new place myself. It's amazing to have enough wall space for once in my life to array my entire *Paris Review* collection and my few art books. Though I am no handyman, I go shopping at Home Depot for tools and materials: lumber, a jigsaw, a drill, an electric sander. When her register gives her trouble, the cashier asks me if I do free tech support. When I return home, I find the drill is missing its power supply.

When I return to the store, the manager refuses my return. I'm apoplectic, but it doesn't help. The next day, I go to another Home Depot. I have no other plan but to return the drill, but habits are easy to make but hard to break. I find the drill's replacement on the shelves but, hearing that primal blind call, I fill my cart with a few other items to return with the receipt I have in hand, just as I used to do in my youth. As soon as I finish my transaction and step into the parking lot, two guys grab me by the shoulder and march me to the back of the store.

In Tamil, there's a word, "*muṭṭāḷ*," which roughly translates into "idiot." Incredibly, having survived the worst years of my life, I've done something to magnify my troubles. The cops are called, and they take the side of the asset protection specialists. I don't even waste my breath trying to explain what happened. I've already learned that the less you say, the better. As a result, I'm arrested on a charge of attempted larceny and told never to step foot in a Home Depot again. I have to call a bail bondsman to bond out. When I tearfully tell my attorney, he calls me an idiot as well.

I could claim racism. I could blame my father for his lifetime of deceptions, large and small. I could evoke my own rage at my perceived treatment at the hands of so many people and blame my compulsive behavior on everything I don't have but desperately want. But, endowed with free will and coming from enormous privilege compared to so many, I have no easy explanation for that reckless streak of craving, for how asleep I've been so many times throughout my life. All I can do is own up to my mistakes and change for the better. To wake up.

After Home Depot, I pray. It is selfish prayer, even while it encompasses my girls, Parker, Julie, Amma, Appa, my sisters, my friends, the men I met in jail, my relatives in India, even the Kevin Rennies of the world. I try to expand my circle of caring ever outward, but the true, secret reason for my newfound spiritual devotion is the wish that my latest transgression goes unnoticed by the media. When I tell Julie, she goes completely silent.

A day passes. Two days. A week. Two weeks. Daily, I check the police blotters and the *Hartford Courant*, but nothing. There are hundreds of alleged crimes each week in greater New England, yet only a minute portion of them are ever reported on. I am nervous yet grow more hopeful by the day. I make promises in my prayers.

Then, one afternoon, a few weeks before the fall semester is set to begin, Julie and I are walking through the Rhode Island School of Design Museum, which is surprisingly world-class for being so small. Legendary geniuses such as Van Gogh and Picasso hang alongside modern masters such as Roy Lichtenstein, Cy Twombly, Richard Serra, and many others. But my favorite artifact is the *Dainichi Nyorai*, the twelfth-century meditating Buddha carved from a roseate wood. It is the largest Japanese wooden sculpture in North America, and, because of the material it has been carved from, it glows. *Dainichi* means "great sun" in Japanese, just as "Ravi" is derived from the Sanksrit word for the same, and this Buddha would have been the central figure in a mandala, the generative force of all creation. Julie and I sit in front of him and feel a warmth and connectedness that is hard to put into words.

When we step outside the museum, the sky gleams. Then, my cell phone vibrates in my pocket. It's a text message from a friend.

"Ravi, you okay? Saw the news. Arrested again??"

Right there, outside the museum, I crumple into a heap on the sidewalk. I feel like someone has kicked me in the gut. I knew this was a real possibility, but after so much time had passed, I had almost started to believe that I could deal with this privately. I can't breathe. I'm curled in a fetal position on the concrete and no longer in my body. I'm floating above it, a wisp of cloud looking down at a crumpled brown sack on the ground. I don't want to reenter my body.

Luckily, I'm with someone who loves me. Julie takes my hand and helps me to my feet. I'm staggering like a boxer with a cauliflower ear. Tears scald my cheeks, and I mutter epithets filled with such immense self-hatred that, if I could, I would take my own life on the spot.

"What are you saying, Ravi?"

"It's not worth it." I gulp to speak. "There's no way back from this."

"Love, there always is. You are a survivor. We just have to get at the root of why you keep sabotaging yourself over and over. Sabotaging us."

"Just leave me alone. You shouldn't be with me. No one should. Please. I just need to kill this pain."

"That's exactly why I *need* to be with you right now. You're scaring me, Ravi. Please don't shut me out in your shame. We can get through this together but right now, you need help, babe."

Woozily, I check myself into Butler Hospital, a private psychiatric hospital on Blackstone Boulevard in Providence. Founded in 1844 along the banks of the Seekonk River, it is Rhode Island's first dedicated mental health hospital, and the main building is magisterial, if a little sinister-looking in a Gothic revival way. At present, it is the major affiliated teaching hospital for behavioral health and psychiatry in Brown University's medical school, a world-renowned center for neuroscience, and a national leader in psychiatric illness and substance abuse research.

Julie sits with me, holding my trembling hand in the waiting room until an attendant nurse takes my vitals. When I confess my suicidal ideations, she admits me as an inpatient. All my possessions, including my phone and wallet, are taken from me. I don't even have a chance to say good-bye to Julie; before she can step out to the car, I'm whisked away, behind a set of double doors that lock behind me. I feel like a porcelain teacup hurled from a balcony.

Once admitted, I'm given a room with a chest of drawers and a spartan bed. The ward resembles nothing so much as a daycare center. Brightly colored drawings of stick figure families are pasted on the wall. There are tubs of watercolors, stacks of construction paper, and containers full of building blocks stacked in the corner. Banners with sayings such as "You are perfect just the way you are," "Stars can't shine without darkness," and "The first step toward getting somewhere is to decide that you are not going to stay where you are" hang from the ceilings.

I spend the entire first day in bed, barely able to emerge when I'm called to join the group. I join a circle seated in chairs. A pretty woman in scrubs leads our discussion.

"Welcome, everyone! Let's take this chance to check in with our bodies. How are we all feeling today? Before we get started, who wants to remind us of our community rules?"

"We listen to each other but don't have to respond. We are respectful and don't interrupt one another," a bruised and obese woman in panther-print spandex volunteers.

"We wait our turn," a gruff male voice appends. I can't be bothered to turn my head, which rests like a rice sack on my neck.

"Good!" the woman in scrubs exclaims. "Now, today we are going to talk about the kinds of foods that make us feel really, really good inside. Who wants to go first?"

The second day in, I meet with a psychiatrist. He's an elderly Chinese American man with bushy eyebrows who comes in with a medical resident and a folder full of papers. He sits in the chair in my room to ask me questions.

"Says here that you have been having thoughts of self-harm. Is that so?"

"Perhaps the world and I would be better off parted. Yes, I've thought that recently."

"Do you still feel this way?"

"No." I'm not sure. I feel nauseous.

"Your paperwork indicates mild depression and anxiety. I'm going to prescribe you some Lexapro for the depression and Lorazepam for the anxiety. I can also get you something to help you sleep if you need it. Also, you know you can't check yourself out of here. Depending on your progress, I will need to sign off on your release, so just stay put."

The next morning, I receive a phone call from Rajni, who has been diligently helping me out behind the scenes. She has let CCSU know that I have been hospitalized and has been in touch with human resources. I've also filed for short-term disability under the federal Family Medical Leave Act, plus I have over a year's worth of sick days that I should be able to use. However, after finding out I was in the hospital, CCSU had gone ahead and scheduled a mandatory meeting with me that they knew I wouldn't be able to attend. Rajni tells me that the outcome of the meeting was that the school has decided to suspend me without pay on the grounds that they consider me "a danger to persons or property." They are also cutting off my health benefits.

Kevin Witkos, the Republican senator from Canton, is in hog heaven. He has written another open letter to the school's administration, this time demanding that I be fired. Rajni reads me an excerpt: "By his continuous disregard for the law, Mr. Shankar has repeatedly demonstrated that he is unfit to discharge his professional responsibilities. The professor is harming the reputation of all in the teaching field and, quite frankly, the administration by its inaction to date." In addition to putting me on unpaid administrative suspension, the university is considering beginning termination proceedings.

When I hang up with her, I'm glad I'm medicated. For the next two weeks, I remain at Butler. I follow the course of events outside detachedly, taking part in our group therapy sessions, eating cherry Jell-O and green beans from little plastic dishes, walking with the other patients throughout the winding grounds. I suffer like Winona Ryder in *Girl, Interrupted*. Amplified. Vulnerable. Swimming in the fog of the Lexapro and Lorazepam. Dropping each facade I have tried so hard to manifest throughout my life. No longer a husband nor father, lover nor son. Neither Indian nor American. Distinguished professor, poet, delinquent, thief—like onion skins, they fall away and sting my eyes with tears. Nothing remains except a gaping void.

As an educator, I had been trained about "trigger warnings"—potentially emotionally distressing content that could affect students. I understood the reasoning but had been skeptical of what such edicts did to free speech and critical discourse. In Butler, I come to understand this phenomenon firsthand. Whenever I hear news of what is happening in the outer world, part of me freezes. All my old mass media friends have been whipped up into a moralizing frenzy and call gleefully for my dismissal. During the infrequent phone calls that I am allowed, I insist that Rajni keep me updated on what's happening, but each bit of news, each new headline, plunges me further into a deep funk. After two weeks, the psychiatrist determines I'm no longer a danger to myself or others.

I am discharged into the partial program and enrolled in cognitive behavior therapy (CBT) classes. CBT is a form of short-term talk therapy that is meant to be pragmatic and goal-oriented, to change unhealthy ideations, and to focus on how we deal with others. I arrive each morning at nine thirty with twenty other enrollees. We begin each day by relating how our previous evenings were. For some, it is a struggle just to get through each night. For others, their anxiety is so debilitating that they are afraid to go out in public. My own troubles, grave as they appear to me, are minimal in comparison. We leave each day with homework, forms to fill out about self-esteem, and charts with which to track our moods.

During the course of the day, we have our choices of different classes: maladaptive behaviors, goal setting, relaxation techniques, anxiety reduction, and combatting negative thoughts. The most useful formula for me is the one that separates out our decision-making process. Say something happens to us (as it does every single day). We respond to the stimuli, which leads us to feel a certain way. This feeling then leads us to do something.

Event → Thought → Feeling → Behavior.

For most people, this entire casual change happens almost instantaneously. Something happens, and then—*boom!*—we react. The CBT idea is that if we slow down and alter our automatic thoughts, we can then change our feelings and, as a result, our behaviors. Though I have other problems with CBT, particularly the assumption that thoughts precede emotions and that any negative ideation is necessarily dysfunctional, this is an elegant formulation. I think about how often I reacted to stimulus without separating out these steps.

My final weeks at Butler are in the interpersonal psychotherapy program (IPT), which is very different from CBT. In these classes, we sit in a circle and talk about how we perceive one another. We talk about body language and gesture, how we appear to be versus how we feel inside. It's not goal-oriented, and oftentimes things arise that are left unresolved. Sometimes the members of the group scream at each other. Other times they blame the therapist, who is meant to be more a member of the group than an authority figure. At the end, we talk about how it felt for us.

How does it feel for me? I'm a wrung-out dishrag left to stiffen on a line.

Once I'm released from Butler, I'm referred to a psychotherapist in town, but there's one small problem. I no longer have medical insurance, nor a salary, even though I'm eligible for medical leave. The head of human resources at CCSU has the last name and distinctive look of a German infantry tank, and she believes I'm fabricating my entire medical condition.

Fortunately, I have a union. I'm a dues-paying member of the American Association of University Professors (AAUP), and one of the first conversations I have when I get out of the hospital is with them. They assure me that they will do everything to advocate on my behalf, including filing a grievance. I also file a complaint with the Connecticut Commission on Human Rights and Opportunities and the US Equal Employment Opportunity Commission. I'm still on the books as an employee of the university, which precludes me from taking another job or even claiming unemployment, yet my salary and benefits are being withheld. It's an untenable and illegal situation.

During this time, I hear that the chair of the English department has arranged for a vote on whether to kick me out of the department. It's a toothless vote, but it's nonetheless meant to be symbolic. In a department of thirty-two full-time members, the measure passes fifteen to thirteen with four abstentions. Still, firing someone who has tenure is difficult. There are a number of steps along the way, many checks and balances, and the union's lawyer tells me that we need to take things step by step.

First, I have a grievance hearing, in which, predictably, the administration agrees with the outcome and the union disagrees. Next, in the very seminar room in which I used to lecture, I have a hearing before the university's mediation committee, a three-person panel of my fellow faculty members, who also meet with the president of the university. Finally, I have to meet before the independent arbitrator.

Along with my attorney and the representatives from the union, I sit on one side of a long oaken table. On the other side sit representatives from the Board of Regents, the CCSU Systems Office, and a sallow trial lawyer from the office of Jackson Lewis—who focuses on employer defense. The arbitrator is a white-haired man with a snowy mustache, and there's a gentleness about his manner that I like immediately.

The next four hours, however, are pure torture.

Whoever else I might be, I'm not the person being painted by the administration's attorney. This grievance is about whether the university had the right to suspend me without pay and deny my medical leave yet keep me on their payroll as an unpaid employee, leaving me unable to claim unemployment and without health insurance at a time when I most desperately needed it. Their attorney presents the litany of charges against me. He reads through my social media posts, my Facebook status updates, and my Twitter feed to make the argument that I have been of sound mind and health, then in the very next breath, he tries to allege that the students had something to fear from me. When the union's attorney tries to introduce a letter from the doctor stating that I suffered from depression and adjustment disorder, and that, in his medical opinion, I should be granted medical leave, he vigorously objects, and his objection is sustained. This key piece of evidence would not be entered into the public record.

It's a straight character assassination, and I can do nothing. My attorney seems to be losing, and losing badly. He barely protests the rambling diatribes by the other lawyer, and his own points are mainly procedural, having to do with the thoroughness of the investigation the university completed to ascertain how I was a "danger to persons and property."

The German tank of a human resources officer is called in to testify. She suspended me without pay after learning I was in the hospital. She neither spoke to my doctors nor did any sort of due diligence to ascertain whether I really had a medical condition. Nor did she speak to me or my attorney. The extent of her investigation was a conversation she claims to have had with the asset protection personnel at Home Depot.

I squirm in my seat, anxious, burning to say a word in my defense. After the hearing, both parties file briefs. The university's brief claims, "When viewed in the context of his prior history, it was clear that the Grievant's theft was the latest of a series of escalating and progressively erratic transgressions. When the Grievant's history was viewed in its entirety, there was only one inescapable conclusion. An individual who has established time and again that he is deceitful, and either cannot or will not control his impulse to act dishonestly, cannot be trusted and is a danger, especially in a University setting."

The union's brief counters, "The record reveals that in fact there was not a scintilla of evidence that Professor Shankar was a danger to persons and property. He may have embarrassed the University (and himself) by exercising extremely poor judgment in his off-campus life, but there is absolutely nothing to suggest he would ever pose a risk to persons or property. Indeed, in his more than 13 years as a productive faculty member at CCSU, there is no evidence that he ever engaged in any inappropriate or even questionable conduct on campus."

The picture that emerges of me from both documents is unflattering, to say the least. The union is confident that we have won the proceedings, simply because a proper investigation was not undertaken and because the university had no right to suspend me without pay, plus deny me the sick days I had earned over the years, but I am uncertain.

During this time, the university offers me a settlement of a semester's pay if I will resign my position. I am advised against it by both friends and experts. In an article published about me and shared over a hundred times in *Inside Higher Ed*, Michael A. Olivas, the William B. Bates Distinguished Chair in Law at the University of Houston and former general counsel for the AAUP, writes, "The crime has to be tied to your core academic professional competencies . . . [Shankar's case] has all the hallmarks of someone who's wildly out of control. But no one has said he's missed class, or not met his obligations of meeting with students. . . . If all of those things are in order, I'd say they'd have a high burden [of proof] before removing him."

Robert O'Neil, the former president of the University of Virginia and professor of law emeritus, is even more explicit: "Despite the disdain shown by the *Courant* editorial and others, Shankar's conduct probably falls toward the low end of that range [to warrant dismissal]. While (in the *Courant*'s view) 'his behavior has shown him to be an extremely poor [role] model [for young people],' even a potpourri of scrapes with the law would seldom warrant a tenured professor's dismissal."

Nonetheless, when the arbitrator rules in my favor and grants me the salary I'm due, the union's attorney suggests that I would be wise to take the settlement the university offers and rebuild my life. I decide he's right. I could continue to fight and go into a termination hearing, but, after what I've been through, which the union attorney has assured me would be mild in comparison, there's no way I could sit through more of the same just for the chance to remain at a school where I have become universally loathed, a blight in a place where I had once been awarded for my teaching and scholarship. If I were to remain, a pariah unwanted by his own department, I would likely never receive another course release or sabbatical.

That's how I end up back in the country from where my parents emigrated. I read from my translations of Āṇṭāḷ, the ninth-century Tamil female bhakti poet and saint, to an audience of more than a thousand people in Jaipur, the Pink City. Just as when I shifted from jail to Hong Kong, the unreality of life swallows me whole. I know I'm neither the humiliated academic I've left behind nor the celebrated author I appear to be here. Neither am I the voice of abnegation and self-loathing that gripped me so intensely while I was at Butler. In spite of what the media might claim, I haven't been convicted of any felonies, nor have I been fired. Not hooking into any of these identities is a start, and my travel back to India teaches me how resilient the human spirit can be.

In New Delhi, a friend's partner tells me about the application of emotional freedom techniques (EFT), also known as tapping, which combines ancient Chinese acupressure and modern psychology. She claims she can help me clear my body's meridians of blockages and that the source of negative emotions is a disruption in the body's energy system. She sits with me on a couch and asks me to admit what I regret and for what I most wish. She uses the fingertips of her index finger and middle finger to tap on meridians at the top of my head, under my eye, on my chin and collarbone, under my arms, and on my wrists. All the while she has me repeat the phrase: "Even though I carry the shame of being arrested, I deeply and completely accept myself."

Then she brings over a mirror and asks me to look into my own eyes. Reminding me that my consistent thoughts will become my reality, she asks me to speak to myself gently, to say, "Even though you weren't honest or skillful enough, I forgive you; you were only doing the best you could." It's the most generically positive, life-affirming sentiment I can imagine, an outlook that seems so childlike and simplistic, yet somehow it helps soothe my nerves.

The highlight of my trip back to India is spending a few days with my ammamma, Amma's mother. She's ninety-three years old and frailer than I remember, but full of warmth and grace. I speak my broken Tamil to her, hold her papery hands in mine, and, when I look into her eyes, I see my ancestors in her. She sits in a sari, and, when she tells me she has not left my aunt's house in almost a year for fear of falling and breaking her hip, I coax her out of the chair. We take gentle steps to the threshold of the old village house with the open courtyard in the middle and stand in the sunlight, holding one another's hands. It would be the last time I saw her alive.

Thiruvananthapuram, the city formerly known as (and still called) Trivandrum, the largest city in Kerala, is on the southern coast of India. It was called the "evergreen city" by Mahatma Gandhi, and loosely translates as the "city of bliss" in Sanskrit. Bounded by the Western Ghats to the east and the Laccadive Sea to the west, the city was an early trading post for sandalwood and ivory, dating back over three thousand years. It's an easygoing, mellow place with nearby beaches and clusters of Victorian museums, although I'm only here to spend time with Ammamma.

Early one morning, I walk with my uncle around the perimeter of Shri Padmanabhaswamy Temple, where armed policemen stand guard, forbidding me from taking even a photograph of its perimeter walls. One of 108 centers of worship dedicated to Lord Vishnu, the temple has indeterminate origins, although it has been rhapsodized in early medieval Tamil literature. It is considered the world's richest house of worship because, in secret subterranean vaults, more than twenty-five billion dollars' worth of loose diamonds, rubies, emeralds, and jewel-encrusted gold chains and more than a hundred thousand gold coins have been found.

There's purportedly even more treasure to be found, but no one has wanted to enter the chamber, which has been sealed with steel doors with two massive cobras entwined upon them, and no latches, keyholes, or any other possible means of entry. Indian astrologers have decreed that the chamber is too sacred and hazardous to open, and that any human who attempts to open it without reciting the proper mantras will result in disasters occurring all over India and perhaps around the world.

The next day, even earlier, at around 3:00 a.m., I leave my aunt's house to make a pilgrimage there on my own. It is Nirmalya Darshan, the first worship of the day, and there is a paltry crowd in attendance. I have borrowed a simple dhoti to tie around my waist and bare my upper body, as per the rules of entrance. It is still dark when I enter to sit cross-legged in front of the enormous reclining Lord Vishnu and pray.

I'm sitting where generations of my ancestors might have sat, where, in the Bhagavad Gita, Krishna's older brother, Balarama, once visited to bathe and to make his offerings. This is an ancient place, the equivalent of which it would be nearly impossible to find in the Western world.

The last few years have been the darkest of my life, there's no doubt about it, and I have demolished an entire lifetime's worth of labor in one fell swoop. Sitting in front of Lord Vishnu, the all-pervasive Supreme Divinity of Creation in Hinduism, I focus my attention on this present moment to the exclusion of these thoughts, and that artless, elemental, irredeemably new age mantra returns to me. I breathe it out into the temple air:

I forgive you; you were only doing the best you could.

Chapter Thirteen

American Larrikin

Once I had resigned from CCSU, all my other legal complications resolved themselves. With respect to Home Depot, I acceded to my attorney's advice to plead no contest to one count of larceny in the fourth degree, a misdemeanor, and to have the matter settled without probation or jail time. In so doing, I followed the example of nine out of ten of those individuals accused of a crime in America who accept a plea bargain.

As Jed Rakoff, a federal district judge, wrote in the *New York Review of Books*, "The suggestion that a plea bargain is a fair and voluntary contractual arrangement between two relatively equal parties is a total myth: It is much more like a 'contract of adhesion' in which one party can effectively force its will on the other party." In my case, I was guilty, so I didn't mind waiving my constitutional right to trial by jury, not that I could have afforded it if I had wanted it.

As my attorney told me, going to trial would cost tens of thousands of dollars, which is why many lower-income defendants, even if they are innocent, accept plea deals. Plus, because mass incarceration has ballooned criminal case dockets, prosecutors often coerce defendants into accepting plea deals by taking advantage of lax discovery procedures that allow for the suppression of critical evidence, and by dangling grossly divergent sentences for those who accept a plea deal versus those who go to trial. According to Rakoff, criminologists who have investigated this phenomenon have found that between 2 and 8 percent of convicted felons who accepted plea deals are actually innocent. With more than 2.2 million people in American prisons, the potential extent of this injustice is staggering.

I was glad to get personal closure, but the trauma of my time in jail and my exposure to the criminal justice system never really disappeared, leaving me picking shrapnel from my limbs in the charred air. Thankfully, I'd only ever been convicted of two misdemeanors this entire agonizing time; a felony conviction would have been tantamount to a life sentence when it came to employment and reintegrating into society. Nonetheless, living in the internet era, the newspaper articles, blog posts, Facebook conversations, and Wikipedia entries about me proliferated, which felt like a latter-day manifestation of the puritanical urge to punish. I didn't feel sorry for myself, but, having paid my debt to society, I just wanted to move forward.

During the onset and resolution of my troubles, the artist Michael Peery from New London, Connecticut, was asked to paint my portrait. It was meant to substitute for the author photo for a new book of collaborative and ekphrastic poems about art, music, and dance. Once every few weeks, over the course of a year, I would sit in his studio in a red vinyl chair that had been marked with masking tape to indicate the posture I needed to take each time I resumed my position. I would stare at the intersection between two crossbeams while he painted me, measuring my face with his brush and forefinger before making a stroke.

"Portraiture," Mike told me once, measuring the length of my face with his brush, "is really a relationship between contours, colors, and distances. How far are your eyes apart? What shape do the edges of your body take in space? What palette is best suited for the complex coloration of your skin? If you can observe those elements precisely, then the soul of the person you are painting starts to materialize."

Sitting there in silence, I wondered if the weight and worry of the last few years were etched on my face and whether the light of my disgrace would be communicable to posterity. Mike discussed the brilliance of Van Gogh as he painted. "Think of his self-portrait at Saint-Rémy, the one in swirling blue that hangs at Musée d'Orsay. He did that after he left an asylum and the painting pulsates with energy. It's the rhythm of his brushstrokes that capture the turbulence inside his mind. You can see he's on the edge of breaking up completely, but how did he achieve that effect? Through color and proportion."

Mike is a talented realist painter, too little known for his technique and artisanship, but his first efforts failed completely. Julie told me I looked like a Malaysian businessman who had gorged himself on too much *nasi lemak*. Mike told me not to worry because his process was to build up layers that would change in time. Eventually, after many months, a portrait emerged that felt haunted and handsome enough to satisfy my vanity. He had captured the liveliness in my eyes and the ease of my jawline. Mike had even included a bookshelf that subtly incorporated a cover from one of my books. I took photos of the finished painting and shared them with friends, receiving their assurances that the portrait was indeed finished. I arranged with Mike to pick up the completed canvas one chilly autumn afternoon.

When I arrived at his studio and mounted the steps, chalky dust rose around me. He had moved to the top of a crumbling warehouse space in downtown New London, once Eugene O'Neill's hometown, and a place that feels forsaken by time, as if its best years might have been before Nathan Hale was hanged by the British. Mike's studio had high ceilings and large windows that looked onto Bank Street. Inside, he kept a collection of vintage folding cameras and hand-cranked movie projectors from the 1930s, and cases of cold PBR in a working 1950s Frigidaire with soft curves.

When I entered his studio this time, however, I was in for a shock. The canvas stood in the corner and, where my face had once been, now there was just a crude brown smear. I had been painted over.

"Mike, what the hell happened?"

"Sorry, Ravi." Mike shrugged. "Wasn't happy. Last time you were in here, I noticed how your head was just too big for your frame. The proportions were off." Six months of work obliterated just like that—like making an intricate sand mandala and then letting the wind disperse it.

But hadn't I done just that to myself? Forty years of my life, painted over.

In classical Japanese philosophy, there's a concept of *mujō*, or impermanence. Our days on earth are like the flux of a river, a succession of discrete moments linked together to give the false impression that it is all continuous and unified. But the narrative we retrospectively apply to being in time is continually belied by time itself, which gives our lives urgency. As the fourteenth-century Buddhist monk and author Yoshida Kenkō puts it in his *Essays in Idleness*, "It does not matter how young or strong you may be, the hour of death comes sooner than you expect. It is an extraordinary miracle that you should have escaped to this day; do you suppose you have even the briefest respite in which to relax?"

When Mike finally finished the portrait a few weeks later, my face had been altered forever. It was still masterfully rendered and certainly more proportional to my body, but the visage I had loved so much had been replaced by an aspect seemingly older and graver than I felt inside. It resembled nothing so much as a pseudo Dorian Gray into whom I might eventually live, and, though I used it on the back cover of my book, I couldn't bear the thought of hanging it in my home. I gave it to Amma and, someday, will pass it on to my daughters.

The Japanese have another aesthetic concept, *wabi-sabi*, which yokes together two words: "wabi," stemming from the root for tranquility and harmony in loneliness, with the added meaning of being humble, unmaterialistic, and in accord with nature; and "sabi," which means the blooming of time, like the effect of a cratered concavity of an oxidized silver spoon, or a crumbling silo so weathered it feels part of the landscape. Taken together, their meanings cross over, the philosophical merging with the aesthetic. Something that possesses wabi-sabi has the imperfection of the handmade in a beauty that deepens with age and incident. It's a celebration of frayed edges and erosion, the melancholic grace of defect, like the chipped lip of a ceramic bowl. As opposed to the mass-produced, wabi-sabi is nothing so much as singular and genuine.

Applied to ourselves, the concept reminds us of our own transience, how our bodies, like the objects in the world around us, are caught in the irreversible process of changing in time. We will all eventually turn to dust, and our faces are also marked by turbulent weather. We wear the visible evidence of repair like a new skin, yet that those healing scars also become a profound source of beauty. We are meant to love ourselves, not just in spite of but because of all our failings and asymmetries, regardless of whether the world conspires to tell us otherwise. As Ernest Hemingway wrote in *A Farewell to Arms*, "The world breaks everyone and afterward many are strong in the broken places." I was determined to be one of those, clinging to an idea of potential redemption like a life raft, because, otherwise, I could so easily drown.

So I focused on what was essential. Tried to strip away what was superfluous. For so long, I had wanted to be adored, and, somehow, the opposite had happened. I had caused that to happen by not following the rules and imagining I could move through the world invisibly. Now I was starkly visible and judged by everyone. In response, I shifted my attention from doing to being, from perfecting to appreciating, from cursing my fate to cultivating gratitude for the small blessings of my family, my lover, my healthy body, my next meal, the natural world, and the universe of books and art. In that way, I found I could begin to face the rubble I had made of my life.

The most despondent outcome, for me, was the dissolution of long-standing friendships dating back to high school and established over my decade in Connecticut. I grew reconciled that I would probably never change the minds of the readers of the *Hartford Courant* or the watchers of Fox News, but, when it came to those mates I felt abandoned by in my time of greatest need, there was no easy cure for the deep gash of betrayal. Seeing photographs on social media of ski trips and vacations to Costa Rica to which I had not been invited was a knife edge. If the hardest thing of all was learning to forgive myself, a close second was granting those I had loved their own fears and letting go of my own bitterness. Ultimately, I would grow to feel lucky to have had them in my life at all. Throughout my life, I've been blessed with dear friends, and if some of them have faded away in time, I have no choice but to mourn them and then move on.

Thankfully, in terms of making a living, I won my case against CCSU. The arbitrator ruled in my favor on every single issue, finding that the university had illegally withheld my salary and health insurance, which allowed me to receive a monetary settlement and claim unemployment. The upshot of these positive decisions, though, was only a temporary financial bridge into whatever I would do next. As someone who had been so visibly besmirched by the media, and who now possessed a criminal record, it was clear that it would be difficult for me to continue my career.

Instead, I cast about wildly, trying to find any way to pay my bills. I did some freelance editing, taught briefly at Sun Yat-sen University in Guangzhou, China, and, when I received a multiyear international research fellowship to study at the University of Sydney, I only hesitated for an instant. It all sounds glamorous and escapist, but to quote *The Adventures of Buckaroo Banzai across the 8th Dimension,* "remember, no matter where you go, there you are." In truth, leaving New England was simultaneously the easiest and toughest decision I ever had to make.

My daughters and Julie still lived there, as did my former students and few remaining friends from the place I had lived for the longest continuous stretch in my entire life. I would miss them massively, just as I would miss those autumn mornings where the forests would transform into a sumptuous banquet of dappled pumpkin orange and apple-skin red. Still, when the universe opened doors, I stepped through them first and asked questions later; plus, Australia seemed as far removed from my troubles as life on Mars.

Travel helped me regain perspective, and, in time, I began to feel less radioactive. I was still in possession of my faculties and family. If chagrined, I nonetheless felt wiser and kinder, more committed to working toward greater mindfulness and social justice. The sense of unbelonging I had felt since being a young boy had led me down furtive and self-destructive pathways, but I understood better than ever before that everything was temporary, continuously changing, and created from habit. I knew now that there were tools that existed to help change the calcified patterns of behavior that most cause suffering.

If I had not spent three months at Hartford Correctional Center, I might have gone through my days blithely unconcerned about the plight of prisoners and the undeniable institutional racism of mass incarceration. If I had not been disfigured in the media, I might not have started to look at journalism with such a critical eye. If I had not been admitted as an inpatient into Butler Hospital, I might have persisted in the illusion that admitting to mental health issues was tantamount to showing weakness. If I had not ruptured my life at its midpoint, I might have floated along inert, unquestioning and half-alive, mildly discontented and disconnected. When you fail spectacularly, you become less afraid of failure and more immune to criticism. Now I had no choice but to dive deeply and reinvent myself.

During one of my first weeks in Australia, I met an indigenous Torres Strait Islander at a bakery in Redfern, a neighborhood that had once been a center of Aboriginal life in Sydney, though its complexion was being altered by gentrification. He overheard me ordering a "smashed avo and feta on sourdough" and wanted to know where I was from, then invited me to join him for lunch. I was suspicious of his motives, because it had been a long time since a stranger had approached me without any agenda. As we began talking, however, I realized my qualms were totally unfounded. He introduced himself to me as Dak and told me he worked as a delivery person for a local pizza joint.

His real interest was in history, and Dak chronicled the early days of Australian colonialization, describing the voyage of Captain James Cook, memorialized in Sydney for having "discovered" Australia, even though it had been inhabited by indigenous people for upwards of sixty-five thousand years. He told me about how the country had been founded as a British penal colony, and how convicts were some of its first European inhabitants; he described the Rum Rebellion, the first and only military coup d'état in the history of White Australia, and how antipodeans took a certain pride in their criminal past. He told me about the 1967 constitutional referendum that allowed Aboriginal people to be counted in the census and improved public services to that community; he also debunked a myth I had heard before, that indigenous people had been officially considered part of the country's local "flora and fauna."

"Doesn't mean fair dinkum's not deeply racist though. Whole of Australia is!" he said with a grin. This man in coveralls and a broad smile could have been a history professor. Instead, Dak delivered pizza on a scooter, and I never got a chance to ask him why that was. It was clear from our conversation that some of the racial discord that existed in the United States also plagued Australia. However, there were clearly some salient differences that I made a mental note to explore.

"Lunch is on me, mate." Dak stood up to screw a red scooter helmet over his shaggy hair. "Never say you got nothing from Oz. Day's good deed for this larrikin!" He sauntered off into the afternoon, leaving me puzzling over his last word.

The slang term first emerged in the late nineteenth century. It meant someone who was rowdy—a hooligan contemptuous of authority, someone who pushed the boundaries of arbitrary social conventions and laws. As historian Manning

Clark defined it, "the larrikin [is] almost archly self-conscious, too smart for his own good, witty rather than humorous, exceeding limits, bending rules and sailing close to the wind, avoiding rather than evading responsibility, playing to an audience, mocking pomposity and smugness, taking the piss out of people, cutting down tall poppies, born of a Wednesday, looking both ways for a Sunday, larger than life, skeptical, iconoclastic, egalitarian yet suffering fools badly, and, above all, defiant."

Even though this term of near endearment has masculine, and even masculinist, inflections, it resonated with me. I thought about the founding of America by Puritans versus the founding of Australia by convicts. Obviously, given my recent history, one of these was more appealing than the other. Learning about the mischievous and the badly behaved streak in the Australian psyche reassured me and helped me feel less guilty. I guess, in the end, I was an American larrikin. As heedless and reckless as I had been, I had never intended to hurt anyone, yet my behavior had nonetheless offended a whole swath of liberal and conservative New Englanders. I fashioned myself a philosophical anarchist and a merry prankster, yet in the eyes of the readers of the Hartford Courant, I was nothing more than a criminal who might contaminate the minds of young people.

Neither attitude was entirely accurate, but I recognized myself in the description of the larrikin and found myself enraptured by Australian culture as well. I found much about being down under appealing: the mandatory and preferential voting system that generally ensured that extremists did not get into power and that the Green Party could be politically represented in a major city like Melbourne; the living wage paid to the working class, which reduced the relative inequity between the very rich and the very poor; the welcome to, and acknowledgment of, the indigenous First Australians that prefaced the public events I attended.

Though many of the Australians I would meet felt that it was mainly lip service, I always found myself deeply moved by the evocation of the traditional custodians of the land. Just having the names of the tribes in the air evoked the colonial violence done to the native inhabitants. I often thought of how amazing—and sadly absurd—it would be if, before a senator spoke in Washington, DC, he or she apologized to the Piscataway Indians who had once lived on the land and asked for the forgiveness of the slaves on whose back the wealth of the nation had been created.

If Americans are said to possess a certain cultural swagger, Australians are said to suffer from a "cultural cringe," a term coined by Melbourne social commentator A. A. Phillips in 1950 to describe an internalized sense of deficiency and inferiority that local writers and artists felt when compared to their European or American counterparts. Phillips believed this phenomenon contributed to a general anti-intellectualism among the antipodeans. I have to disagree, as most Australians I have met, if refreshingly diffident, are nonetheless cosmopolitan and well read, even if they love their sports and their beer. In Australia, I regained my voice and began, hesitantly at first, then more confidently, to be able to talk and write about everything I had been through.

This is how, in the end, the worst years of my life became my greatest blessing. I never imagined I'd do time, and yet, if I hadn't, I would never have discovered the shadow self that reflects the disregarded underside of an entire country. I would never have met Chaos or Lenny, Domo or Junkie John; never have seen the grace in the ugliest side of all of us; never have understood how trouble also holds the most promise for redemption. Looking back at those surreal years of my life, I find that a plank has loosened. I'm better able to forgive myself those reckless impulses that nearly undid my life. I harbor no more ill will to those by whom I have felt wronged. Like in the Japanese craft of *kintsugi*, which is the art of repairing broken ceramics with glue and gold dust, strengthening it while calling attention to its imperfections, I am rebuilding my life, making it stronger at the very places where it had been broken.

The most important takeaway of my experience is the conviction that the raw, unvarnished truth of the American carceral system can no longer be a dirty secret. Those who have gone through it, whatever their trespass, deserve a second chance. Maybe if we can suspend our chastisement and stop shaming others, then the principle of transformative repair can work on us collectively as well as individually.

Imagine humanity identifying its flaws and then using such recognition as the guiding principle to evolve as a species. Imagine us acknowledging the predatory principles at the root of colonialism but also the philosophical elegance of modern democracy. Imagine all of us treating one another with altruism, regardless of skin color; each of us recognizing in one another our unique subjectivity and the awareness that there are many sides to every story, and many stories on every side; and that to typecast people as heroes and villains might work in the movies, but that it doesn't pass muster in real life.

American exceptionalism doesn't make sense either. The Native American tribe of the Iroquois, who lived in what is now northern New York State and knew themselves as Hau De-no Sau-nee (People of the Long Houses), possess an older continuous participatory democracy, one that has lasted more than eight hundred years. The Iroquois joined together with the Cayugas, Mohawks, Oneidas,

Onondagas, and Seneca Native Americans to form the Six Nations, a system of consensus governance that had a written constitution and provided inspiration to Benjamin Franklin and Thomas Jefferson, who used their model in the framing of the United States Constitution. The Faroe Islands have an even older parliamentary system and Vaishali, the capital city of Licchavi in the eastern Indian province of Bihar, had a functional democracy as early as the sixth century B.C. But that history is not taught in American schools.

I am exceedingly lucky to have been born in the United States of America in the late twentieth century. Yet I recognize that the men and women who shaped the country were flawed slave owners and native killers who did not believe in equal rights for everyone. The legacy of their thinking has persisted in the form of relative privilege manifest in a criminal justice system that unequally imprisons its citizens, in journalism that reduces complex individuals to a lead and a sound bite (*if it bleeds, it leads*), and in the minds of even the most well-meaning liberal progressive whose eager solicitousness feels like condescension. We are all constituted with such contradictions—shadow and light—and, if we could practice *upeska*, that Sanskrit word meaning "equanimity" or "nonjudgment," perhaps it will become possible for us to make an evolutionary leap.

In John Winthrop's "City on a Hill" sermon, which galvanized the Puritans of the early seventeenth century, and which continues to resonate in the American sensibility and shape its domestic and foreign policy, there's another, less-cited passage, which reads, "We must delight in each other, make other's conditions our own, rejoice together, mourn together, labor and suffer together, always having before our eyes our commission and community in the work, our community as members of the same body." Even though he and the people to whom he was preaching didn't choose to put it into practice, I don't know if there's a better expression of the work we have been put on earth to do.

We all live in the same body. Each one of us is a single stitch in a vast, expanding tapestry, the edges of which unfurl in space and time far beyond what we are capable of seeing. We all contribute to that living image, which is the very essence of divinity. Instead of Arthur Rimbaud's famous statement *je est un autre*, let's strive for *je vous suis*. I am you. You are me. We are each other. Some mornings when I wake now, thankful to draw another breath, to be a free man, to have created and gone through my own trauma with enough spirit and support to begin to transform it, I can feel clearly, with compassion and without judgment, our indelible ineradicable interconnectedness.

PinPani (*Prevernal*)

This is my letter to the World that never wrote to Me.

—Emily Dickinson

Dear Creation,

I jacked up my life because I once saw god. Up on a mountaintop, with one of my best friends as a witness, I felt the ripple of the energy that keeps us connected harmonizing with my own intent and possible futures. There were deer involved and a thunderstorm, but it's a revelation that will only feel mundane, even in the deployment of the most refined language. It's simply enough that it happened. I was provided that afternoon a destiny to which I failed to measure up, given a family I could have kept intact, if not for my personal menagerie of pig, cock, and snake. That's what I find hardest to forgive myself for, since I'll never know what was down that other diverging road. Instead, I took the one less traveled by, the more painful, self-revealing path, and that has made all the difference.

Robert Frost continues to be my American freshmen college students' favorite poet, which always astonishes me because they don't seem to exhibit much in common with his bleak, overdetermined stoicism. I'm always glad to introduce those students to other poets, running the gamut from Etheridge Knight and Claudia Rankine to Emily Dickinson and John Keats, whose advice to "tell all the truth but tell it slant," or whose concept of negative capability, "being in uncertainties, mysteries, doubts, without any irritable reaching after fact and reason," remains so germane. The world is never quite as monochromatic as we might hope, and the divisions between us are just in our minds.

None of us are born wanting to marginalize another human being. Yet when, in history, an entire economy is fabricated upon the enslavement of others, and some people continue to benefit disproportionately from that fact, we need to point that out, even if it makes us uncomfortable. When we see the outdated Puritan mechanism of shaming being used, we need to respond with compassion. For Buddhists, shame, if understood properly for what it is—an impoverished mentality, the terror of being judged, a state of lacking, the condition of perpetual insufficiency—can actually become a transformative principle. It can provide a gateway to a larger, more inclusive sense of belonging and help open us up compassionately to others. It shows how empty the egoism with which we invest ourselves really is, compared to the vastness of our luminous true natures.

In Madras, South India, where my father's family comes from, there's a singsong taunt that you will hear in the dusty schoolyards. *Shame, shame, puppy shame, all the monkeys know your name!* The chant means to jeer that you've been found out: been exposed bare-ass as a newly born cur! The fact that one of the slang connotations of the word "puppy" in Tamil is "penis" only adds delectably to the cutting double entendre. This is the kind of phrase my bow-tied adversaries would intone in unison at my convent school when one of the younger students had peed himself in fright after being set upon by bullies wielding tiffin-carriers. That nursery rhyme chorus is a way of othering, of making a distinction between a group and an individual, of drawing a line in the sand, of saying you are there and I am here with the others. You live on the other side of this border from us.

Isn't that what it means when a group or individual is cast "beyond the pale"? That linguistic phrase for impropriety absorbs connotations as it moves through time. Etymologically, the idiom refers to an archaic definition of the word "pale," that is, a region lying within an imposed boundary, like a staked fence, as part of Ireland was for fourteenth-century English administrators, so that going beyond it was doing something outside those lines. It began to mean acting bizarrely or slightly abhorrently: literally leaving civilization behind. And yet, when we hear that phrase now, we can't help but see color: pale-face, as in possessing a White complexion, as in conforming and being civilized. Overlay that sense with the act of colonizing a territory or policing the grounds of propriety, and we have a very different signification indeed. Today, it is the prison population who are beyond the pale.

Personally, though, I've always been more interested in the shadow: that part of ourselves that we are ashamed of and that we feel guilty about, the part that has the propensity to grow if ignored. The shadow is dangerous. Primitive. Irrational. Reeks of the public lavatory. The taboo. If, collectively, we don't pay it the attention it deserves, it could swallow up an entire epoch. This is the place where shame might be productively used. Carl Jung has written that "shame is a soul eating emotion," and it is that for sure, but in its corrosive capacity, it can completely hollow us out, so that in the empty space cleared out, we have greater capacity for empathy toward those around us. Connecting with the part of ourselves we hope others don't see is to begin to dissolve the very mindset that harbors that hope in the first place. In the process of learning to forgive ourselves, we can also forgive others.

Here I stand, your Keatsian example of negative capability. I've been a professor and a prisoner. A thief and a saint. A citizen and an anarchist. Mentally gifted and mentally ill. Consciously and inadvertently, I've inflicted harm on other living creatures, and I've sacrificed myself completely for their well-being many times over. I've been your mother, and you've been my daughter for so many lifetimes, all of us spinning together on this marvelous planet, orbiting a star in an unfathomable universe of stars. Let's actively—not abstractly—love each other and work to change this world we share to be more magnanimous, for, in such daily acts of connectedness, grace resounds more permanently than the sound of a judge's gavel against a wooden bench. It's a reverberation to ripple us awake.

Epilogue

I hoped to end this book by emerging newborn, bathed in the baptismal waters of my misfortune to emerge a new man, ready to start again, a phoenix with his scars for a crest. I never expected to be sideswiped by yet another controversy, again due much to my own making. This cost me fellowships, contracts, friendships, community, even, at times, my mental and physical health. I realize now that I've also been given a chance to step back and view my own male privilege within the larger context of the double patriarchy, American and Indian, in which I was raised.

While teaching in China, diagramming relative clauses for engineering students from Guangzhou, straining to stay connected to my own daughters through Skype, unsure what I would do to survive when I returned, a successful female poet, whom I had met a half-dozen times in my life, wrote an essay about "sexual assault in the literary world," in which she accused a number of men, including me. The basis for my inclusion was an alleged unsolicited kiss in the middle of a crowded hotel lobby more than a decade earlier. She identified all the men by their first name and last initial, providing a cloak of cover for the Don F.'s and John P.'s of the world, and casting a spotlight onto the unmistakable Ravi S., already in exile halfway across the world.

Within days, the few lifelines I had back in the United States—the class visits and readings scheduled months before, the tenuous bridges back to the community on which I depended to survive—began to crumble. If being convicted of a misdemeanor in Connecticut cost me my academic career, then being accused of this unwanted kiss nearly cost me the rest of my reputation. I received hate mail from a graduate student encouraging me to castrate myself. The editor of *Drunken Boat*, the journal I had founded decades earlier, attempted to use the controversy to usurp the journal to fulfill their own political agenda and remove me from the board. Stunned, still unable to remember the grievance in question, and galled by what I perceived as irresponsibility in calling whatever might have transpired between us "sexual assault" without first contacting me to have a private conversation, I made the grave error of responding publicly to the author. I wanted sincerely to enter into a dialogue, however difficult, and to apologize. I also acknowledged the gap in my own memory that, unbeknownst to me at the time, negated the apology in the minds of many.

If I had ever imagined that lessons about impulsivity could be easily mastered, whether in relation to an unremembered kiss, a power tool at Home Depot, another whiskey, or my blind urge to clear my name and walk headlong into a forum for which I had no operating instructions, nor the wisdom to know I needed them, I was sadly mistaken. In writing this response, I had opened myself up to further charges, this time of gaslighting and mansplaining. It was a panicked and—in hindsight—defensive maneuver, and it helped no one. Rather than obtaining clarification and forgiveness, I had done nothing but present myself as one who, now more than ever, ought to be condemned and cast beyond the pale. A few female friends nevertheless wrote to me privately to express their support, drawing attention to the often-overlooked degrees of distinction in what is defined as sexual misconduct. They were nevertheless unwilling to respond publicly in my defense for fear of provoking further outrage. Acting from sheer desperation, and with my friends' permission, I collaged together their sentiments under a few pseudonyms and posted them as comments on my accuser's blog to show there was indeed a countervailing point of view. Not a single day passes without me wishing that I had simply remained silent.

Yet how problematic that using silence would have served me so much better than attempting to engage in dialogue. I wanted at the time—and still want—to engage male fragility. While a byproduct of patriarchal culture myself, up to that point I had always envisioned myself as an active feminist. I had made donations to the South Asian Women's Centre, volunteered at the Charlottesville Women's Shelter, marched alongside my sisters at Take Back the Night, and published anthologies and journals that have always included more women than men. Moreover, I am convinced that, if anything, the often debated, highly politicized, "1 in 5" statistic of women who have been sexually assaulted on college campuses likely undersells the actual percentage.

The women in my life have felt firsthand, in large and small ways, the abuses of power within our patriarchy, and even us men who want no part of that system have to own our own complicity within it. This is part of what compels me to get it right. We live in a world in which toxic masculinity is as ubiquitous as reflexive racism; women still have to fight for permission to be faithful interpreters of their own experiences and are often refused equal agency to create their own sexual subjectivity and financial independence. Moreover, women who are minorities, immigrants, poor, indentured, all those who stand to have more to lose, or who might lack the very language to name their own experiences, are probably not accounted for in that figure.

I entered into a private conversation with the person who made the allegations against me. She forgave me, writing, "I would love to do something to help alleviate the problems you are having and to help the fallout on you to die down. . . . It hurts me as a person every time I see that it is causing problems for you." This was accompanied, on WhatsApp, by a heart and a butterfly. I was grateful for this expression of forgiveness but remained upset and angered by the circumstances of the allegation and how it had affected my life. This should have been a moment of calm introspection, but I felt voiceless and embittered. Real restorative justice can't come in the form of a hit-and-run that, through blaming and shaming, seeks simply to flip the balance of power, not eradicate it.

How I wish I simply ignored this person, yet I refuse to believe that silence will ever be the best way to heal trauma, because what does that teach my daughters or my stepson? If I regret my flailing attempts at apologizing, I don't regret the larger conversation those attempts hoped to engender. Making an example of any one man does nothing to redress the larger problem of pervasive toxic masculinity, the harm that the imperatives "be a man" or "don't cry" do to any young boy, the way that the lines between the biological and the social have become so blurry that we scarcely have a language to reflect what we ourselves don't yet understand in terms of gender and power. We need to transpose "1 in 5" with the "1 in 4" boys who report being bullied (and the much greater number who never report it), the 99 percent who report playing video games (when 90 percent of all video games are found to have violent content), and the ones committing homicides and suicides at a rate greater than three times their female peers. Then we might understand our culture's role in forming masculine (and feminine) identity. From the casual misogyny and reflexive violence all around me, being incarcerated exposed me to what a microscopic and concentrated version of hypermasculine society might look like. We need to address the underlying disconnection, objectification, and brutality (which is largely unexpressed grief) that have been normalized by late-stage capitalism, the way masculinity becomes an ideal modeled on a lack of empathy, and on the rejection of—and domination over—the feminine, because it is far easier to market and sell that way.

I know that I will write more about this subject in the future, considering it from the perspective of American and Tamilian Brahmin culture, asking whose point of view is sanctioned and supported in any given community, and what role language plays in policing and punishing those who transgress against those agreed-upon norms. Like many men, I've also fallen prey to the idea that masculinity is based on how much money you make, how many goals you score, and how many women you bed. So long as these are the measures by which half the population are encouraged to assert their self-worth in society, the violence will never diminish. This is a conversation that all of us, regardless of sex, gender, and sexual identity, need to take part in, as it's a task bigger than any one person can take on alone, for the difficulty is symptomatic of a larger disease.

I am sorry for having hurt any person, female or male, queer or trans, alive or dead, and I am dedicated to a lifetime of service and excavation, digging until I've gotten the rot out at the root. I've got to dig myself out of Appa, and Appa out from his father before him, not just in regard to the American masculinity that prizes greed, mastery, aggression, and self-gratification over authentic connection and emotional expression but also ancient Indian customs in which women were treated as the property of men who gifted them to other men. Trauma, according to therapist Resmaa Menakem, "can cause us to react to present events in ways that seem wildly inappropriate, overly charged, or otherwise out of proportion . . . [and] over time can become embedded in the body as standard ways of surviving and protecting itself." These often-subconscious coping strategies are passed on from generation to generation until they become "the standard response in families, communities, and cultures." Yet there is always the opportunity for healing and growth that arises from genuine vulnerability and a breaking down of defensiveness.

Brazilian educator and philosopher Paulo Freire defines humanitarian generosity as being motivated by a dehumanizing sense of paternalism and the egoistic interests of the oppressor. It's the reason why there are so many college courses on Marxism, racism, and the abolition of the prison-industrial complex taught by professors who benefit from the very institutions they claim to critique. When Julie teaches classes in homeless shelters, she invites conversation that is inclusive, unafraid, difficult, messy, and courageous (sometimes she will even invite her students home), and I believe we have to dare to be just as vulnerable in our own discussions about race and gender if we want to build a more equitable social order. When a sense of victimization is used as a bludgeon to perpetrate violence on another and thereby gain relevancy, there cannot be true transformation or healing.

The allegations made against me affected me deeply. As every aspect of my life continued to come under attack, for my own recuperation, I felt the need to return to Hartford Correctional, five years after I had spent ninety days of my life there. I wanted to breathe in the sweat and moldy cinderblock masked over by industrial cleaner, sit in the visiting room in which Julie had waited for hours to speak to me through Plexiglas (nearly being denied the opportunity due to wearing a sleeveless summer dress), and perhaps reconnect with some of the men who might still be there. I had kept their pain alive even as I had secured my freedom, and still had their inmate numbers and their nicknames. I suppose I wanted to experience something akin to what veterans of war might feel upon revisiting a village that they had occupied years before.

But it was not to be.

All my letters to the men whose inmate numbers I still had went unanswered, the Connecticut chief state attorney and commissioner of the Department of Corrections ignored my requests to speak to them, and then all correctional facilities went into lockdown due to the outbreak of COVID-19, a disease that first emerged late in 2019 in China and spread to the rest of the world the following year. The risk of infection and transmission was particularly high in jails because of inferior healthcare, little access to proper hygiene, overcrowding, a general lack of testing, and a flux of bodies going in and out. There was no way that I was going to be able to visit.

Faced with the dilemma of wanting to reenter a carceral space but being prohibited from doing so, I was forced to confront my own motivations in wanting to return to jail in the first place. Was I an anthropological tourist who had gone through an unfortunate time and wanted to capitalize on those experiences by writing this very book? Certainly, my personal circumstances were very different than most of the men I had met while incarcerated. I had come from a life of relative privilege and returned to that life, even if I had constant reminders of what I had been through and how much I had lost. Formerly a tenured professor, now I couldn't even be hired as an adjunct to teach expository writing. Even when I had ten times as many positive evaluations and recommendations to the two misdemeanors on my record that show up with every background check, the latter were all that seemed to matter.

Julie told me that, in the aftermath of my incarceration and the enduring, reverberating public shaming, I had changed shape and was now a round peg, still trying to force my way into a square hole. To lose my tribe was devastating, but it compelled me to connect to real people, such as those working in criminal justice reform. I connected with a gardener in Providence who uses the cultivation of vegetables as one way to teach inmates actual skills that would allow them to become apprentice gardeners upon their release. I ran a writing workshop for a professional chef who teaches culinary techniques to young adults in the Department of Youth Services in Rhode Island. I met a former Florida cop who had risen all the way up the ranks to become a member of President Obama's task force on twenty-first-century policing and who described how overpolicing certain communities and the incestuous relationship between some prosecutors' offices and police departments has led to a corroding distrust in democracy.

Well aware of my own difficulties finding employment, I made an appointment with the director of a nonprofit organization that helps prisoners reintegrate into society. What she told me confirmed my worst fears: "We are not a forgiving society, Mr. Shankar. The rates of unemployment are over five times higher for those who have a criminal record than those who do not. Prisoners are stereotyped on the basis of a conviction, and the kinds of jobs that I help them get are the lowest of the low. If I can get someone hired as a dishwasher or a janitor, it's considered a great success. If they can become a skilled laborer, a plumber, or a barber, we celebrate it like we've landed a rocket on the moon."

"The irony is," she paused a long time, "that these men and women are some of the hardest workers, the cleverest people I have ever met—and I have been on Capitol Hill and at lunch at Harvard. They are sorry for their mistakes and want to contribute to society. But no one wants to give them a second chance. And that's why the rates of recidivism are so high. These men and women *want* to work when they get out and have a stable family life, but guess what? If they can't pull down a steady paycheck, how the *pinche* are they supposed to resist the streets?"

The most transformative thing I did was join And Still We Rise, a Boston-based company run by Dev Luthra, a classically trained Shakespeare actor, dedicated to telling the stories of those whose lives have been affected by incarceration. We get together every Thursday online, though I'm told that, in the past, it was in a black box theater where everyone would improv and tableau. Now we put together ensemble theater pieces through video, and, even as we generate new material and practice our blocking, we support one another through a crisis of housing or family difficulty, uplifting one another through art and companionship. It's the kind of community theater group that I would never have dreamed of joining while I was at Columbia, yet I feel more invested and alive with them than ever. While I have been beleaguered and beaten down many times over the past decade, being part of this group reminds me weekly that even in my darkest moments, my privilege has inoculated me to a certain extent from the daily injustices faced by the Black and Latino communities, women, and the poor. Above all, this group reminds me to be humble and grateful: a lesson that is never finished but which takes the work of a lifetime to remember and to enact.

Lois, a grandmother and reformed drug addict, who falls on stage and screen into character so convincingly that it takes my breath clear down to my beating heart, tells me about her family.

I'm a mother of four sons and each one of them has been in and out of jail since they were little. First, youth services then the state penitentiary then halfway houses. But they are good boys. I raised them to know right from wrong. I had to work three jobs to pay the rent when they were growing up, so wasn't around as much as I wanted to be. Sometimes I blame myself. But then, other times, I think that's just the price of being Black in America. We didn't ask to be here, but here we are. I guess I just feel blessed that they are still alive.

In December 2020, in a year that saw the death of George Floyd, Rayshard Brooks, Daniel Prude, and Breonna Taylor at the hands of police, a crane lifted a nearly three-thousand-pound bronze statue from its granite pedestal not far from where I live in Boston's Park Square, where it had stood since 1879. The Emancipation Group memorial, itself a replica of a Washington, DC, statue, depicted a godlike, fully attired Abraham Lincoln standing over a kneeling, near-naked, still-shackled Black man. The man is, according to historian Kirk Savage, "the very archetype of slavery: he is stripped, literally and figuratively, bereft of personal agency, social position, and accouterments of culture. . . . Frozen forever in this unfortunate juxtaposition, the monument is not really about emancipation but about its opposite—domination." If a better visual embodiment of White savior complex has ever been crafted, I don't know what it could be. Moreover, as cited in the *Washington Post* in 2011, of the more than five thousand public statues depicting historical figures in public squares and parks throughout the United States, less than four hundred of these monuments are of women. We don't have to look that hard to see how racism and sexism color our governmental institutions and permeate our consciousness.

Spearheaded by Boston artist Tory Bullock, the Boston Art Commission decided in 2020 to take down the statue, giving it the same fate as other Confederate and colonist monuments around the country. Statues, unfortunately, are easier to move than minds. All it takes is a crane to hoist an offensive reminder of our history onto the back of a flatbed truck to be buried in some official depot's basement. But the reverberations of that colonialist mentality continue in the inner workings of everyday life and stay buried within our institutions. Just by making a statue disappear, or by entombing an entire class of people in prison, we'll never heal the original wound that arises from the fact that nation building has been a brutal, racist, inequitable practice that unjustly shapes the lives of generations of citizens. For true reparation to happen, we must acknowledge the enduring legacy of injustice by confronting those who've been wronged—and ourselves—directly, while also doing the policy work behind the scenes to transform policing, adjudication, sentencing, parole, and reintegration.

My own life only overlaps briefly with these larger social justice imperatives, though my experiences have made it impossible for me to avert my gaze while those around me suffer, and while others around me—either intentionally or complicitly—help cause that suffering. Those generations who come after us may well look at mass incarceration and social media shaming the way we regard medieval bishops who, while building exquisite cathedrals, also came up with ingenious ways to torture their fellow human beings. We refuse each other's subjectivity because we are scared of difference, but your pursuit of life, liberty, and happiness doesn't threaten mine, so long as we can agree on the assumption of privilege that puts that goal at unequal distances for each of us.

I began work on this book because I promised the men of Dorm #4 in Hartford Correctional that I would help share their stories. They might never have the chance to get their voice back from their court documents and psychiatric records, but I can use mine to loosen their closed fists and reveal our shared humanity. Those men are all around us. I am one of them. I have had to reclaim my own voice from the *Hartford Courant* and from the blogosphere, from Amma and Appa, and from the lies I told myself because I was hurting and did not know how to confront the pain. I knew how to mask it but never could quite drink or drug or fuck it away.

There is so much I wish I could whisper in the ear of that awe-stricken boy, lying on his back on a rooftop in Madras, watching the swirl of stars overhead in a delicious moment of respite from the sweltering summer heat. Everything seemed imbued with such magical possibility. My cousins and I were separated by oceans, but we were family! You could eat sweet *pongal* with your hands or cornflakes with a spoon for breakfast! Somehow Pac-Man had reached the shores of India but not Donkey Kong! It all made such perfect sense. Now I wake up each morning with the intention of perceiving again with such nonjudgmental curiosity. Some days, when I wrap my arms around my beloved, laughing, after getting off the phone with my daughters, our dogs sniffing and wagging around our feet, miso soup on the stove and the Japanese maple flaring darkly crimson in the window, everything seems so tender and possible and alive and intended. I never imagined that I would have to lose so much to come this close to feeling free again.

Acknowledgments

Throughout the writing of this memoir, I have received a great deal of support and assistance from numerous organizations and individuals. First, I'd like to thank the University of Sydney International Scholarship (USydIS), without which I would never have had the liberty to undertake this work.

I'm deeply indebted to my faculty advisors, Dr. Fiona Giles and Dr. Bunty Avieson from the University of Sydney's Media & Communications Department. I would also like to thank the Higher Degree by Research Administration Centre, and the rest of the faculty at MECO, particularly Dr. Benedetta Brevini, Dr. Megan Le Masurier, and Adam Aitkin for their invaluable assistance throughout my fellowship.

I also would like the thank the MacDowell Colony, the Corporation of Yaddo, the Djerassi Resident Artists Program, and the I-Park Foundation for the gift of time and space to work on different aspects of this project. Additionally, I would like to thank the Rhode Island State Council on the Arts, the South Asian Arts Resiliency Fund from the India Center Foundation Inc., the Kerkyasharian and Kayikian Fund for Armenian Studies, and PEN America for funding that has helped support me and my family during the composition of this work and during the COVID-19 pandemic.

My sincere appreciation also goes to Dennis Lloyd and the entire staff at the University of Wisconsin Press for sharing and sharpening my vision for *Correctional*. Thanks to all the other editors and publications in which excerpts from this work have previously appeared or are forthcoming, including the *New York Times*, *Hartford Courant*, NPR, *Michigan Quarterly Review*, The Marshall Project, and *The Common*, particularly Susan Chiara and Lawrence Brantley for their openness and Akiba Soloman, Reginald Dwayne Betts, Aaron Stone, and Jennifer Acker for their keen edits. Thanks also to the Australasian Association of Writing Programs, Auckland University, Columbia University, New York

University Shanghai, and the University of Macau, where I presented aspects of this memoir in different forms.

Much gratitude to Jen Stott and Harvest Kitchen and Dev Luthra, Vincent Siders, and Zahra Belleya and the entire community of And Still We Rise for making me feel a part of their gastronomical and theatrical families, respectively. I'm obliged to the U.S. Studies Centre at the University of Sydney, the New York Writers Workshop, and the Cambridge Center for Adult Education for allowing me to support my writing process through teaching. Thanks also to Matwaala, the Asia Pacific Writers & Translators, especially Dr. Sally Breen, Dr. Julia Prendergast, and Aaron Chapman, University of Arkansas Press, and Recent Works Press, who have been invaluable in providing support and community in moments I needed it most.

Many people have read and commented on this creative work in its various stages. Some of you have spoken to me as recently as last week, and others of you I have not spoken to in years, but the assistance you provided me will not be soon forgotten and will live on in the legacy of *Correctional*. Thanks to my agent Sarah Jane Freymann, as well as my colleagues and friends, including Usha Akella, Indran Amirthanayagam, Rob Arnold, Reginald Dwayne Betts, Michelle Cahill, Tina Chang, Rand Richards Cooper, Jake Donovan, Dr. Robert Dowling, Evan Fallenberg, Dai Fan, Luis Francia, Dr. H. Bruce Franklin, Jessica Hall, Nathalie Handal, Dr. Marcus Hermes, Linda Jaivin, Peter Kahn, Rakesh Kaul, Dr. Neil Maclean, Khaled Mattawa, David Mura, Russell Palmer, Gregory Pardlo, Lisa Samuels, Sarah Schulman, James Scudamore, Sudeep Sen, Yuyutsu RD Sharma, Dr. Caleb Smith, Dr. Shane Strange, Shreerekha Pillai Subramanian, George Szrites, Andy Thibault, Tim and Deedle Tomlinson, Sarah Vallance, Pramila Venkateswaran, Peter Walsh, Frances Kai-Hwa Wang, and Mags Webster. I would like to particularly highlight the contributions of Dr. Rozanna Lilley, who not only provided critical feedback but made me part of her family while I was in Sydney; Tim and Deedle Tomlinson, whose support and encouragement have been a perpetual lifeline; and agent extraordinaire Bill Clegg, who did not choose to represent my manuscript but gave me such detailed and generous feedback that it utterly transformed the book. Editorial assistance in the form of copyediting was provided by Anne McPeak, Dan Crissman, and Dr. William Ives, Research Fellow at the University of St Andrews. My gratitude as well to all those other librarians, friends, researchers, and colleagues who I have neglected to mention. Special thanks to Sarah Drepaul, who worked as the book's Creative Producer with a shared passion for equal justice initiatives, and my publicist, Lissa Warren, for her timely correspondence and connections.

Thank you to my eternal cheerleaders, my amma, Rajeswari Shankar, and my sisters, Dr. Rajni Shankar-Brown and Rahini Shankar. Without all of you, including K. H. Shankar, none of this would have been possible.

I am also grateful to those who will encounter this book, hoping that it might inspire them to continue developing on the thinking I've begun here and make genuine transformations to create a more equitable society. I'm appreciative of all my future readers, including my own daughters, Samara and Talia Shankar, who I hope will come to read this in time and recognize how much I love them both.

And finally, last but by no means least, thanks to my partner and lover, Julie Anne Batten, whose conversations into the nature of shame, race, bibliotherapy, incarceration, and life writing helped shape the framework and essence of this work. It's been said that we have entered a moment of reckoning where we can set right generations worth of racism and colonialism and environmental justice, and it's toward that goal that this work contributes.